Paying the Price

Paying the Price

Ending the Great Recession and Beginning a New American Century

Mark Zandi

Vice President, Publisher: Tim Moore

Associate Publisher and Director of Marketing: Amy Neidlinger

Executive Editor: Jim Boyd

Editorial Assistant: Pamela Boland

Development Editor: Russ Hall

Operations Specialist: Jodi Kemper

Marketing Manager: Megan Graue

Cover Designer: Chuti Prasertsith

Managing Editor: Kristy Hart

Project Editor: Betsy Harris

Copy Editor: Apostrophe Editing Services

Proofreader: Williams Woods Publishing Services

Senior Indexer: Cheryl Lenser

Senior Compositor: Gloria Schurick

Manufacturing Buyer: Dan Uhrig

© 2013 by Pearson Education, Inc.

Publishing as FT Press

Upper Saddle River, New Jersey 07458

This book is sold with the understanding that neither the author nor the publisher is engaged in rendering legal, accounting, or other professional services or advice by publishing this book. Each individual situation is unique. Thus, if legal or financial advice or other expert assistance is required in a specific situation, the services of a competent professional should be sought to ensure that the situation has been evaluated carefully and appropriately. The author and the publisher disclaim any liability, loss, or risk resulting directly or indirectly, from the use or application of any of the contents of this book.

FT Press offers excellent discounts on this book when ordered in quantity for bulk purchases or special sales. For more information, please contact U.S. Corporate and Government Sales, 1-800-382-3419, corpsales@pearsontechgroup.com. For sales outside the U.S., please contact International Sales at international@pearsoned.com.

Company and product names mentioned herein are the trademarks or registered trademarks of their respective owners.

Printed in the United States of America

First Printing September 2012

ISBN-10: 0-13-704798-3

ISBN-13: 978-0-13-704798-7

Pearson Education LTD.

Pearson Education Australia PTY, Limited.

Pearson Education Singapore, Pte. Ltd.

Pearson Education Asia, Ltd.

Pearson Education Canada, Ltd.

Pearson Educación de Mexico, S.A. de C.V.

Pearson Education—Japan

Pearson Education Malaysia, Pte. Ltd.

The Library of Congress Cataloging-in-Publication data is on file.

This book is dedicated to my loving family,
Ava, Bill, Anna, and Lily.

Contents

Introduction xiii

Chapter 1   Financial Shock to Financial Panic 1

   Tidal Wave 4

   Monetary Accelerator 6

   Broken Pipes 8

   Regulatory Failure 10

   Financial Shock 12

   Fannie and Freddie 16

   Financial Panic 19

   Endnotes 21

Chapter 2   Bank Bailout 23

   Confidence Game 26

   Lender of Last Resort 28

   Insurer of Last Resort 31

   TARP: The Bailout Fund 34

   Stressful Stress Testing 39

   Chaos to Calm 42

   Endnotes 43

Chapter 3   Outside the Monetary Box 47

   Battling Asset Bubbles 51

   Bernanke's Education 54

   ZIRP, QE, and the Twist 58

   Exit Strategy 66

   Endnotes 68

Chapter 4   As GM Goes, So Goes the Economy......71

Headed for a Crash.........................75

The Rationale 78

The Bailout 82

Auto-Led Recovery........................86

Endnotes 88

Chapter 5   Stimulus Is Not a Dirty Word 91

Stimulus Logic...........................96

Temporary Tax Cuts 99

Emergency UI and the Multiplier 102

Municipal Bailout 105

Shovel Ready............................107

Strong Evidence 108

Exit Strategy 112

Endnotes 114

Chapter 6   The Foreclosure Fiasco...............119

Housing Boom and Bust...................125

Dazed and Confused......................130

Bold and Foolhardy 132

Quelling the Chaos 135

Emptying the Pipeline 137

Endnotes 141

Chapter 7   Fixing the Financial Plumbing 145

Systemwide Failure. 150

Systemic Risk. 153

Resolution Authority. 155

Too Big to Fail. 158

Out of the Shadows. 161

What If?. 164

Road to Redemption. 166

Endnotes 167

Chapter 8   The Fallout. 171

Buying Binge to Bust 175

Homeownership Overreach 178

Two Americas 182

European Existentialism. 189

Dark Pessimism. 193

Endnotes 194

Chapter 9   Getting Our Groove Back 197

This Time Is Different 200

Of Sharks and Black Swans. 207

Regulators and Lawyers 210

Approaching the Fiscal Cliff. 213

Endnotes 215

Chapter 10   Don't Bet Against the United States.....219

Righting the Fiscal Ship 222

Navigating the Monetary Shoals. 228

Getting Out of the Mortgage Business 231

Where Will the Jobs Come From?. 235

Endnotes 240

Index 243

Acknowledgments

Ava, my dear wife, is critical to making everything work in my life. Without her tireless support and advice, I would not have been able to write this book or accomplish much of anything else.

Paul Getman, my best friend and colleague, constantly challenges my perspectives, making my views sharper and better balanced. He also worries about all the many things that make our company successful, so that I don't have to.

I'm also very grateful to Andy Cassel for his brilliant editing. He somehow figures out a way to breathe life into my dense prose. I'm sorry I keep making the same mistakes, but perhaps that makes editing my work easier.

Thank you to my dad. Your empathy is inspirational and your sometimes unconventional views always make me think.

To Richard, Meriam, Karl, and Peter, I will always cherish our times together. There is nothing as durable as an opinion formed in the crucible of a Zandi debate. I miss our mom; she was a key ingredient in how I see the world.

Moody's Corporation also deserves a big thank you for allowing me to think about whatever interests me and saying whatever I think. I suspect there aren't many companies that foster this kind of intellectual freedom.

About the Author

Mark Zandi is the Chief Economist of Moody's Analytics. He is the cofounder of an economic consulting firm that was purchased by the Moody's Corporation in late 2005. His recent research has focused on assessing the economic impacts of tax and government spending policies, the appropriate monetary policy response to asset market bubbles, the determinants of foreclosure and personal bankruptcy, and housing and mortgage market policies. He is on the board of directors of MGIC, the nation's largest mortgage insurer, and The Reinvestment Fund, a non-profit that combines public and private capital to make investments in grocery stores, charter schools, health centers, and other facilities in inner cities in the Northeast. A trusted adviser to policymakers and an influential source of economic analysis for businesses, journalists, and the public, he often testifies before Congress and appears on CNBC, NPR, CNN, and *Meet the Press*. He is the author of *Financial Shock*.

Introduction

"One of my largest suppliers was just cut off by his bank...he says he won't be able [to] deliver at the end of the month." It was early October, 2008, and the financial markets were in chaos. The CEO of one of the nation's largest retailers was panicked; unless his vendor quickly found another bank, it wouldn't pay its employees and suppliers and would leave the retailer without an important shipment. The CEO was asking if I could help.

At that moment the implications of the financial shock that had begun only a few weeks earlier became clear. What it meant for Wall Street was already obvious: Hysteria had taken hold of the financial system as venerable institutions teetered and collapsed. But the implications for Main Street weren't so clear, until that phone call. Now I realized if retailers were having this kind of trouble, the entire economy was in a perilous state.

In the end the economy escaped collapse, but only barely. Wall Street's descent into chaos inflicted catastrophic economic damage, both in the United States and beyond. In January 2009, the apex of the Great Recession as well as the month President Obama was inaugurated, U.S. payrolls shrank by a stunning 820,000 jobs. The unemployment rate was rising by one-half percentage point each month, as CEOs in every industry and region of the country slashed payrolls. The bloodletting continued for another year, and when it was finished, an incredible 8.75 million jobs had been lost, by people in all walks of life. The unemployment rate was in double digits.

The financial carnage also cost millions their homes. Many Americans had bought houses with big mortgages as the housing bubble rapidly inflated in the mid-2000s. When house prices subsequently collapsed, millions of homeowners found they owed more than their homes were worth. For the typical underwater homeowner, "negative equity" amounted to almost $50,000. For many who had lost jobs, or even found themselves with a leaky roof to repair, foreclosure quickly followed. The crisis this provoked would ultimately displace more than 10 million households.

Those fortunate enough to keep their homes saw real-estate prices fall and their wealth shrink. A house is still most Americans' most important asset, and the typical U.S. home lost more than one-third of its pre-crash value. Stock portfolios were also hammered, as prices fell 50% at the worst of the selloff. Stocks partially recovered, but by 2012, the typical American nest egg was still only about as large, after inflation, as it had been in the mid-1990s. And wild swings in stock prices were making it hard to be sure of even that.

Resentment of the wealthy had also, understandably, intensified. Although the gap between the richest Americans and the rest had been widening for decades, prolonged joblessness made the pain of poverty more acute. And most trends suggested that the gulf would only widen. The Occupy Wall Street movement was the most dramatic expression of this frustration; it would not be the last.

The economy's turmoil reshaped lives, particularly among the young. Those who came of working age during the bust years struggled to find jobs and were often paid less than their predecessors. Twenty-first century 20-somethings couldn't think about spending, borrowing, investing, and risk-taking the way their parents' generation—the baby boomers—had. This was in part for the good; future American families would spend and borrow less aggressively and save more. But they would also be less inclined to seize opportunities or start the new ventures the economy would need to keep growing.

Young or old, in early 2012 we were still shell-shocked. Numerous surveys of consumer sentiment showed the same thing; although no longer terrified, Americans remained extraordinarily skittish. It took little to puncture our fragile confidence; $4 gasoline or a downgrade of the U.S. Treasury's AAA rating could cause consumers and businesses to pull back. Fearful that the economy would unravel again, we reacted quickly to bad news, spending or hiring more cautiously. The psychological weight of our recent economic trauma was the most significant impediment to a stronger economy.

And yet, although much remained to be nervous and frustrated about, impressive progress had been made righting the wrongs that got us into this mess. American businesses had dramatically reduced their cost structures to become more globally competitive than at any time in the previous 50 years. Although smaller firms weren't doing as well as large ones, businesses as a group had never been as profitable, nor their balance sheets as strong. Main Street had spruced itself up; increasingly the question was no longer of whether businesses could expand, but whether they were willing to do so—a big distinction.

Financial institutions, big and small, also found their bearings. Bank failures had abated, and the rest of the financial system had dramatically shored up its foundations. Banks' capital buffers against loan losses had never been as large. Although financial institutions weren't nearly as profitable as they had been before the shock—and were unlikely to be again, given stiffer capital requirements and regulatory oversight—they were solidly profitable. The credit spigot was slowly opening as banks worked through the regulatory and legal issues that remained from the disastrous lending they made during the housing frenzy.

Even households who had piled on debt in the boom times were digging out from under. Foreclosures remained a problem, although a gradually shrinking one, and households had successfully lightened their debt burdens. Some 100 million credit cards were cut up during the Great Recession. Households had defaulted and banks had written off their debts—but this, too, was economically therapeutic.

Homeowners who struggled to meet monthly mortgage payments experienced wrenching foreclosures but often ended up with lower monthly rental bills, leaving them more to spend or save.

The economy still faced a long climb but was well on its way to recovery. Job growth had resumed and was broadening across industries, occupations, and regions. The unemployment rate, although still painfully high, was receding. The pace of layoffs eased; businesses indeed found they might have cut too deeply during the recession. Hiring, which had been painfully weak, began to revive. With the housing crash over, house prices were stabilizing, and stock prices had had a remarkable run. The average American was still poorer than before, but the value of U.S. homes and stock portfolios was no longer being artificially pumped up by flippers and day-traders.

The economy's dramatic turn from free fall to growth was no accident. It wouldn't have happened as quickly, or at all, without the government's help. What policymakers did to stem the financial panic and combat the effects of the Great Recession remains intensely controversial but must ultimately be judged a success.

The vital first step was an emergency rescue of the financial system. The Federal Reserve was especially active, providing liquidity to all corners of the system. Financial institutions had all but stopped lending to each other, fearful of being dragged over the brink by failing counterparties. It was a reasonable fear. Lehman Brothers had collapsed after its creditors effectively cut it off from additional credit by demanding more collateral. The Fed flooded the financial system with cheap money, throwing lifelines not only to banks, but also to money-market funds, commercial paper issuers, broker-dealers, insurance companies, and investment banks.

The Fed's efforts were valiant but not sufficient. Congress needed to act as well, and after much hand-wringing it did, establishing a $700 billion bailout fund that became known, infamously, as the TARP, for Troubled Asset Relief Program. The TARP was voted down at first, but after stock traders furiously dumped shares in reaction, Congress was forced to quickly reverse itself. The TARP remained political poison for years—no member of Congress wanted to be known for bailing out the Wall Street institutions that were at the root of the crisis—but doing so had been essential. The TARP's real purpose, moreover, wasn't to save Wall Street, but Main Street. The retailer who asked me for help ultimately received his delivery only because the TARP saved the banks and the retailer's supplier secured a new line of credit. The bank bailout eventually turned a profit for the government, moreover. A few banks that had received TARP money weren't able to pay it back, but most did, with dividends.

But the financial panic wasn't fully subdued until the big banks were forced to recapitalize. Regulators demanded that banks figure out how much capital they needed in order to withstand losses on par with those they suffered in the 1930s. Then bankers had to go out and raise the necessary capital. This procedure, called *stress-testing*, seemed a gimmick to me until I heard the loud screaming from bank executives. Many of them had hired my firm and others to help with the stress-testing, and I was hearing their pain firsthand. Every banker thought his bank was well capitalized and complained that raising additional capital would only reduce the stakes of current shareholders. They were right about dilution, but the pain was well worth it. The extra capital, some of it from the TARP, immediately re-established confidence. Lending among the banks resumed, their stock prices rose, and the financial system quickly stabilized, although deep wounds remained.

Policymakers then turned their attention to the faltering economy. The Federal Reserve jettisoned its historically go-slow approach, slashing short-term interest rates to zero. The Fed also brought out monetary tools that had previously existed only in theory. Most notably the Fed purchased trillions of dollars in Treasury and government-backed mortgage securities—a procedure that readers of the financial press came to know well as *quantitative easing*, or QE for short. QE had its downsides, but it effectively lowered long-term interest rates. Within a short time, homebuyers with good jobs and high credit scores could obtain mortgages at record low rates. QE also lifted stock prices. The Fed had misjudged events leading up to the financial shock, but committed to avoiding the same mistakes afterward.

Away from Wall Street and the banks, the U.S. auto industry posed an especially vexing problem for Congress and for both the Bush and Obama administrations. Rising unemployment and shrinking credit had made it much harder for Americans to afford new cars, and vehicle sales had collapsed. Profits had suffered even more, as the automakers tried desperately to keep up sales volumes by offering aggressive discounts and easier financing terms. By early 2009, GM and Chrysler were careening toward bankruptcy. Worse, the turmoil in financial markets meant the crippled auto companies would not be able to keep their factories running during the months or years of restructuring that a bankruptcy would require. The alternative was liquidation. If Chrysler and GM closed down, hundreds of auto dealers and suppliers would follow. The list of potential casualties included Ford, the vast network of parts suppliers, and dealerships in every community in America. Millions of jobs were at stake, especially in the Midwest and South. Washington's auto bailout wasn't pretty, but it forestalled something much uglier, and was essential to the subsequent revival in U.S. manufacturing.

The most controversial but ultimately the most successful effort to end the recession was Washington's fiscal stimulus. The logic behind a stimulus is straightforward: With businesses and consumers hunkered down, government steps in by temporarily increasing spending and cutting taxes. The objective of an economic stimulus is to end recessions and jump-start recovery. It is not to provide a source of longer-term growth. Using a fiscal stimulus to combat a recession isn't novel; it has been part of the response to every recession since World War II, and the size of the stimulus was always tied to the severity of the recession. The amount of fiscal stimulus used to fight the Great

Recession was massive—equal to almost 10% of GDP—but that was appropriate given the downturn's depth.

Several rounds of fiscal stimulus were fired at the Great Recession. The first consisted of tax rebates, sent out near the end of the Bush administration. The largest and most controversial was the American Recovery and Reinvestment Act, passed soon after Obama took office. The Recovery Act included nearly $800 billion in stimulus over 4 years, roughly two-thirds temporary spending increases and the other third tax cuts. It worked. The act was passed in February 2009, the Great Recession ended in June, and job growth resumed a year later, in February 2010.

The stimulus was not a hit politically, however. Skepticism about its effectiveness was widespread, fueled in part by the Obama administration's blunder in marketing the program. Selling the Recovery Act to a suspicious Congress, the administration argued that it would keep the unemployment rate from rising above 8%. In fact, the unemployment rate was already above 8% when the administration made its claim; only nobody knew that. The economy had been shrinking so rapidly that the data couldn't keep up; policymakers were working from forecasts that severely underestimated how bad things actually were. It was a rookie mistake by the new president and his staff, but it handed the administration's opponents a political tool with which they proceeded, inappropriately but effectively, to undermine the merits of the stimulus.

Policymakers also focused on the disastrous housing market, rightly thinking that because housing was ground zero for the recession, nothing good would happen until housing hit bottom. A large number of policy steps had already been taken, dating back to the Bush administration, which temporarily eliminated the tax liability on mortgage debt forgiven in a short sale. The Obama administration acted much more aggressively, empowering government lenders Fannie Mae, Freddie Mac, and the Federal Housing Administration to fill the hole created by the collapse in private mortgage lending.

The FHA's response was especially forceful. When credit was shut off to nearly all borrowers during the financial shock, it remained available to mortgage borrowers because of the FHA. This was precisely what the agency's New Deal-era designers had in mind when they set it up in the 1930s. Without a steady flow of credit from the FHA, the housing market would have completely collapsed, taking the already reeling economy with it.

Government policy also succeeded in breaking a vicious deflationary psychology that had gripped the housing market. Tax credits for homebuyers that lasted only a few months gave buyers a compelling reason to act rather than wait for prices to fall further. The tax savings went a long way to compensating buyers for any additional price declines. Home sales gyrated as the credits were extended, withdrawn and then extended again, but the free fall in home sales and prices stopped.

Probably the least effective policy responses to the housing crash involved mortgage loan modifications and refinancing. Because foreclosure is costly to both homeowners and financial institutions, government planners hoped to persuade banks to change the terms of troubled mortgage loans, lowering either the interest rate or the principal owed, to keep homeowners in their homes. Loosening the rules on refinancing to let troubled homeowners lower their monthly payments also seemed promising. But these ideas worked better in theory than in practice. The Home Affordable Mortgage Program, introduced by President Obama in mid-2009, was designed to push both modifications and refinancing. The program helped but fell well short of expectations.

With housing no longer in free fall and the economy in recovery, policymakers turned to the daunting task of financial regulatory reform. The financial system's catastrophic failure demanded a reworking of its legal and regulatory plumbing. Dodd-Frank, the reform legislation that became law in summer 2010, after a torturous trip through Congress, made a vast number of changes to the financial system. Some did not initially seem to work well, but overall the law seemed to ensure that future financial crises would be less cataclysmic than those of the recent past.

A key to this optimism was Dodd-Frank's clearly defined process for dealing with too-big-to-fail financial institutions. Regulators had been confused about how to handle the institutions that failed in 2008; their confusion allowed the initial financial shock to spread. Dodd-Frank didn't solve the too-big-to fail problem—there will always be institutions whose failure would rock the system—but the law made it more likely that such failures would be manageable. Requiring big institutions to formulate "living wills"—guiding regulators as they unwind the firms' operations if they fail—also seemed likely to help.

Further easing the too-big-to-fail risk, Dodd-Frank institutionalized the bank stress tests that had so successfully ended the financial turmoil. The largest and most important financial institutions would have to simulate adverse economic scenarios and study the effect on their balance sheets and income statements, rigorously and consistently. In 2012, stress tests were employed to assess the threat of a severe European debt crisis.

Dodd-Frank's most controversial provision was the establishment of the Consumer Financial Protection Bureau. Although critics were justified in worrying about the added regulatory burden this created, the CFPB rightly put financial consumers' interests front and center. The CFPB was to ensure that consumers were offered financial products appropriate to their needs, and that they had enough information to adequately evaluate these products. Given the dizzying complexity of financial services and the woeful state of consumer financial literacy—many homebuyers had a hard time understanding adjustable rate mortgages—the CFPB was sorely needed.

Dodd-Frank had its blemishes. A rule named for former Federal Reserve Chairman Paul Volcker, which required large banks to split off trading for their own profit from trading on customers' behalf, proved difficult to implement. Dodd-Frank correctly required that derivatives trading be done on exchanges—not knowing who was doing the trading in what Warren Buffet so colorfully called "weapons of mass destruction" created a tangled mess during the financial chaos in 2008—but the law went too far. Rules to require that issuers of mortgage securities hold some of the risk in their securities also seemed unworkable, despite their laudable intent.

Perhaps the most serious downside to Dodd-Frank was the uncertainty it created. Already stressed, the financial system was forced to make complex changes quickly, amid a blizzard of other regulatory and legal issues. Nervous and confused, bankers didn't know how much capital they would need, nor the cost of that capital, and were unsure of their legal liabilities and regulatory costs. Bankers hunkered down in response, lending sparsely and conservatively. Dodd-Frank intended to ensure that credit would flow less recklessly than it did during the housing bubble; but the law's effect, at least at first, was to slow credit from flowing freely enough.

While the financial system was grappling with Dodd-Frank, non-financial businesses were growing anxious about other big changes emanating from Washington. In early 2010 the Obama administration passed a massive overhaul of the healthcare system. Its main intent was to provide health insurance to the millions of uninsured Americans. But although many of the law's provisions wouldn't come into effect for years, small businesses struggled to understand what it meant for them. New environmental and labor regulations, and tougher enforcement of those already on the books, also contributed to business angst. In normal times all this might have been seen as just a cost of doing business, not a major problem—but these weren't normal times. Policy uncertainty cast a pall over the economy. Skittish businesses grew more cautious, slowing down investment and hiring.

People were also unnerved by the government's ballooning budget deficits. The nation's debt, as a proportion of GDP, doubled in only 5 years to its highest point since just after World War II. The federal government had significant fiscal problems even before the

Great Recession; now tax revenues plunged with falling employment and corporate profits, and government spending surged along with the unemployment rate. The tab for the government's efforts to save the economy from calamity came on top of all that. To bail out Wall Street, the auto industry and housing, provide enough capital to keep Fannie and Freddie afloat, and then launch successive fiscal stimulus efforts, cost $1.8 trillion—more than the wars in Iraq and Afghanistan combined (see Table I.1).

Table I.1 Federal Government Response to the Financial Crisis (*Billions $*)

	Originally Committed	Ultimate Cost
Total	**12,430**	**1,804**
Federal Reserve	**6,699**	**15**
Term auction credit	900	0
Other loans	Unlimited	3
Primary credit	Unlimited	0
Secondary credit	Unlimited	0
Seasonal credit	Unlimited	0
Primary Dealer Credit Facility (expired 2/1/2010)	Unlimited	0
Asset-Backed Commercial Paper Money Market Mutual Fund	Unlimited	0
AIG	26	2
AIG (for SPVs)	9	0
AIG (for ALICO, AIA)	26	1
Rescue of Bear Stearns (Maiden Lane)°°	27	4
AIG-RMBS purchase program (Maiden Lane II)°°	23	1
AIG-CDO purchase program (Maiden Lane III)°°	30	4
Term Securities Lending Facility (expired 2/1/2010)	200	0

	Originally Committed	Ultimate Cost
Commercial Paper Funding Facility°° (expired 2/1/2010)	1,800	0
TALF	1,000	0
Money Market Investor Funding Facility (expired 10/30/2009)	540	0
Currency swap lines (expired 2/1/2010)	Unlimited	0
Purchase of GSE debt and MBS (3/31/2010)	1,425	0
Guarantee of Citigroup assets (terminated 12/23/2009)	286	0
Guarantee of Bank of America assets (terminated)	108	0
Purchase of long-term Treasuries	300	0
Treasury	**1,160**	**255**
TARP	700	57
Fed supplementary financing account	560	0
Fannie Mae and Freddie Mac	Unlimited	198
FDIC	**2,913**	**75**
Guarantee of U.S. banks' debt°	1,400	4
Guarantee of Citigroup debt	10	0
Guarantee of Bank of America debt	3	0
Transaction deposit accounts	500	0
Public-Private Investment Fund Guarantee	1,000	0
Bank resolutions	Unlimited	71
Federal Housing Administration	**100**	**26**
Refinancing of mortgages, Hope for Homeowners	100	0
Expanded Mortgage Lending	Unlimited	26
Congress	**1,458**	**1,433**
Economic Stimulus Act of 2008	170	170

	Originally Committed	Ultimate Cost
American Recovery and Reinvestment Act of 2009***	808	783
Cash for Clunkers	3	3
Worker, Homeownership, and Business Act of 2009	91	91
Education, Jobs, and Medicaid Assistant Act of 2010	26	26
Hire Act (Job Tax Credit)	17	17
Tax Relief, Unemployment Insurance Reauthorization, and Job Creation Act of 2010	189	189
Temporary Payroll Tax Cut Continuation Act of 2011	29	29
Middle Class Tax Relief and Job Creation Act of 2012	125	125

*Includes foreign denominated debt

**Net portfolio holdings

***Excludes AMT patch

Sources: Federal Reserve, Treasury, FDIC, FHA, Moody's Analytics

Growing budget deficits set off alarm bells about the federal government's role in the economy. By 2010, federal spending accounted for more than one-fourth of U.S. GDP, and an increasing number of Americans felt the government was out of control. Washington appeared to be forcing its way into nearly every aspect of life; becoming a shareholder in the nation's largest banks, insurers, and auto companies, and making most new housing and small-business loans. On top of all that were looming mandates for health insurance and security pat-downs at airports. For many it was too much.

Some claimed all this was turning America into Europe, and more derisively into France, where government regulation and safety nets are wider and deeper. It wasn't the American way, critics argued, and Europe's debt crisis seemed to underscore the point. Some opponents of the Obama administration's initiatives insisted that failure was a necessary part of capitalism. Businesses and individuals who had made mistakes should pay a price—typically bankruptcy or fore-closure—or they would have little incentive to avoid those same mis-takes in the future.

Others saw the government's actions as unfair. Why were execu-tives at Bank of America or Goldman Sachs—who had arguably been to blame for the financial shock—more worthy of help than underwa-ter homeowners? Why should taxpayers come to the aid of a delin-quent homeowner who had borrowed and spent too much in the boom, but not the more prudent neighbor who also struggled with mortgage payments? Why should GM or Chrysler receive handouts when hundreds of thousands of small businesses were also flounder-ing? Questions like these heated the crucibles in which the Tea Party and Occupy Wall Street movements were forged.

Still others accused the government of crony capitalism, favoring some groups over others for political reasons. The Bush administra-tion was chastised for helping, among others, Goldman Sachs, where Treasury Secretary Hank Paulson had been CEO. The Obama admin-istration was hammered over the GM and Chrysler workouts, which seemed to favor labor unions over bondholders. The fiscal stimulus bill was roundly criticized for funding costly but marginal infrastruc-ture projects, such as a barely used regional airport in the middle of Pennsylvania, and giving energy tax breaks to shaky businesses such as solar-panel manufacturer Solyndra.

Concerns about big budget deficits and big government were valid but missed the point. Although policymakers clearly made mistakes, they had no choice but to step into the breach created by a collapsing financial system and rapidly sinking economy. Debate over the gov-ernment's appropriate role in the economy is as old as the nation, but few question the need for government to respond in a crisis. Govern-ment must act for us collectively when we are unable or too scared to act on our own. What qualifies as a crisis is a reasonable question, but most fair-minded observers would include in that category the closest brush with a full-blown depression since the 1930s.

Although the policy response to the Great Recession was costly, taxpayers would have been forced to ante up much more if policymakers had not acted so aggressively. In a new depression, tax revenues would have plunged along with employment, corporate profits, stock prices, housing values, and retail sales. The government's safety net would have been stretched thin as vast numbers of American households sought help. The government's involvement in the economy would have grown even more than it has, the opposite of what critics said they wanted.

Much of the criticism was fueled by popular ignorance of the many ways the U.S. government has backstopped the economy for decades. Consider the 30-year, fixed-rate mortgage, a staple of the housing market that most homebuyers take for granted. It exists largely because the federal government began assuring mortgage investors as far back as the 1930s that it would step in in a crisis. Without such assurance, lenders could not offer 30-year fixed-rate mortgages at affordable rates. Some housing experts argue, plausibly, that the government undercharged private lenders for this guarantee; others say the government should never have provided it in the first place. But for millions of American homeowners, the fixed-rate mortgage is the preferred way to finance a home, freeing families from worry about interest rates and credit availability. The 30-year mortgage was invented to fix what had been a big problem during the Great Depression, and it succeeded.

Entrepreneurship and risk-taking, key foundations of economic growth, also depend on government being there in a crisis. Who would start a business, particularly one based on a new idea or technology, if he feared being caught in a sudden economic downturn? Without an adequate sense of economic security, caution can inhibit capitalism. Of course there is a line between encouraging prudent risk-taking and igniting counterproductive speculation, and at times the government has crossed it—but not often enough to believe that reasonably skilled policymakers can't tell the difference.

At the same time, the battle over the government's appropriate role in our economy is therapeutic and necessary. Founding fathers Alexander Hamilton and Thomas Jefferson debated how much power the federal government should have over the nation's finances. Should the federal government assume the states' war debt after the American Revolution? And if so, what sort of taxing authority was appropriate to repay it? The argument was settled in a historic bargain: The states joined in a stronger fiscal union, as Hamilton wanted, while the nation's capital was placed near Jefferson's home state of Virginia. Was this cronyism? A modern version of this debate played out in 2012 Europe over the fate of the euro zone.

Years of battle over the American government's role in the Great Depression of the 1930s produced the New Deal. The Roosevelt administration's policy ideas, which formed the basis of our modern economic safety net, included unemployment insurance, food stamps, the FHA, and Social Security, arguably the government's most successful and popular initiative ever. Such programs would not be nearly as effective if they had not been tested against the objections of their opponents. Indeed, other Roosevelt administration initiatives, such as price-fixing and production limits in a range of industries, failed those tests and disappeared before they could cause lasting harm.

The fierce debates sparked by the Great Recession and its aftermath have also made policy better. Political acrimony during the Treasury's debt ceiling in summer 2011 was unpleasant to watch, and likely cost the United States its top credit rating, but the tussle ended up helping create the political dynamics necessary to address long-term fiscal challenges. Washington's mud-wrestling produced a consensus among Democrats and Republicans that the deficit should shrink by some $4 trillion over the next decade. Lawmakers also agreed to cut spending by more than $2 trillion to achieve this. Although even more fiscal discipline would be needed to make the government's finances sustainable over the long term, even skeptics of the government suggested it was likely to happen.

At this point, a bit of personal history might help explain my perspective. I'm an economist by training, but also an entrepreneur and manager. During the recession of the early 1990s, I co-founded an economic consulting company along with my brother, Karl, and my best friend, Paul Getman. The firm grew into a good-sized small business, employing more than 100 when we sold it to the Moody's Corporation. That was in November, 2005—the peak of the housing bubble. I've experienced the business from many angles—as a startup, as a small business, and now as part of a multinational corporation. Moody's operates in every corner of the globe. My clients include companies in nearly every industry as well as federal, state, and local government. I've had the opportunity to observe the economy through many different prisms.

I'm not part of the Moody's rating agency, but a separate subsidiary called Moody's Analytics that provides research, tools, software, and data to financial institutions across the globe. We produce stress-test models used by European banks, software that helps Chinese banks underwrite business loans, and analytics and data used by the FDIC and Federal Reserve to oversee American financial institutions. I have no direct input into the ratings process and no inside information on the U.S. credit rating; although I do listen carefully to what the analysts at the rating agency say (and hope they listen to me occasionally as well). The opinions expressed in this book are my own and not necessarily those of my employer, Moody's Corporation.

I also played a small role in government policymaking during this tumultuous period. I helped the Obama team evaluate the impact of various fiscal stimulus proposals before the administration took office, and did the same for various stimulus and housing policies during Obama's first term. I advised Congress on the auto bailout, housing policies, and fiscal stimulus. And I have been involved in bank stress-testing. My firm has not been paid for the policy work; I view it as an important public service, and payment could undermine our perceived if not our actual objectivity. Some may say I benefited from the high-profile nature of my policy work, but this cuts both ways—my role has also drawn significant criticism. In the same spirit, I plan to give any royalties from this book to my son's 501(c)3 "Students Helping Students," whose mission is to recycle books and furnishings from donor schools to needy schools.

This account of recent history takes an optimistic view of our economic future. Indeed, I believe the U.S. outlook has never been brighter. We have experienced a painful episode, and many of us are still paying for the egregious mistakes made during the housing bubble, but a great deal has been done to repair and restore our economy. Much work remains, and our progress could easily be derailed; but if so it will not be because our economy is flawed, but because we have lost faith in ourselves. My optimism may not represent the consensus view, but if our nation's history provides any guide, we optimists will ultimately be proven right.

1

Financial Shock to Financial Panic

"What does this mean?" asked Moody's CEO. "And how should we respond to it?" It was Sunday afternoon, September 7, 2008, and the U.S. Treasury had just nationalized Fannie Mae and Freddie Mac, the twin behemoths of U.S. housing finance. On a hastily scheduled call, the CEO was asking Moody's executives to consider how this previously unimaginable event might affect their research and ratings. Although Moody's was on the front line of the financial system, CEOs across America would soon be asking their executives these same questions.

Even before that fateful weekend, Wall Street had been experiencing a bear market—the S&P 500 stock index was more than 20% beneath the all-time high it had achieved the previous year. Investors were nervous about falling house prices, rising mortgage defaults, and big losses at financial institutions. Housing had gone from boom to bust and the broader economy was struggling, with unemployment on the rise.

At the heart of the problem was a colossal failure of the vaunted U.S. financial system. Trillions of dollars had poured into the United States from emerging economies flush with trade surpluses. Fearful of deflation after the 2000 technology bust, central banks such as the Federal Reserve added to the flood by pushing interest rates to record lows. Cash was everywhere, and financial institutions weren't sure what to do with it all.

Wall Street came up with an answer: securities backed by residential mortgages, credit cards, auto loans, and more. But the market

1

for securitized loans was deeply flawed. Although securitization had been around for decades, it had been mainly limited to top-quality loans, to borrowers who were carefully screened for income and payment history. Attempts to securitize loans to lesser-quality borrowers had failed, but these were small scale experiments, so the financial damage was limited. Now with house prices booming, lenders and investment banks were securitizing trillions of dollars in loans to borrowers of all types, even to those with poor credit histories and little or no income. Securitization empowered increasingly risky lending, prompting lenders to invent ever-more exotic types of mortgages with confusing names such as "subprime," "alt-A," and "option-ARMs."

The government regulators and credit agencies charged with policing the securitization process seemed to be asleep. At the Federal Reserve, the nation's principal financial regulator, officials believed investors' own self-interest would ensure the process worked. The rating agencies used information from the investment banks to evaluate their securities and applied models that failed to account for their complexity.

As sketchy borrowers stopped paying on their loans, the securities they backed fell in value, putting severe pressure on the financial institutions that owned them. The problem began to surface early in 2007 when HSBC, one of the world's largest banks and a major subprime mortgage lender, reported shocking losses. Other lenders soon produced their own dismal reports. That summer Bear Stearns, a blue-chip investment house, had to shore up some hedge funds that had bet wrong on mortgage-backed securities. By spring 2008, Bear's own capital was largely depleted and, and as other banks abandoned it, the firm collapsed.

At this point, Wall Street's troubles were newsworthy but not particularly catastrophic. The U.S. financial system had been through worse, in the form of failing banks, slumping markets and even economic recessions. The selloff through the summer of 2008 was orderly. Even Bear Stearns' collapse, while surprising, seemed manageable; the U.S. Treasury and Federal Reserve had stepped in and successfully sold the investment firm's assets to the banking giant JPMorgan Chase. Something similar had occurred a decade earlier when regulators engineered an orderly break-up of hedge fund Long Term Capital Management. Bear Stearns vanished, leaving not much more than a ripple.

But the takeover of Fannie Mae and Freddie Mac set off a tsunami that, within a few days, hit the next weakest institution on Wall Street, investment house Lehman Brothers. Although Lehman's failure is often blamed for starting the financial panic, it probably had its genesis the previous week, with the forced takeover of Fannie and Freddie. As shareholders in the two mortgage finance firms were all but wiped out, all investors in financial institutions were put on notice; no institution was too big to fail. And when the government refused to protect Lehman's creditors as it had Fannie's and Freddie's, investors' worst fears were realized.

The result was financial panic. Stock prices cratered, bond markets and money markets froze, and a string of institutions previously seen as rock-solid evaporated over the next few weeks. Wachovia, Washington Mutual, Countrywide Mortgage, and Merrill Lynch were among the fallen.

The decision not to save Fannie and Freddie set off a chain of events that ultimately gave policymakers no choice but to bail out the entire financial system. Only when the government went all-in, acquiring stakes and guaranteeing the debt and deposits of the biggest U.S. financial institutions, did the system's free fall stop. Without such action the system would have collapsed and taken the economy with it. As it was, the financial system was brought to its knees and the U.S. economy was enveloped in what came to be known as the Great Recession—the sharpest economic contraction since the Great Depression of the 1930s.

Tidal Wave

A financial system exists to connect savers with borrowers, prudently investing a nation's capital for the future. For decades, the U.S. system did this better than any in the world, efficiently putting the savings of American households to its best uses, producing benefits for savers, borrowers, and the broader economy.

The system had had its ups and downs. Pressed by competition and unshackled by regulators, bankers had tended to let their guard down in good times, making loans that even under reasonable assumptions were unlikely to be repaid. For a while, freely flowing credit masked the mistakes made by borrowers. But when defaults mounted, bankers pulled back, sometimes suddenly and all at once, triggering financial crises and recessions. Yet most times, the pain was short-lived and manageable.

Not so in the 2000s. For one thing, the scale of the financial system had grown. Along with the savings of American households, U.S.-based banks now managed a growing mountain of cash for savers in China, India, Brazil, and other developing economies. These nations were earning hundreds of billions of dollars per year in trade, as U.S. consumers snapped up the lower-priced apparel, furniture, toys, consumer electronics, and other goods they made.

Adding to the emerging world's cash hoard was the surge in global demand for energy, agriculture, and other commodities. Oil, which sold for $20 per barrel in 2000, surged to a record high of $120 per barrel by summer 2008. Commodity producers in the Middle East, South America, and Asia received a windfall, most of it in U.S. dollars.

All these dollars needed to be invested. At first, cautious emerging-world investors bought U.S. Treasury bonds, the safest of all investments. High returns weren't as important as safety for these investors. Foreign holdings of Treasury bonds increased more than three-fold in the 2000s to $3 trillion, about half of all publicly held

U.S. bonds. By the end of the decade, China alone owned nearly $1 trillion in Treasuries (see Figure 1.1).

Foreign Investors Flock to the Safety of Treasuries

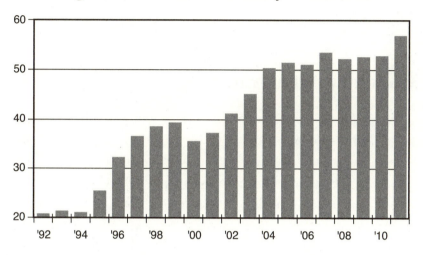

Figure 1.1 Share of publicly traded Treasury debt owned by foreigners, %.

Source: U.S. Treasury Department

Yet as their Treasury holdings mounted, global investors grew more interested in achieving higher returns. They had little appetite for stocks, remembering the technology bust a few years earlier, when stock prices had fallen nearly in half. Real assets, such as businesses or office buildings, offered an alternative, but these investments required expertise that non-U.S. investors didn't possess, and the political barriers were formidable. U.S. lawmakers had no problem selling the Chinese a Treasury bond but were queasy about allowing foreign ownership of large U.S. companies.

For overseas investors, the next best thing appeared to be bonds backed by mortgages. These seemed reasonably safe: U.S. house prices had not fallen since the 1930s Great Depression, and delinquency rates on mortgages were consistently low, even during recessions. Foreclosures were rare. Global investors also took comfort in the U.S. government's participation in the housing market, directly through the FHA and implicitly through Fannie Mae and Freddie

Mac. From U.S. Treasury bonds, it wasn't much of a leap to investing in mortgage bonds issued and backed by Fannie and Freddie, and from there it seemed natural to move into privately issued securities backed by U.S. homeowners.

Monetary Accelerator

Helping cash pour into the financial system were global central bankers, who were pressing hard on the monetary accelerator. None pressed harder than Alan Greenspan, Chairman of the U.S. Federal Reserve. The Fed had grown nervous about the U.S. economy's prospects after the 9/11 terrorist attacks and the tech bust. The central bank's concerns grew as the economy flirted with deflation after the 2001 recession. The Fed knew how to fight off excessive inflation, but it had fewer options and little experience handling the economic dislocations that occur when prices fall too much. The central bank began by sharply cutting its key interest rate from above 6% to 1%, a level not seen since the late 1950s (see Figure 1.2).

The Fed Goes on High Alert

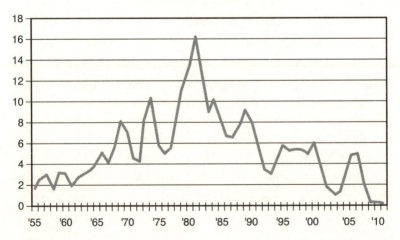

Figure 1.2 Federal funds rate, %.

Source: Federal Reserve Board

Lower interest rates were like a shot of adrenalin for the housing market; as mortgages became cheaper, buyers could afford more and larger homes. This was by design; Greenspan hoped housing would drive the economy out of its funk and diffuse the deflation threat. He publicly urged homeowners to take out adjustable-rate mortgages, suggesting they would be cheaper in the long run than more popular fixed-rate loans.[1] Many took his advice, and the use of ARMs took off, even among borrowers with checkered credit histories and limited means—the soon-to-be-infamous subprime market.

Greenspan accomplished his goal; home sales, housing construction, and house prices all rose. In the 4 years following 9/11, national house prices surged nearly 50%. The effect was profound; homeowners felt much wealthier and acted like it, borrowing aggressively against their homes and spending the proceeds. Homeowners extracted a stunning $3.1 trillion through home equity loans and cash-out refinancings between 2002 and 2006.[2] The economy's growth accelerated and the deflation threat faded away.

But the boom became a bubble. Years of strong price gains attracted speculators looking to flip homes for quick profits. As long as prices were rising, the house flippers could make big bucks using borrowed money, and their activities helped drive prices even higher, particularly in Arizona, California, Florida, and Nevada. Builders responded to what looked like booming demand by putting up more new homes. By 2006, both housing construction and house prices were exceeding all records (see Figure 1.3).

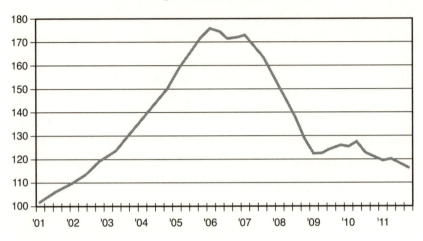

Figure 1.3 Case Shiller repeat-sales house price index: 2000Q4=100.

Source: Fiserv Case Shiller

Broken Pipes

The tidal wave of cash coming from the emerging world and from nervous central bankers overwhelmed the financial system. Wall Street's preferred channel for funneling all this liquidity—the securitization market—had worked in the pre-boom era, but couldn't scale up easily to handle the flood.

Securitization involves combining lots of loans and using the principal and interest payments to back bonds, which are then sold to investors. The first security backed by residential mortgage loans was issued in 1970 by Ginnie Mae, a federal government creation. In its infancy, securitization had been a straightforward business, handling only high-quality loans or those guaranteed by the federal government. Principal and interest payments were passed directly through to investors. There were no frills and few moving parts.

The benefit of securitization is similarly straightforward; it lets capital flow where it's needed. For borrowers this means cheaper loans because more institutions are providing them; for investors it means the ability to diversify their portfolios. And regulators liked the idea of letting financial institutions offload some risk to other investors.

Yet as we learned, securitization has its problems. Because financial institutions that originated loans could sell them off quickly to Wall Street, they suffered little if the loans went bad and therefore had less incentive to be sure they were sound. This problem became evident in the late 1990s, in the market for securitized mobile-home loans. Banks made hundreds of thousands of such loans to lower-income households who were ill-prepared to repay them. The resulting defaults sank the manufactured housing market.

Securitization also turned out to be susceptible to a kind of bank run, similar to those that had ravaged the economy in the early 1930s. In those years, when depositors thought a bank was in trouble, they would rush to withdraw funds all at once, causing the failure they feared. Investors in securitized loans could panic as well, it turned out, causing cash to stop flowing suddenly. The credit-card securitization market was hit by this kind of panic briefly during the Asian crisis in the late 1990s.

But the lessons of the mobile-home and credit-card securitization markets were quickly forgotten in the boom of the mid-2000s. Wall Street bundled trillions in residential mortgage loans and sold them to global investors in structures that grew increasingly complex and opaque (see Figure 1.4). The proceeds flowed back into housing in a flood of new mortgages offered to increasingly risky borrowers. At the peak of the lending frenzy in 2006, approximately one-half of all new mortgages required no down payments, little documentation of employment or income, and only a cursory building appraisal.

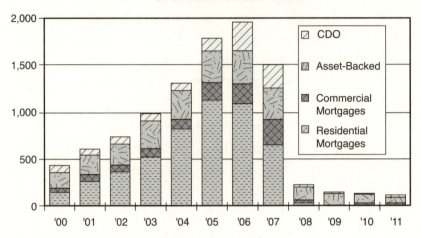

Figure 1.4 Issuance of securitized instruments, bil $.

Source: Moody's Investor Service

Regulatory Failure

All this should have set off alarms among the nation's financial watchdogs. Some regulators were clearly uncomfortable, particularly those at the Federal Deposit Insurance Corporation.[3] But few took action to rein in the runaway lending.

The silence was most deafening at the principal regulator of the financial system, the Federal Reserve. Fed officials believed in letting the market police itself; investors would make sure the bonds they bought were sound, or at least priced appropriately. If some home-owners were liable to default, their loans would carry higher interest rates, compensating investors for the added risk. The Fed, beginning with Chairman Greenspan, was philosophically predisposed to believe that markets worked efficiently if left alone; there was no need for heavy-handed oversight.

After the crisis, some argued that regulators lacked the legal authority to intervene more aggressively in the mortgage market; this is untrue. Congress had given the Fed authority to act against unfair or deceptive mortgage lending as far back as the early 1990s.[4] But regulators did not begin to use this power until late 2006, too late to stop the housing bubble from imperiling the economy.[5]

Regulators were hampered to some extent by the complexity of their own system—an alphabet soup of agencies with partial and overlapping responsibilities. In addition to the Fed and FDIC, these included the OCC, the OTS, and the NCUA. The Federal Trade Commission, Securities and Exchange Commission, and FHFA also had a say.[6] With so many voices, it was hard to reach consensus on any action that would cut across all financial institutions. Many financial institutions, and arguably the ones that did the most egregious lending, were the most lightly regulated. These were finance companies with names like New Century Financial, Ameriquest, and Novastar.

That the credit rating agencies weren't on high alert over mortgage-backed securities was also in a sense a regulatory failure. The agencies had significant power over bond markets because of capital and liquidity standards that required banks to use ratings in their risk management. Wall Street banks needed ratings to sell any bonds, and particularly mortgage-backed securities. Few investors were equipped to evaluate these extraordinarily complex debt instruments; gathering the data needed to understand their component parts and untangle their structures would have been an overwhelming task.

The agencies issued tens of thousands of ratings on mortgage-related securities during the housing boom, and in hindsight it's clear that many of those ratings were too positive. In many cases, agencies began downgrading their opinions not long after they were issued; it had quickly become clear that the securities were much riskier than their original ratings implied.

Several types of errors skewed the agencies' opinions, starting with the quality of the underlying data they were given to evaluate. Rating agencies typically assume the information they receive from issuers is correct, and historically it mostly has been. So when the agencies received data from mortgage lenders—about homebuyers' debt levels, income, purchase prices, and so on—the agencies took it as true. The agencies made no secret of this; they didn't consider it their responsibility to verify such data, and thus couldn't tell when homebuyers were stretching the facts or lying outright. As a result, ratings on mortgage securities worth trillions of dollars were based on falsified data.

The rating agencies missed the mark badly enough on many mortgage securities to stoke some long-smoldering criticism of their basic business model. For years critics had said the agencies were subject to a conflict of interest, because they are paid by people who issue bonds (as opposed to the investors who buy them). The agencies thus allegedly have an incentive to produce favorable opinions, regardless of their accuracy. The higher the rating, the higher the price issuers can obtain for their securities. Some critics charged that bond issuers routinely shop for good ratings, steering business to the agency offering the sunniest opinion.

There is little evidence for this. Ratings are based on statistical models, which constrains analysts' ability to rate bonds for spurious reasons. Still, because issuers pay the agencies to rate their securities, there is at least an appearance of a conflict.

Financial Shock

The foundation of a systemic financial crisis was in place by early 2007. The securitization frenzy had been in full swing for several years, pumping out trillions of dollars in debt backed by increasingly shaky mortgages. Excessive lending was fueling both homebuilding and buying, pushing prices to levels that made single-family housing unaffordable to more and more families. The market was increasingly dominated by speculators.

A type of euphoria had taken hold. After several decades of almost continual economic growth, punctuated by only brief and shallow recessions, many believed the business cycle had been tamed. Globalization, sophisticated financial markets, and expertly managed monetary policy meant any financial crises and recessions would be mild and short-lived. Some dubbed this new era the Great Moderation.

Such thinking empowered more risk-taking, not just in the mortgage and housing markets but throughout the financial system. Credit spreads—the difference between interest rates on riskier bonds and on risk-free Treasury securities—narrowed dramatically as investors bought risky assets with increasing abandon. Representative of this was the extraordinarily thin 2.5 percentage-point gap between the interest rate on lower rated or "junk" corporate bonds and that on 10-year Treasuries (see Figure 1.5). In normal times, this spread would be closer to 5 percentage points. During the financial panic it was more than 20 percentage points.

Investors Were Euphoric Before the Panic

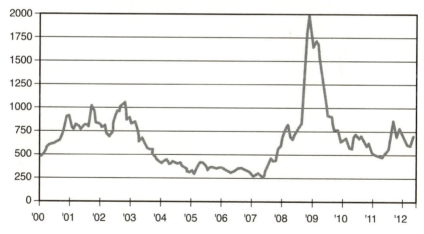

Figure 1.5 High-yield corporate bond spread to 10-year Treasuries, basis points.

Sources: Federal Reserve, Bloomberg, Moody's Analytics

The euphoria held the seeds of its own destruction. Investors had become overextended in every direction, and increasingly confused by the dizzying complexity of the things they were blindly investing in. Securities were broken into pieces or *tranches*, each holding a different amount of risk. Tranches of different securities were packaged together to form *collateralized debt obligations*, and insurance policies known as *credit default swaps* were written to pay off in case these securities defaulted. CDOs made up of CDSs were becoming popular.

The financial system had become so opaque that more sophisticated investors began to take advantage of those who couldn't keep up, selling securities with the expectation that their prices would fall. Some investors even bought the riskiest tranches of securities simply to make sure the rest could be sold and then bet big that the securities would fall apart. This Alice-in-Wonderland strategy reaped enormous profits, as the money lost on the riskiest tranches was more than made up by bets against the rest.[7]

The first clear cracks in the financial system appeared in early 2007, as mortgage lenders began reporting mounting delinquencies and defaults. In early March, global banking behemoth HSBC warned that it faced large losses on mortgage investments. HSBC had purchased subprime lender Household Finance not long before, hoping to cash in on the U.S. housing boom. Instead, HSBC became the first big victim.[8] Smaller finance companies were also reporting dismal earnings, driven by souring mortgage loans, but HSBC was the first big firm to acknowledge a problem.[9] Subprime mortgage lending became a dirty word on Wall Street.

By summer, the blue-chip investment house Bear Stearns was also in trouble. Bear was a big player in the mortgage world, originating loans, securitizing them, and selling them to investors, or to itself through hedge funds it controlled. Two of Bear's funds had run into trouble as the value of their mortgage securities began to fall. Bear put additional money into the funds to shore them up and secured loans from other banks collateralized by the funds' assets, but it all came undone in just a few weeks as house prices and the value of mortgage securities continued to plunge.

Bear's problems began to threaten the wider financial system. Spreads began to widen between Libor—the London Interbank Offered Rate, which large banks pay when they loan each other money—and Treasury yields (see Figure 1.6). This signaled mounting angst in the financial system. Banks were even charging their biggest peers more for loans, out of fear they wouldn't be repaid. Sensing trouble, the Federal Reserve finally began to cut its benchmark interest rate in August but did so too slowly and too late.[10]

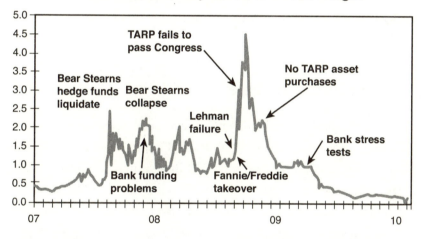

Bear Stearns Collapse Raises Investor Angst

Figure 1.6 Difference between three-month Libor and Treasury bill yields.

Source: Federal Reserve Board

Bear Stearns was forced to sell itself at a fire-sale price in March 2008. By then, no one was willing to lend it money, and with cash running out, the firm turned to the Federal Reserve for help. But Bear received less help than it had hoped for. Rather than bailing it out, the Fed arranged a sale of the firm, offering JPMorgan Chase an attractive loan to sweeten the deal. It was a classic response by the central bank: Instead of allowing a large financial firm to collapse in a disorderly bankruptcy that could disrupt the system, the government stepped in. Bear was not the first big Wall Street firm to be deemed too big to fail: hedge fund Long-Term Capital Management had received similar treatment during the Asian crisis in 1998. So had Citigroup when it faced trouble over bum commercial real estate deals in the early 1990s. Bear shareholders took a big hit, but the company's creditors were made whole.

The government's intervention helped, at least for a while. The Fed grew more aggressive, lowering interest rates and offering financial institutions cheap loans to try to settle the financial system. The Libor-Treasury spread narrowed, signaling the financial crisis had eased. The Bush administration offered a fiscal stimulus in the form of a sizable tax rebate. The housing market continued to deflate, but the economy seemed to stabilize. It was only a brief respite.

Fannie and Freddie

By 2008, markets were growing concerned about the government-sponsored housing-finance institutions Fannie Mae and Freddie Mac, whose financial health appeared increasingly tenuous. Fannie and Freddie weren't to blame for the U.S. housing bubble, although the two firms had made many mistakes over the decades. But their takeover in summer 2008 triggered a worldwide financial panic.

Fannie and Freddie were actually minor players in the crazed lending of the 2000s, which was dominated by the private sector. Between 2004 and 2007 during the height of most crazed mortgage lending, private lenders originated three-quarters of all subprime and alt-A mortgage loans (see Figure 1.7).[11] The rest came from government agencies, including Fannie, Freddie, and the Federal Housing Authority.

Private Mortgage Lenders Inflated the Bubble

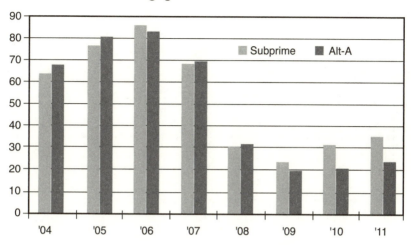

Figure 1.7 Share of mortgage originations by nongovernment lenders, %.

Sources: Equifax, Moody's Analytics

In 2006, the dollar amount of those private subprime and alt-A loans had reached a jaw-dropping $600 billion—about as much as all Americans collectively owe on bank credit cards. By contrast, government lenders made more than $100 billion in subprime and alt-A loans in 2006. Even in 2007, when the housing market was starting to crack, private lenders still originated more than $300 billion in subprime and alt-A mortgages.

This had the effect of shrinking the share of total residential mortgage debt insured or owned by Fannie Mae and Freddie Mac. At the start of 2002, the two agencies issued or guaranteed almost 54% of all mortgage debt. By summer 2006, their share had fallen to 40% (see Figure 1.8). That shrinking market share undercuts arguments that the agencies had inflated the housing bubble. In fact, it shows the opposite: The bubble was diminishing Fannie's and Freddie's position in the housing market.

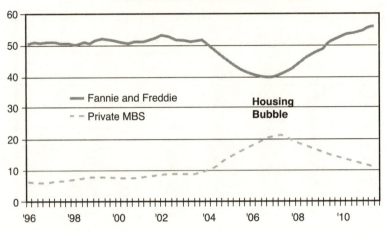

Figure 1.8 Share of mortgage debt, %.

Sources: Federal Reserve Board Flow of Funds, Moody's Analytics

Fannie and Freddie weren't making prescient strategic decisions to pull back on mortgage lending; their government regulator had forced them to rein in growth after the agencies committed various accounting irregularities. Moreover, the two firms couldn't compete with rapacious private lenders, who, thanks to securitization, could offer extra-low rates and irresistible terms to borrowers. In 2006, almost half the loans made by private lenders required no down payment and no documentation. Fannie and Freddie simply couldn't play in that league, even though Congress had given them aggressive lending targets to help boost homeownership among lower-income and minority households.

Fannie and Freddie did play a significant part in the financial panic. As conditions began to weaken in 2007 and the private mortgage industry pulled back, the agencies attempted to get back in the game. The memory of their accounting scandals had faded and policymakers hoped they could prevent the housing market from unraveling. Fannie's and Freddie's originations of sketchy loans actually peaked near $160 billion in 2008, the year regulators placed them into conservatorship. The two agencies had jumped back into the housing market at precisely the wrong time.

Loss rates on Fannie's and Freddie's loans were still low by industry standards, but they were rising and starting to threaten the institutions' thin capital cushions. The average commercial bank held $10 in assets for every $1 of capital; Fannie and Freddie's ratio was as high as 70 to 1. Regulators never demanded the two firms hold as much capital as ordinary banks because their loans went to top borrowers. Now that they were lending to the less creditworthy, their capital was woefully inadequate.

As investors began to worry they might fail, Fannie's and Freddie's share prices plunged, and their borrowing costs rose. This made it harder for the two firms to extend mortgage credit just when policymakers were counting on them to help stabilize the housing market. Instead, mortgage rates began to rise.

Treasury Secretary Henry Paulson aimed to shore up investor confidence when in July 2008 he reaffirmed and expanded Fannie's and Freddie's federal credit lines. Investors were appeased only briefly; after that they grew even more convinced that Fannie and Freddie were headed toward insolvency. In early September 2008, with the backing of the Treasury Department, the FHFA placed Fannie and Freddie in conservatorship, effectively nationalizing them.[12] Where before they had been public-private hybrids known as "government sponsored enterprises," now they were firmly part of the federal government. Their debt holders were safe, but their shareholders were effectively wiped out.

Financial Panic

The government's takeover of Fannie and Freddie arguably ignited the global financial panic. The Treasury Department's decision to wipe out shareholders of two of the largest financial institutions on the planet shocked markets, making it apparent that no institution was safe. Investors in all financial institutions questioned the value of their shares, bonds, and loans.

The weakest link in the financial system was investment house Lehman Brothers; it came under immediate pressure as shareholders dumped stock and short-sellers took advantage of the downdraft. Lehman had access to cash, thanks to the Fed, but one by one, Lehman's business partners dropped away, seeing the firm as too risky to do business with. The company spiraled toward bankruptcy.

The Treasury and the Fed worked feverishly to find a buyer for Lehman but came up short for several reasons. One was Lehman's extensive operations in London, which meant British banking officials needed to be involved. Treasury officials ultimately decided not to intervene, arguing that they couldn't bail out every financial institution and that Lehman's counterparties had had plenty of time to prepare after the Bear Stearns collapse 6 months earlier. The Fed went along, arguing that it could not by law loan Lehman any more without collateral.

This was a grievous mistake. The Fed and Treasury misjudged what a Lehman bankruptcy would mean. One of the nation's oldest money-market funds, the Reserve Primary Fund, held a sizeable amount in Lehman paper. As that investment collapsed, the Reserve Fund "broke the buck"—the value of its assets fell below what it owed its investors—which in turn broke the confidence of small investors who thought of a money fund as one step removed from a mattress. Other money-market funds saw redemptions surge, forcing them to sell off short-term IOUs called commercial paper, which many large firms issued for ordinary working cash needs. The market seized up, terrifying investors: If firms couldn't issue commercial paper, many couldn't meet payrolls, finance inventories, or pay vendors. A huge amount of commerce would simply cease.

Other major financial institutions were teetering. The venerable investment house Merrill Lynch, fearing Lehman's fate, hastily sold itself to Bank of America. Shakier banks suffered silent runs as scared depositors with more than the FDIC-insurance limit of $100,000 moved funds. Wachovia, a top-five commercial bank, was forced to sell itself to rival Wells Fargo, and Washington Mutual, the nation's largest savings and loan, was seized by bank regulators and sold to JPMorgan Chase.

In the midst of this turmoil, insurance colossus American International Group told policymakers that it, too, was in serious financial trouble. The company had been aggressively writing insurance on mortgage-backed securities via the credit default swap market. As the value of those securities declined and the cost of the insurance it was providing rose, AIG debt was downgraded by the credit rating agencies. Other financial institutions that had bought credit insurance demanded more collateral, which AIG didn't have. AIG was nearly broke and the financial system was shutting down.

Endnotes

1. Federal Reserve Chairman Alan Greenspan explicitly exhorted mortgage lenders to provide new alternatives to fixed rate mortgages in a February 23, 2004 speech to credit union executives. See "Understanding Household Debt Obligations," http://www.federalreserve.gov/boarddocs/speeches/2004/20040223/default.htm.

2. This is the net amount of homeowners' equity extracted and is based on estimates constructed by Alan Greenspan and Jim Kennedy, a Federal Reserve economist. The $3.1 trillion in extracted equity amounts to approximately 6% of consumer spending over the 5-year period.

3. FDIC Chairwoman Sheila Bair, who oversaw the regulator during much of this period, spoke out early and forcefully on the threats to the financial system posed by the mounting housing bubble and increasingly risky mortgage lending.

4. The Home Ownership Equity and Protection Act (HOEPA) of 1994 granted the Federal Reserve significant powers to regulate predatory mortgage lending.

5. Regulators' first coordinated attempt to rein in some of the most egregious mortgage lending didn't occur until September 2006. http://www.federalreserve.gov/newsevents/press/bcreg/20060929a.htm.

6. The Office of the Comptroller of Currency regulated national banks; the Office of Thrift Supervision regulated savings and loan institutions; the National Credit Union Association monitored credit unions. The Federal Housing Finance Agency oversees Fannie Mae and Freddie Mac.

7. Hedge fund Magnetar was a particularly egregious example of financial institutions that followed this strategy. See ProPublica, http://www.propublica.org/special/the-timeline-of-magnetars-deals.

8. A press account of HSBC's subprime warning can be found here: http://articles.marketwatch.com/2007-02-08/news/30714711_1_alt-a-loans-fixed-rate-loans-regular-mortgage.

9. A thorough list of mortgage companies that have failed since 2007 can be found at Mortgage implode-o-meter: http://ml-implode.com/fulllist.html#lists.

10. Calls to lower interest rates had been mounting since very early in the year. CNBC's Jim Cramer issued a much publicized call for the Fed to cut rates on August 3, 2007.

11. Subprime loans are defined as loans to financially fragile homeowners with credit scores under 660. The U.S. average is closer to 700.

12. The FHFA's directive putting the GSEs into conservatorship can be found here: http://www.fhfa.gov/webfiles/23/FHFAStatement9708final.pdf.

2

Bank Bailout

"The feds have no *** idea what they are doing." The chief credit officer at one of the nation's largest banks had worked himself into a lather over the Federal Reserve's demand that financial institutions stress-test their portfolios. It was early 2009 and the nation's banking system had just suffered a near-death experience. A government bailout had saved his bank and many others from almost sure extinction, but the banker was apoplectic that the government was now requiring his institution to examine itself to see how well it could survive a major economic shock.

It wasn't just the mechanics of stress testing, though those weren't exactly pleasant. What bothered this banker was the thought that he and his colleagues might need to go to investors, hat-in-hand, for more capital. His bank was on solid financial ground, or so he thought, and didn't need the extra capital cushion. Perhaps other banks did, but not his.

I heard the same refrain, if less crudely put, from most of my banking clients. My firm was helping banks translate the economic assumptions of the Fed's stress tests into dollars and cents terms, so they could weigh the hypothetical damage to their books. The Fed wanted to know how much the banks would lose on mortgages, credit cards, and other loans if the economy deteriorated more. The economy had already performed much worse than expected, of course. But what if the crisis deepened? The question wasn't unreasonable, given how badly forecasters had underestimated the downturn thus far.

The bankers' objections to the stress tests weren't surprising—bankers generally object to anything regulators propose—but their vitriol was. That was a good sign because it meant those tests weren't just a show, something to reassure the banks' stock- and bondholders that all was well. The banks had to determine how bad things could get under the worst of circumstances and raise enough capital to survive that. The capital would come from investors, or, if they wouldn't provide it, from the government. Either way, bankers would see lower returns on capital and be accountable to more stakeholders in the future. Hence their unhappiness.

Of all the government's many responses to the financial panic and ensuing Great Recession, the bank stress tests were arguably the most important. They helped persuade investors that the banks were sound, but much more critically they convinced the bankers themselves. Bankers knew that if their competitors were put through the same workout, they could survive almost anything. Banks began lending to each other again, a necessary step before lending to households and businesses. Just a few months after the financial system had shut down, it was revving back to life.

Even before the financial crisis erupted in late 2007, Federal Reserve officials realized they had to find a creative way to help the banks. The Fed manages the nation's monetary policy and is the banking system's most important regulator, but perhaps its most vital role is as the lender of last resort. In a crisis, with confidence and lending evaporating, the Fed can step in to provide as much cash as needed.

Traditionally, the Fed did this by lending freely to the banks on easy terms. But there was a problem with this approach: Banks feared that if they were seen receiving Fed help, they'd be tarred as unsafe and would have even worse trouble raising funds. So the Fed devised ways to inject cash anonymously into the stricken financial system, beginning a series of ingenious responses as the financial crisis grew into a panic.

The Federal Deposit Insurance Corp., the government agency charged with resolving failing banks, also went into action. The FDIC had been created to prevent bank runs, which had destroyed many financial institutions in the Great Depression. It succeeded so well that by the 2000s, the image of panicked bank depositors lining up to demand their cash existed only in old photos and period movies. FDIC insurance had convinced most Americans that any money they put into a bank was safe.

That changed in the financial crisis. The FDIC's insurance was capped, and many wealthy depositors had deposit accounts well above the limit. As the panic spread, the depositors began to bail out—but 21st-century technology meant there was no need to stand in line. Money now fled the banks through millions of mouse clicks. Not all involved depositors, moreover: Banks also had trouble issuing debt to fund loans. No interest rate was high enough to convince bond investors that they would get their money back after they gave it to the banks. The banks were literally running out of cash.

Empowered by Congress, the FDIC ended these so-called silent runs by raising deposit insurance limits and guaranteeing the banks' debt. The full faith and credit of the government now backed institutions such as J.P. Morgan, Bank of America, and even Goldman Sachs, the giant investment bank that had nominally become a depository institution to qualify for government help.

None of this would have worked, however, without the government making a bigger commitment to bail out the financial system. It did this through the $700 billion Troubled Asset Relief Program. The TARP was the equivalent of a Hail Mary pass—a dramatic move by Treasury Secretary Paulson and Fed Chairman Bernanke to stem the rapidly mounting financial panic. What the program lacked in definition, it made up for in size—big enough, they hoped, to convince scared markets that the government would do whatever was necessary to keep the financial system together.

Congress initially balked at putting up so much money with little notion of what it was for, but went along when it became clear that something had to be done quickly. TARP money ended up being used for many purposes, but most important it provided the capital necessary to keep the banking system afloat. The government had completely reversed its position over just a few weeks, from refusing to save Lehman Brothers to bailing out the entire system.

Confidence Game

Bankers like to portray their institutions as rock-solid stable, but the financial system as a whole is anything but. It often experiences wide mood swings, with sentiment shifting from wild optimism to abject pessimism and the availability and flow of credit moving in tandem with it. At the start of 2007, the financial system was overflowing with hubris and credit. It appeared the good times would never end.

Sentiment was surprisingly bright in the stock market, which had fallen sharply as the technology bubble burst only a few years earlier. Share prices were once again setting new highs, but instead of Internet and telecommunication companies, the leaders were financial institutions, homebuilders, and retailers. The bond market was even more euphoric, as investors flocked to lower-rated debt, the riskiest kind. Besides corporate and emerging-market debt, particularly popular were asset-backed bonds, where the returns came from payments on ordinary American mortgages, credit cards, auto loans, and student loans. Wall Street investment banks were more than happy to supply these, cranking the bond-making machinery up to full speed. During the first 6 months of 2007, an astounding $1 trillion in asset-backed bonds were sold to investors, half of them backed by payments on first mortgage loans.[1]

To feed this machine, all types of financial institutions were effectively conscripted to originate new loans. They had little choice but to participate or be driven out of business by their competitors.[2] Many commercial banks and savings and loans got into the act, but the most aggressive lenders were newly minted and lightly regulated finance companies, which often had been financially empowered by the Wall Street investment banks.

Mounting evidence that the housing market had already topped out did little to dent the optimism, at least for a while. Home sales had peaked in summer 2005, house prices a few months later. Homeowners were already going delinquent on their mortgages at a faster pace; even more worrisome, some borrowers were going straight from being current with their payments to defaulting. Many of these "house flippers" had made quick profits during the housing frenzy; as those opportunities vanished, they turned in their house keys back to their lenders.

Despite the cracks in the market, Wall Street doubled down. After erecting this massive machinery to originate, securitize, and sell loans to investors, the financial system couldn't just turn it off or even slow it down. Instead, to keep the money flowing, lenders dropped their standards to borrowers even further. Some of the poorest quality loans—loans with the highest probability of not being repaid—were made during this period.

There were some naysayers at the time (including the author), but their pessimistic message was dismissed, even ridiculed.[3] It was difficult to ground objections in hard numbers given how rapidly the securitization machine was operating and how complex and opaque the financial markets had become. Securities were divided up into many tranches, or slices, and combined with tranches of other securities to form collateralized debt obligations. Credit default swaps were written on these CDOs and repackaged into even more complex securities. It was difficult to determine precisely what was going on, let alone explain why it felt wrong. And many naysayers had lost credibility after warning about calamities that hadn't happened.

No one seemed to be listening, until suddenly they were. Precisely when sentiment flipped is hard to pin down; there was no particular event or data point, rather just a growing string of bad news that eventually became impossible to ignore. From HSBC warning that it would take a hit from losses on its subprime lending, to the meltdown at Bear Stearns' mortgage funds, to the accelerating decline in house prices and increase in mortgage defaults—by late summer 2007, confidence was wobbling and the preconditions for a shock were in place.[4]

Stock and bond investors began to capitulate. Even more worrisome, banks began to grow reticent to lend to each other, uncertain about which institutions were most exposed to the tumbling housing market. The difference between the 3-month interbank lending rate known as Libor and rates on 3-month Treasury bills—an important barometer of confidence in the banking system—ballooned from 20 basis points at the start of 2007, to 200 basis points by year's end.

Credit is vital to a well-functioning economy. Businesses need it to pay vendors before they can collect from customers. They also need credit to expand because the payback period for a new machine or office building could be years away. Households need credit to buy homes, cars, and appliances. And governments need credit to build roads, fight wars, battle recessions, rebuild after disasters, and educate their populations. But too much credit leads to bad loans and poor investments. As bankers say, "If it grows like a weed, it probably is one." On the other hand, not enough credit chokes hiring, investment, and growth. As 2007 ended, confidence was evaporating, the credit spigot was closing, and the economy was struggling.

Lender of Last Resort

The Federal Reserve's responsibilities include monetary policy and regulating the banking system, but its most fundamental charge is to be the financial system's lender of last resort. Regardless how dark the financial outlook, the Fed must ensure that lending continues and credit flows freely.

The Fed was born out of the debilitating panic of 1907, when a number of New York banks collapsed, credit dried up, and the nation entered a severe recession. Many such panics had afflicted the United States since its inception. The Federal Reserve was established in 1913 to end them.[5]

The Bernanke-led Federal Reserve knew this history and knew its responsibilities. Although initially slow to respond—it wasn't until August 2007 that the Fed began to ease monetary policy—it grew increasingly aggressive. Interest rates were pushed to effectively zero by the end of 2008, and the Fed looked for ways to aid cash-starved banks.

The banks had cash problems because they were nervous, not only about borrowing and lending among themselves, but also about borrowing from the Fed. In times past, if a creditworthy bank had trouble raising cash, it would borrow from the Fed's discount window. But now, no bank wanted to be seen going to the Fed, lest others conclude it was in financial trouble and cut it off from future interbank funds.

The Fed's solution to this problem was the Term Auction Facility. The TAF was a new way for depository institutions to borrow from the Fed through an auction. The banks had to put up the same collateral required at the discount window, but the bidding process made it difficult to discern why a bank was borrowing. It could be because a bank needed cash or because the TAF offered an advantageous interest rate. Thus there was no stigma attached to participating in a TAF auction.

Non-U.S. banks also struggled to raise dollars. Foreign businesses and households need dollars for commerce and travel, but tighter credit meant there weren't enough dollars to go around. The Fed responded by establishing swap lines with its counterparts in Canada, Europe, and Japan, trading dollars for other currencies with an agreement to reverse the trades at some point in the future. Such deals are all but risk-free because the Fed is dealing with other central banks.

The Fed's creativity alleviated the cash crunch in the banking system but could not keep credit conditions from tightening elsewhere in the broader financial system. When the Fed was established, the financial system had consisted almost exclusively of banks and similar depository institutions. Now, nearly half of all credit was provided by the so-called shadow banking system, a term encompassing a variety of institutions that did not take traditional deposits or make traditional loans.[6] What the shadow banking system had in common with traditional banks was that it was in trouble and needed the Fed to help it, quickly.

Investment banks were particularly desperate.[7] The Bear Stearns collapse raised serious questions about such institutions—not only those known to be in trouble such as Lehman Brothers, but also previously irreproachable firms such as Merrill Lynch, Morgan Stanley, and even Goldman Sachs. The Fed responded by creating the Primary Dealer Credit Facility and the Term Securities Lending Facility, two credit arrangements that enabled these institutions to raise cash on favorable terms. The PDCF and TSLF never grew very large, but by simply creating them, the Fed sent a clear signal that it would do what was necessary to backstop the shadow banking system.

Any doubts about the Fed's commitment to its role as lender of last resort were dispelled following the Fannie and Freddie takeover and the Lehman bankruptcy. The Fed flooded the financial system with cash, particularly the commercial paper market, money market funds, and the asset-backed securities market.[8] All three were important sources of short-term cash for businesses, households, and small banks; indeed, they formed the most direct link between Wall Street and Main Street. If they had shut down or were even significantly impaired, the economic damage would have been great.

By the end of 2008, the Fed had extended more than $1.6 trillion to the financial system (see Figure 2.1). As the financial panic faded, so did the flows of cash. By early 2010, the Fed's credit facilities had been allowed to expire, save for the swap lines, which were revived in late 2011 after the European debt crisis boiled over.

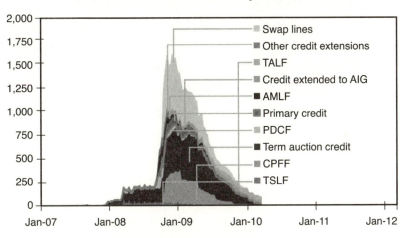

Fed Floods the Financial System with Cash

Figure 2.1 Federal Reserve's short-term lending operations, bil $.

Sources: Federal Reserve, Moody's Analytics

There can be reasonable debate about the efficacy of any of the Fed's initiatives during this period, but in total its actions were impressive.[9] In short order and under extreme duress, the Bernanke-led Fed devised and installed a new set of pipes in the financial system's plumbing. And as liquidity reached all corners of the system, confidence returned and credit began to flow again. The Fed's actions were exceptionally creative and ultimately successful.

Insurer of Last Resort

The Federal Reserve is a mystery to most Americans, but nearly everyone has heard of the FDIC. It provides the banking system's Good Housekeeping seal of approval, displayed prominently in every bank branch in the country.[10] If you put your money in an FDIC-insured bank and the bank fails, you will get your money back. The confidence this creates is vital to a well-functioning financial system.

Yet the FDIC's seal wasn't enough when the financial crisis hit. Not because depositors thought the agency wouldn't do its part if a bank failed—the FDIC is fully backed by the U.S. Treasury—but because the FDIC could insure deposits only up to $100,000. This limit had been in place since 1980, and many wealthier households had bank deposits exceeding this limit. As the crisis intensified and one blue-chip financial institution failed after another, big depositors grew increasingly nervous that their banks might be next.

In the 1930s scared depositors lined up outside banks to pull their funds; this time the runs occurred on the Internet. With only a few thousand mouse clicks, a rumor that a bank was in trouble could become reality. The nation's largest savings and loan, Washington Mutual, and commercial bank giant Wachovia were the biggest casualties of these silent electronic runs. Both institutions were big mortgage lenders during the housing boom, and both saw big losses as the bust spread. Their customers began to bail out, with increasing speed. That sent the FDIC into action.

For banks, the quid pro quo of FDIC deposit insurance is FDIC oversight, which makes the agency the second most important financial regulator after the Fed. The FDIC has the power—and the obligation because taxpayer money is on the line—to seize an institution if it appears headed toward failure. The FDIC's long history is filled with such takeovers. FDIC examiners typically swoop in on a Friday, after a troubled bank closes for the week, and on Monday the bank reopens under another name. Usually it has been sold to a sounder bank. Customers may not even know of the change unless they read the financial news.

This time, the FDIC pushed Washington Mutual into the hands of JPMorgan Chase. Wachovia ended up as part of Wells Fargo. The two bank transactions were the largest in U.S. history, and the FDIC pulled them off with barely a hitch,[11] showing again that it could efficiently deal with even the most complex and troubled financial institutions.

Bank takeovers don't engender confidence, however, and as the crisis continued, the bank runs threatened to intensify. Congress responded by raising the deposit insurance limit to $250,000, which helped. Wealthy depositors could divide their cash among institutions to remain under the cap. Although the increase was supposed to be temporary, the Dodd-Frank financial regulatory reform bill later made it permanent.

Restoring confidence among depositors was important because deposits are one essential source of funds for banks to lend. But so is bank debt; thus it was equally vital to convince bond investors that their money too was safe. These investors were staging their own kind of bank run, demanding sky-high interest or refusing to invest in financial institution paper at all.

The FDIC responded with an initiative called the Term Liquidity Guarantee Program, guaranteeing that investors in bank debt would be repaid.[12] Judging by interbank lending rates, the financial panic reached its apex on Friday, October 10, 2008; The FDIC announced the TLGP the following Monday. A few months later, the FDIC was guaranteeing some $350 billion in bank debt, putting the full faith and credit of the U.S. government behind the banks' obligations (see Figure 2.2). There was no longer a question that bank depositors' and investors' money would be safe.

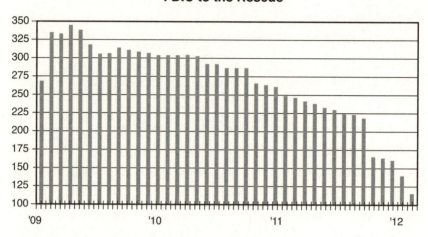

Figure 2.2 Term liquidity guarantee debt outstanding, bil $.

Source: FDIC

TARP: The Bailout Fund

The Fed's and FDIC's actions during this period were valiant, but not sufficient. The panic that gripped the financial system had become too pervasive. Financial institutions were failing, markets were gyrating, and the entire system was teetering. Policymakers had more work to do.

The Troubled Asset Relief Program was devised by President Bush's Treasury Secretary Henry Paulson at the height of the panic in September 2008. With the help of Fed Chairman Bernanke, Paulson sold the sketchy idea to a skeptical Congress, and the TARP become law a few weeks later.[13]

House Speaker Nancy Pelosi tells a harrowing story of how Paulson and Bernanke met with her, Senate Majority Leader Harry Reid and other Congressional leaders to introduce the TARP proposal. Bernanke began by describing in stark terms how close the financial system was to collapse. Congress had only a few days to act, appropriating several hundred billion dollars to forestall the cataclysm.

An incredulous Senator Reid questioned Paulson. "How many hundreds of billions are you talking about, Hank, one or two?" Paulson didn't answer and went on in more detail regarding the financial system's troubles. A now agitated Senator Reid tried again. "Do you need three or four hundred billion?" That wasn't enough, the Treasury Secretary said. "Well, how much are we talking about?" Reid asked. Paulson answered: "Ben and I think we need $700 billion." The room was silent.

Paulson and Bernanke have never publicly explained how they reached that number. In later testimony before Congress, Bernanke justified the TARP's size with a back-of-the-envelope calculation involving expected loss rates on various types of bank loans. More likely, the $700 billion was less the result of a precise financial calculation than a realization that the TARP had to be big—really big—to convince financial markets that the government was committed to preserving the system. Only then would panic abate. If calm returned, moreover, there was a good chance the ultimate cost would be less than $700 billion.

As initially proposed, the TARP was to purchase troubled mortgage loans and securities, whose value had collapsed when homeowners stopped paying on their loans. The price drop was exacerbated by the forced asset sales as institutions complied with stringent accounting rules that required banks' books to reflect current market prices. Such rules worked reasonably well in normal times but created big distortions when prices went into free fall.[14] Even if they weren't interested in selling assets, banks had to mark them to market, reducing their own capital and often forcing sales that drove prices even lower. Unchecked, the process could become a vicious cycle to financial oblivion.

The TARP was intended to break this cycle. The Treasury would run reverse auctions, buying troubled assets to shore up prices in a way that would entice other private buyers back into the market. It was a reasonable theory, but there were many practical issues to work out and little time.[15]

Any hope of using the TARP as originally envisaged was dashed when Congress balked, initially voting the whole plan down. Legislators were appalled at the cost; many thought it was simply a back-door handout to the banks. That the 2008 election was only weeks away didn't help. As it became clear that Congress couldn't muster the needed votes, financial markets crumbled. The Dow Jones Industrial Average suffered its largest daily point loss—nearly 800 points—the day Congress said no to the TARP.[16] That was enough to convince legislators they had no choice, and they quickly reversed course a few days later, approving a slightly reworked TARP. But the delay had consequences; there was no time for the Treasury to work out a process to buy banks' troubled assets.

Treasury Secretary Paulson quickly pivoted. Instead of buying troubled assets, the government would use the TARP to take equity stakes in the nation's largest financial institutions.[17] In just a few weeks, policymakers went from allowing Lehman Brothers to fail, signaling the government would not backstop the financial system, to becoming a huge shareholder in the nation's financial system and taking whatever steps were needed to keep the system from failing.

Through what became the Capital Purchase Program, the Treasury ultimately took equity stakes worth more than $200 billion in close to 700 institutions, including all the nation's largest bank holding companies.[18] A few of the strongest banks didn't want the TARP money—they knew it would come with strings, including limits on executive compensation. But the Treasury gave them no choice. Officials didn't want TARP to distinguish between strong and weak banks, lest it fuel more bank runs. On the other side, many institutions (mostly nonbanks) wanted the money, but didn't qualify. The

Treasury turned them down for various reasons, including the likelihood they would fail even with government help. Institutions that managed to survive without TARP money now hold this up as a badge of honor.

There were calls at the time for the government to fully nationalize banks, as it had Fannie Mae, Freddie Mac, and the insurance firm AIG. Some felt that the financial system would unravel otherwise, and others believed shareholders in these institutions should be wiped out as punishment. Policymakers admirably resisted these calls. The government took big stakes in Bank of America and Citigroup because these institutions had stumbled badly and required more TARP help, but these were still minority positions. The government's stakes in other TARP-aided institutions were much smaller.

TARP will remain politically tainted for a long time, being popularly associated with the distasteful bank bailout. Indeed it was a bailout fund used to prop up the same Wall Street institutions whose actions had led to the financial panic and Great Recession in the first place. Yet while no one likes to think that some financial institutions are too big to fail, TARP is proof that our financial system is littered with them. It is no wonder that Congress would vote for it only after it became clear that the alternative was collapse—of the financial system, and ultimately of the real economy.

TARP money ultimately funded a range of economic rescues aside from the banking system. It provided the cash that helped save GM and Chrysler, stem the housing crash, restore lending to small businesses and revive the asset-backed securities markets (see Table 2.1). Not only was the TARP vital to stabilizing the financial system, but it ended up costing taxpayers almost nothing: Nearly all financial institutions ultimately repaid their TARP loans with interest. The decision to keep financial institutions private was instrumental in allowing the government to quickly exit the banking business. Management and shareholders had strong incentives to buy back the government's stake and regain control of their institutions.

Table 2.1 Troubled Asset Relief Program (*Billions $*)

	Originally Committed	Ultimate Cost
Total	**700**	**57**
Bank Bailout	550	10
CPP (Financial institutions)	250	-27
Tarp Repayments		
Losses		
Dividends, Warrant proceeds		
AIG	70	36
Citi (TIP)	20	0
Bank of America (TIP)	20	0
Citi debt guarantee	5	0
Federal Reserve (TALF)	55	0
Public-Private Investment Fund (PPIP)	30	1
Auto Bailout	85	22
GMAC	15	4
GM	50	17
GM (for GMAC)	1	0
Chrysler	13	1
Chrysler Financial Loan	1.5	0
Auto suppliers	5	0
Small Business Aid	15	0
Housing Bailout	52	25
Homeowner Affordability and Stability Plan	52	25
FHA Short Refinance program	2	0

Sources: Federal Reserve, Treasury, FDIC, FHA, Moody's Analytics

Stressful Stress Testing

Before the government could withdraw, however, the banks had to prove they had sufficient private capital to survive. As 2008 came to an end, it was clear the financial system was short on capital, but just how short was unclear.

The stress tests were supposed to provide the answers. The nation's 19 largest financial institutions, each with assets of more than $100 billion, would have to determine the losses they would suffer if the economy sank more than anticipated.[19] They would then be required to raise enough capital to withstand those losses, either from private investors, or from the government through the TARP.

The stress tests were met with significant skepticism. They seemed like window dressing—a way to convince everyone that banks were solid even if they weren't. Would the Fed actually allow major banks to fail? Historians recalled that President Roosevelt had used sleight-of-hand to restore confidence in the banks when he took office in 1933. Roosevelt had told Americans he was declaring a "bank holiday," after which only the good banks would reopen. There would thus be no reason to pull money out of good banks—and it would be smart to return earlier withdrawals. The ruse worked; the bank runs ended. It later turned out that the administration wasn't sure the reopened banks were solid and indeed knew some were not. The president of the San Francisco Fed had insisted that Bank of America, the largest bank on the west coast, was insolvent. But the Roosevelt administration feared widespread panic if BofA didn't reopen, so it did.

In early 2009 the government wasn't stress-testing banks for show. Banks that year were required to consider what would happen if unemployment averaged more than 10% in 2010, and if house prices, which had already fallen 30%, fell 30% more. What they found was a stunning 2-year cumulative loss rate above 9%—that is, the 19 institutions tested would lose more than 9% of their assets by the end

of 2010. This was comparable to what the banks lost during 1933 and
1934, the worst 2 years of the Great Depression (see Figure 2.3).[20]
The banks found they would need $75 billion in new capital to survive
such a new depression.

Bank Stress Tests Were Very Stressful

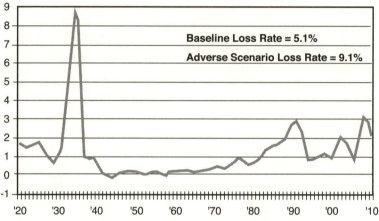

Figure 2.3 Cumulative two-year commercial bank loan loss rate.

Source: Federal Reserve Board

To further allay concerns that they might be coddling the banks,
regulators publicly detailed each institution's test result. Anyone
could examine the hypothetical loss rate of American Express' credit
card portfolio or Citigroup's commercial real estate loans. Many participating banks objected to the Fed releasing so much detail, fearful
it would spook investors or give away too much information to their
competitors. But the transparency of the process convinced everyone,
including the banks, that raising more capital would put them on solid
ground. Interbank lending rates fell quickly back to where they were
prior to the financial crisis. The system had suffered a great deal of
damage, but the crisis was over.

The bank stress tests set the U.S. apart from nations that had suffered similar meltdowns in the past. After Japan's real estate market
collapsed in the early 1990s, banks there were never forced to publicly acknowledge their losses and raise more capital. Nearly a quarter

century later, Japanese banks remain moribund, reluctant to provide credit, dooming the Japanese economy to slow and halting growth.

The European debt crisis was in part a banking crisis, as European banks never fully fessed up to their bad lending in real estate and to fiscally profligate European governments. Europe's financial regulators attempted U.S.-style stress tests in mid-2010, but these fell well short. Soon after the tests ostensibly cleared the banks of problems, much of Ireland's banking system failed. A second round of tests in mid-2011 again concluded the banks were in good shape; soon afterward, the French-Belgian banking giant Dexia went belly-up. Europe's tests were opaque, with each nation's regulators determining how much information to disclose. German and Spanish regulators were particularly unforthcoming. Only massive cheap lending by the European Central Bank, dwarfing anything the Federal Reserve did during the U.S. financial crisis, kept Europe's banks afloat.

European regulators had a much more difficult job than did their American counterparts. Getting regulators from nations with such different banking systems to read from the same page was a yeoman's task. More important, for a long time the Europeans had no analog to the TARP.[21] The giant pot of money made it possible for the U.S. stress tests to be tough because failure didn't mean a bank was doomed, only that it would be required to take capital from the TARP. TARP capital was expensive and came with lots of strings, but it was there if the banks needed it.

The Europeans had no such backstop in place when they conducted their tests. If a bank were found deficient, there was no place for it to go for capital and it would fail, complicating matters for the system and for the governments burdened with the banks' obligations. Ireland's banking collapse forced the Irish government to seek a bailout from the European Union. Unlike in the United States, where the TARP was established before the banks were run through their stress tests, the Europeans had mistakenly put the cart before the horse.

Stress testing has since become a standard part of U.S. bank regulation. The nation's largest financial institutions go through it each year, and the tests' demands have grown more complex and arguably more stressful.[22] But banks are no longer complaining loudly. They too view the tests as therapeutic for their own risk management and as a signal to their shareholders, bondholders, and other stakeholders that they are well managed. In no small part due to the stress tests, U.S. banks are as highly capitalized as they have ever been (see Figure 2.4).

Banks Are as Well Capitalized as Ever

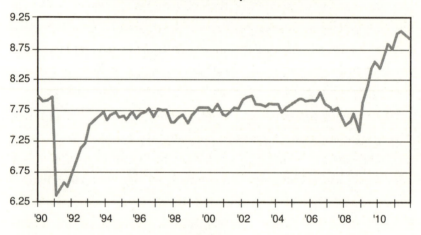

Figure 2.4 Commercial bank core capital ratio.

Source: FDIC

Chaos to Calm

The bank bailout was an historic turning point. The U.S. financial system, once the envy of the world, was shown to be clearly flawed. It had failed in its core mission—to channel the savings of households, businesses, and government into good investments and prudent loans. Banks had instead made millions of bad loans, triggering a serious economic crisis as borrowers reneged.

So much bad lending would have provoked a significant crisis under almost any scenario. It turned into a near-disaster this time because policymakers mishandled institutions they thought were too big to fail. Bear Stearns was gracefully folded into J.P. Morgan Chase with government help. Shareholders in Fannie and Freddie were wiped out, but bondholders were made whole. Lehman was allowed to go bankrupt, crushing its stakeholders. Creditors in financial institutions thus had no idea where they stood. They ran for the proverbial door, panic ensued, and the financial system nearly collapsed.

Some would call this an exaggeration, arguing that the financial system, although obviously under severe strain, would have quickly recovered on its own, without a major government bailout. This view is misplaced. Yes, the ATMs would have still worked, given FDIC insurance, but little else would have been normal. Lending and borrowing would have come to a dead stop, and with it the economy. It is not clear how or when it would have restarted.

The government's bailout was massive and in its totality masterful. From the Fed's creative efforts providing liquidity to the financial system, to the FDIC insuring deposits and bank debt to end the bank runs, to the TARP and the bank stress tests, the effort succeeded. The chaos of September 2008 had given way to calm by spring 2009. The financial system was bowed, but not broken, and only a few years later was arguably as strong as it had ever been.

Endnotes

1. This includes only private label securities—bonds issued by private financial institutions—and not bonds issued by the government-sponsored institutions Fannie Mae, Freddie Mac, and Ginnie Mae.

2. This follows Gresham's Law, in which poor lending drives out sound lending. Lenders who did not lower standards to match their competitors would be quickly driven out of business.

3. I am one of those naysayers. Relevant articles I wrote in the lead up to the housing crash include "Housing Correction or Crash," February 2006, *Regional Financial Review*; "Housing from Boom to Bust," August 2006, *Regional Financial Review*; "Housing at the Tipping Point," October 2006, special Moody's Analytics study; and "Into the Woods: Mortgage Credit Quality, Its Prospects, and Implications," July 2007, special Moody's Analytics study.

4. See my quote in "Global Markets Tumble as Credit Worries Deepen," *The New York Times*, July 27, 2007. http://www.nytimes.com/2007/07/27/business/27stox.html

5. The First Bank of the United States was chartered under the nation's first treasury secretary, Alexander Hamilton, and lasted 20 years. It was instrumental in establishing the new country's credit. The Second Bank of the United States also lasted 20 years and was key to establishing the dollar as a sound currency and reining in inflation. But the bank's operations became politically controversial, and President Andrew Jackson allowed its charter to expire in 1836. Financial panics and bouts of inflation and deflation occurred periodically until the Federal Reserve was established in 1913.

6. According to the Federal Reserve Board's Flow of Funds, traditional depository institutions such as commercial banks, savings and loans, and credit unions provided nearly all the economy's credit after World War II, but only about half by the mid-2000s.

7. Investment banks are nondepository institutions that generally serve as primary dealers of U.S. Treasury securities.

8. The Commercial Paper Funding Facility was established on October 27, 2008, the Money Market Investor Funding Facility opened its doors on November 24, 2008, and the Term Asset-Backed Securities Loan Facility began on November 25, 2008.

9. For example, Stanford Professor John Taylor has been highly critical of the TAF program. See "A Black Swan in the Money Market," NBER Working Paper, April 2008. http://www.nber.org/papers/w13943

10. The FDIC was founded in 1933 as part of the Glass Steagall Act. Financial institutions that take deposits are required to pay for FDIC deposit insurance and put the FDIC's seal in their branches. Banks have been happy to comply.

11. The FDIC did stumble when it initially agreed to sell Wachovia to Citigroup but switched when Wells Fargo made a higher bid. This was fortuitous as Citi ran into financial difficulties not long after.

12. The TLGP also guaranteed noninterest bearing deposits with no limit. This was also made permanent as part of the Dodd-Frank financial regulatory reform legislation.

13. The Emergency Economic Stabilization Act was signed into law on October 3, 2008. http://www.gpo.gov/fdsys/pkg/PLAW-110publ343/content-detail.html

14. Mark-to-market accounting rules are designed to make institutions recognize mistakes in their lending and investment decisions, act quickly to clean them up, and thus return to sounder financial ground. The rules make sense for assets that institutions plan to sell in the near future, but less for those it plans to hold for a long time.

15. I proposed a similar idea in testimony before the House Financial Services Committee in early 2008. http://www.economy.com/mark-zandi/documents/Financial_Services_2_26_08.pdf

16. Congress voted down the TARP on September 29, 2008. Selling in the stock market intensified as the roll call was being taken, and investors realized the vote would fail.

17. Policymakers didn't completely give up on using the TARP to buy troubled bank assets. On March 23, 2009, newly appointed Treasury Secretary Tim Geithner announced the Public-Private Investment Program for Legacy Assets or PPIP. PPIP married TARP money with funds from private investors to buy troubled assets, but the program never lived up to expectations.

18. The Capital Purchase Program was authorized to provide up to $250 billion of the $700 billion in TARP funds as capital to financial institutions. At the peak, the CPP had extended $205 billion. The banks were permitted to treat the TARP money as Tier 1 capital, making it much easier for them to achieve their regulatory capital standards.

19. Regulators announced the stress tests, also called the Supervisory Capital Assessment Program (SCAP) on February 25, 2009. http://www.federalreserve.gov/newsevents/press/bcreg/20090225a.htm. The 19 large financial institutions included regional banks such as SunTrust and BB&T, investment banks such as Goldman Sachs and Morgan Stanley, insurance giant Metropolitan Life, and GMAC, the finance division of auto maker General Motors.

20. A detailed discussion of the methodology used to conduct the bank stress tests and their results was released on May 7, 2009. http://www.federalreserve.gov/newsevents/press/bcreg/bcreg20090507a1.pdf

21. The euro zone ultimately established a bailout fund known as the European Financial Stability Facility, but it was initially too small and ended up providing help to troubled governments.

22. The bank stress tests announced in early 2012, known as the Comprehensive Capital Assessment and Review or CCAR, required the banks to have enough capital to survive 13% unemployment, a 50% fall in stock prices and another major drop in house prices. http://www.federalreserve.gov/newsevents/press/bcreg/bcreg20120313a1.pdf

3

Outside the Monetary Box

"Well, Congressman, these specific allegations you've made I think are absolutely bizarre, and I have absolutely no knowledge of anything remotely like what you just described."[1] Federal Reserve Chairman Ben Bernanke was clearly taken aback by questioning from Texas Congressman Ron Paul. Paul had asked if Bernanke knew whether the Federal Reserve had provided funds to the Watergate burglars and illegally funneled billions of dollars in loans to Iraq's Saddam Hussein.

The allegations were fantastical, but they came from a U.S. Congressman, who mustered significant support in his subsequent run for the Republican presidential nomination. Much of Paul's stump speech focused on the Fed, and what he claimed was the central bank's egregious abuse of power. Paul's suspicions weren't in the mainstream, but they were symptomatic of a simmering hostility that has plagued the idea of central banking in the United States since Congress chartered the first such institution soon after the nation's founding.[2] That emotion, in 21st-century form, nearly boiled over when the Fed responded to the Great Recession.

The Fed had fueled some of the hostility on its own. Lax monetary policy had contributed to inflating the housing bubble, and policymakers were slow to recognize what was happening after the bubble was pricked. Chairman Bernanke showed how badly he misjudged the developing subprime mortgage crisis in a speech in May 2007. "Given the fundamental factors in place that should support the demand for housing," he said, "we believe the effect of the troubles in the subprime sector on the broader housing market will likely be limited, and we do not expect significant spillovers from the subprime market to the rest of the economy or to the financial system."[3]

Just weeks later, this view appeared silly. By August, CNBC personality Jim Cramer was waxing apoplectic on his show, raging that the Fed was either inept or indifferent to the cracks developing in the financial system.[4] There was no doubt that Wall Street thought the Fed should ease monetary policy, but it wasn't until mid-September that the Fed began to do so, lowering its key interest rate a timid quarter percentage point to 5%.

Fed policymakers thought they were merely being prudent, following a rule book written when Alan Greenspan was chairman. These rules say monetary policy should be determined mainly by how near inflation and unemployment are to the central bank's targets. The Fed should lower interest rates only if inflation was approximately 2% or lower, and the unemployment rate was significantly above 5%.[5] Even in late summer 2007, these limits hadn't been breached.

But the Fed failed to take account of the growing carnage in financial markets as the housing bubble deflated. Fed officials believed monetary policy should not respond directly to asset bubbles, which reflected the judgment of the markets: Millions of people were buying stock and houses, who was the Fed to say they were paying too much? The rule was to respond only when the bubble caused big changes in inflation or unemployment. That approach seemed to work out when the stock market bubble imploded early in the 2000s. But the limitations—or the folly—of this thinking were growing increasingly clear as 2007 ended.

Through 2008, the Fed scrambled to get ahead of events. By the end of that year, it had pushed the federal funds rate effectively to zero, and just a few months later policymakers were using monetary policy tools previously untried. Some had been discussed earlier in the decade when deflation briefly appeared to be a threat after the tech stock bubble burst.[6] The Fed also had the chance to observe Japan, which had been stuck in a deep economic slump since the early 1990s, even though officials lowered interest rates to zero. But until the 2007 financial panic, such discussions had been entirely theoretical.[7]

No one was better suited than Fed Chairman Bernanke to translate theory into practice. Much of his academic career had been spent studying periods of extreme financial stress, such as the 1930s Great Depression and 1990s Japan. Bernanke believed that in such times, central banks had to act with overwhelming monetary force. He half-seriously suggested that if all else failed, central bankers could still drop money from helicopters.[8] His point was that the Fed had the power, if it were willing, to ensure that the economy didn't remain stuck in a deflationary trap.

What this meant became vividly evident when the Fed began a program of quantitative easing (QE), purchasing trillions of dollars in Treasury bonds and mortgage securities. The program immediately became controversial; critics charged the Fed was effectively printing money, a policy that could ignite runway inflation. Some invoked the hyperinflation of the Weimar Republic, saying the Fed's actions would produce a similar result here. Others complained that by working to bring down mortgage rates, the Fed was making fiscal policy, something only Congress could do. Outside the United States, central bankers and finance ministers were annoyed that the Fed's policies were likely to lower the value of the U.S. dollar against in Europe, Asia, and Latin America enough to stunt those regions' exports and economic growth.

QE did bring some uncomfortable side effects, but its economic benefits were meaningful. Bringing down mortgage rates dovetailed with other fiscal policy efforts to stimulate mortgage refinancing, which allowed financially stressed homeowners to lower their monthly house payments. QE also encouraged risk-taking, something that had been crushed by the Great Recession. With interest rates falling toward zero, investors had more incentive to buy stocks and corporate bonds in hopes of higher returns. Indeed, financial markets rallied whenever the Fed even hinted that it might launch more QE.

Also controversial was the Fed's solid commitment to its zero-interest-rate policy. In late 2011, when the European debt crisis appeared liable to derail the still fragile U.S. recovery, the Fed made an extraordinary pledge to keep rates "exceptionally low" well into the middle of the decade. For this to be convincing, the Fed needed to lay bare its thinking regarding future interest-rate policy. This was out of character; the central bank had historically been quite secretive, one reason it drew so much suspicion. Not until Greenspan took the reins did the Fed even announce its changes to interest rates. Investors previously had to divine what the Fed was up to by monitoring the effect of its actions on financial markets. The Bernanke Fed wasn't exactly an open book, but it provided regular forecasts of the economy's performance and the federal funds rate; it no longer required clairvoyant interpreters to tell the world where monetary policy was headed.

The late 2011 announcement was as clear as it could be: Interest rates would remain very low for a long time. Investors had additional incentives to take chances with their money. Simply parking it in FDIC-insured certificates of deposit wouldn't be a winning strategy; inflation would erode investors' wealth. Retirees who relied on CDs and bonds for income were perturbed, and they had a point; it didn't make much sense for older people to be chancing stocks or other high-risk investments.

Yet despite the controversies and complaints, the Bernanke-led Federal Reserve prevented a new depression. Rock-bottom interest rates allowed debt-laden households and businesses to lighten their loads, and gave the banking system a path back to profitability. Low borrowing costs encouraged firms to invest more and prevented an even greater crash in home and vehicle sales. Stock and bond prices were given a boost, softening the sting from weak house prices. Bernanke put all the Fed's weight into ending the financial panic and Great Recession, and it worked.

Whether monetary policy during this period was ultimately judged a success, however, would depend on how gracefully the Fed ended its extraordinary intervention in the economy. The Fed had flooded the financial system with trillions of dollars of liquidity, which would have to be drained once the economy began growing faster, or inflation would flare up. Policymakers had time: A number of dominoes must fall after the Fed creates money before it begins to fuel inflation. Policymakers had carefully thought through their exit strategy, devising and testing new financial tools to aid in the withdrawal. Lest there was any confusion regarding its goals, Fed officials eventually made explicit their previously implicit 2% inflation target.

But pulling this off wouldn't be easy, particularly given the Fed's zero-interest rate policy. This wasn't a commitment—the Fed would raise interest rates sooner than planned if inflation revived—but it meant the Fed would be slower to respond to inflation pressure than in times past. The Bernanke Fed did an admirable job expanding its reach into the economy and saving it from calamity, but its success would ultimately be judged on how it retreated.

Battling Asset Bubbles

The Federal Reserve is a creation of Congress, and although Congress is often critical of its creation, it has given the Fed little guidance on how to do its job. Congress is clear that it wants the Fed to engineer low inflation and unemployment but is silent about precisely what "low" means, about whether inflation is more important than unemployment or vice versa, or even whether these should be the only goals the Fed considers when setting interest rates.[9] This silence is largely by design because even most members of Congress understand that monetary policy must remain independent. History is littered with countries whose economies were shipwrecked by politicized central banks.

Although the Fed has wide leeway to set monetary policy, it generally remains true to its congressional guidepost. Policymakers often talk about the appropriate federal funds rate target in the context of the Taylor rule—a formula that explicitly relates the funds rate to inflation and unemployment.[10] If inflation is above the Fed's target and unemployment is below it, then the Fed should raise interest rates, and vice versa. It's not that the Fed simply plugs unemployment and inflation statistics into a Taylor rule calculator, and sees the correct federal funds rate pop out. But during the past quarter century the Fed has come close to effectively doing just that (see Figure 3.1).

The Fed Sticks Close to the Taylor Rule

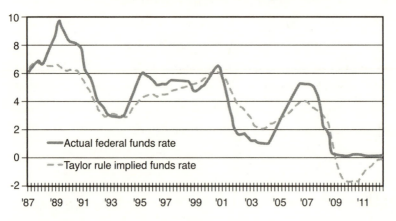

Figure 3.1 Federal funds rate, %.

Sources: Federal Reserve Board, Moody's Analytics

The exceptions have been times of financial stress. During the dizzying 1987 stock market crash, the recently arrived Fed Chairman Alan Greenspan slashed interest rates even though inflation was above target and unemployment was low. Greenspan did the same thing after the 1998 collapse of the Long-Term Capital Management hedge fund, and again after the bursting of the technology stock bubble and the 9/11 terrorist attacks. The Fed's policy of aggressively lowering interest rates to cushion the blow from financial turmoil became known as "the Greenspan put"—a signal from the central bank that it would limit investors' downside risk.[11]

Greenspan was willing to use monetary policy to stabilize free-falling financial markets, but he was more circumspect about using policy when markets were shooting upward, even when they appeared to be driven by reckless speculation. Unlike investors who buy assets expecting them to appreciate for fundamental reasons—economic growth, technological change and so on—speculators buy simply *because* prices are rising, in hopes of quickly selling at a profit, perhaps to other speculators. Day traders swapping technology stocks in the late 1990s were speculators, as were house flippers in the mid-2000s. Speculators also often attempt to boost their returns by buying with borrowed money. Day traders used margin credit, and house flippers took on mortgage loans with little or nothing down. When speculators overrun a market, prices can spiral higher and a bubble can form, as in the stock market around 2000 and the housing market circa 2005.

Just months before the stock bubble burst, Greenspan opined that although it would be nice if the Federal Reserve could deflate asset bubbles, it was ill-equipped to do so:

> Obviously, if we could find a way to prevent or deflate emerging bubbles, we would be better off. But identifying a bubble in the process of inflating may be among the most formidable challenges confronting a central bank, pitting its own assessment of fundamentals against the combined judgment of millions of investors.[12]

It was better, Greenspan said, for the Fed to ease the economic damage after a bubble burst:

> The bursting of the Japanese bubble a decade ago did not lead immediately to sharp contractions in output or a significant rise in unemployment. Arguably, it was the subsequent failure to address the damage to the financial system in a timely manner that caused Japan's current economic problems. Likewise, while the stock market crash of 1929 was destabilizing, most analysts attribute the Great Depression to ensuing failures of policy. And certainly the crash of October 1987 left little lasting imprint on the American economy.[13]

Greenspan's monetary game plan was thus lopsided: The Fed should do little when a bubble was forming except to follow the Taylor rule and maintain low inflation and unemployment. When a bubble burst, however, the Fed should respond aggressively. The strategy worked reasonably well—until the housing crash. Indeed, the housing bubble may have grown in part because of the Fed's asymmetric strategy. Although the Fed had not literally bailed out the day traders in tech stocks, it had kept the fallout from that market crash to a minimum, arguably encouraging investors to attach higher values to mortgages and other financial securities. If the Fed were willing to limit the downside, any investment was arguably safer and thus worth more. Lower interest rates and easier credit fueled the crazed demand for homes and inflated the housing bubble.

Bernanke's Education

Ben Bernanke was sympathetic to Greenspan's view of asset bubbles but did not fully agree with it. As a member of the Fed Board of Governors from 2002 to 2005, Bernanke's thinking had surely been influenced by Greenspan; much more important to molding Bernanke's views, however, was his own academic research on the Great Depression of the 1930s and the deflation that gripped Japan in the early 1990s. Both economic cataclysms had origins in bursting stock-market bubbles.

From his studies, Bernanke knew the Great Depression had largely been caused by the Federal Reserve. The Fed of the late 1920s had been unnerved by that era's rip-roaring stock market, with its rampant speculation fueled by easy credit. Policymakers concluded that the bubble needed to be pricked, even with an economy still recovering from recession and not a whiff of inflation. The Fed had hiked interest rates, precipitating the 1929 stock market crash and ushering in the Depression.[14, 15]

The economy's slide had been exacerbated when, instead of easing monetary policy after the crash, the Fed tightened in a lame defense of the gold standard. Market speculators had forced Great Britain off the gold standard in 1931; they looked next across the Atlantic, betting the U.S., too, would have to abandon fixing the currency to the precious metal. As speculators sold dollars and bought gold, banks saw nervous depositors withdraw funds. The Fed responded by pushing up interest rates even more, preserving the fixed dollar price of gold but nearly wrecking the banking system. Speculators took another run at the dollar in 1933 just prior to Franklin Roosevelt's inauguration, expecting that the new president would dump the gold standard. The Fed raised interest rates again, inducing even more bank failures and further undermining the economy.

The Fed also botched its role of lender of last resort. Central bank officials believed that the only way to strengthen the banking system was to weed out the weaker banks.[16] Moreover, the Fed felt no obligation to help smaller banks, which were not part of the Federal Reserve system. Neither did the big banks, which before the creation of the Fed system, would often work together in times of crisis to shore up their smaller colleagues. Now, some bigger banks preferred to wait and pick up the assets and deposits of their failing smaller competitors. Such thinking only encouraged bank runs, which culminated in Roosevelt's bank holiday in March 1933. As the entire banking system shut temporarily, the economy cratered and deflation became endemic.

Japan's long-running struggles with deflation also provided Bernanke plenty of examples of how not to deal with that economic disease. Deflation is especially pernicious when interest rates have collapsed to zero, as occurred in Japan in the mid-1990s. Indebted households and businesses are hit hard as they try to make debt payments amid declining wages and profits. Many default, hurting banks and other creditors, forcing a general pullback in lending. The economy weakens further, deflation intensifies, and a vicious cycle sets in.

Conceptually, the cure for deflation is simple: Increase the supply of money. Like gold, money's value is inversely proportional to its supply.[17] But central banks such as the Bank of Japan or Federal Reserve can produce an infinite amount of money at essentially no cost. As Bernanke put it:

> ...the U.S. government has a technology, called a printing press (or, today, its electronic equivalent), that allows it to produce as many U.S. dollars as it wishes at essentially no cost. By increasing the number of U.S. dollars in circulation, or even by credibly threatening to do so, the U.S. government can also reduce the value of a dollar in terms of goods and services, which is equivalent to raising the prices in dollars of those goods and services. We conclude that, under a paper-money system, a determined government can always generate higher spending and hence positive inflation.

If the deflation cycle could be broken so easily, then why couldn't Japan break it? Bernanke concluded that Japan's problem was political; policymakers lacked the political will to do what was needed:

> ...Japan's deflation problem is real and serious; but, in my view, political constraints, rather than a lack of policy instruments, explain why its deflation has persisted for as long as it has. Thus, I do not view the Japanese experience as evidence against the general conclusion that U.S. policymakers have the tools they need to prevent, and, if necessary, to cure a deflationary recession in the United States.

Bernanke suggested a range of policy instruments, many of which he ultimately implemented. Most notably he proposed large-scale asset purchases, also known as quantitative easing.[18] Although the Fed normally creates money by purchasing modest amounts of Treasury bonds, there is no reason it couldn't buy other bonds—mortgage securities, corporate debt—as well as stocks, or even fine art if that would make a significant difference.[19]

Bernanke's ideas later provoked sharp criticism of his policies. The Fed chairman earned the pejorative nickname "helicopter Ben" because of his suggestion that the government could end deflation with a tax cut financed by additional Fed asset purchases—that is, by the Federal Reserve printing money. Bernanke explained that this "money-financed tax cut is essentially equivalent to Milton Friedman's famous 'helicopter drop' of money."

Bernanke also spoke approvingly of lowering the dollar's value if the United States ever found itself trapped in a deflationary cycle. He held up Franklin Roosevelt's decision to take the country off the gold standard in 1933—a move that devalued the dollar 40% against gold—as an example. Not surprisingly, foreign central bankers and finance ministers feared that Bernanke had something similar in mind with quantitative easing. Some of these officials—uncharacteristically for central bankers—openly criticized the Fed. Yet despite their worries, the dollar's foreign-exchange value barely budged throughout the financial turmoil, as the United States remained a safe haven for skittish global investors.[20]

Bernanke drew another important lesson from history, namely that although monetary policy wasn't good at preventing asset bubbles, the Fed wasn't powerless to address them. Indeed, the Fed's responsibility as principal regulator of the nation's financial system gave it a powerful lever to do just that:[21]

> Understandably, as a society, we would like to find ways to mitigate the potential instabilities associated with asset-price booms and busts. Monetary policy is not a useful tool for achieving this objective, however. Even putting aside the great difficulty of identifying bubbles in asset prices, monetary policy cannot be directed finely enough to guide asset prices without risking severe collateral damage to the economy.... A far better approach, I believe, is to use micro-level policies to reduce the incidence of bubbles and to protect the financial system against their effects. I have already mentioned a variety of possible measures, including supervisory action to ensure capital adequacy in the banking system, stress-testing of portfolios, increased transparency in accounting and disclosure practices, improved financial literacy, greater care in

the process of financial liberalization, and a willingness to play the role of lender of last resort when needed.

This is where Bernanke and Greenspan divided intellectually. Greenspan seems to have held the Fed's regulatory functions in disregard or even contempt, insisting that self-interested investors would figure everything out much better than government bureaucrats. Bernanke thought solid regulation was necessary to head off future bubbles. His perspective would be important when policymakers eventually considered financial regulatory reform.

There was arguably no person better prepared to lead economic policymaking during the Great Recession than Ben Bernanke. His scholarly research and training were tailor-made to deal with just such a scary economic scenario. When it became a reality, he already had thought through how to deal with it.

ZIRP, QE, and the Twist

Bernanke's Fed began executing this game plan as the financial crisis and economic downturn intensified in 2008. The federal funds rate target was 4.25% when the year began; by the end of the year it was effectively zero, the lowest funds rate on record. There was some concern that this zero-interest rate policy would be a problem for the money-market mutual fund industry—firms wouldn't earn enough interest income to cover their costs—but these worries were quickly put to rest.[22]

The real funds rate—the difference between the funds rate and inflation expectations—was negative by the spring (see Figure 3.2).[23] It is typical during recessions for the Fed to lower the funds rate below the inflation rate to jump-start recovery. With a negative real rate, debtors can repay what they owe more easily, investors and creditors have an incentive to take more risk, and households and businesses are motivated to spend and invest more aggressively.

Fed Presses on the Monetary Accelerator

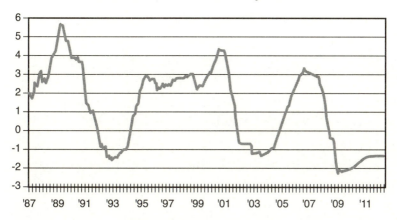

Figure 3.2 Real federal funds rate, %.

Sources: Federal Reserve Board, BLS, Moody's Analytics

But with inflation expectations already near 2% when the economy slid into recession, the Fed had little choice but to bring rates effectively to zero. There was no other way to generate a meaningful negative real rate. This highlights a problem central banks potentially face when they set their inflation targets too low. The lower the inflation target, the more likely the central bank will hit the zero bound for nominal rates when times get tough.[24] This is an uncomfortable place for a central bank. It also limits how negative a real rate can become. Even when the Fed had pushed the funds rate to zero during the worst of the Great Recession in early 2009, the real funds rate was still only –2%, not much different than during other, much milder recessions.

The zero-interest rate bound is also why central banks are deathly afraid of deflation. If nominal rates are zero and prices are falling, it means real interest rates are positive by whatever the rate of deflation. This is precisely the opposite of what central banks want when their economies are reeling. And this was the specter the Fed faced in early 2009: The federal funds rate was effectively zero, and low inflation threatened to give way to outright deflation.

In response, the Bernanke Fed took the next logical step in its game plan, beginning quantitative easing. Before the recession, the Fed owned approximately $800 billion in Treasury bonds and no mortgage-backed securities. It began buying both on a large scale in late 2008 and by June 2009 held $2.1 trillion in these securities (see Figure 3.3). The Fed continued to buy during the following months, just to replace its maturing securities, but in late 2010 it announced a second round of new purchases, which became known as QE2. By mid-2011, the Fed held nearly $3 trillion in Treasury and mortgage securities on its balance sheet.

Fed's Balance Sheet Balloons

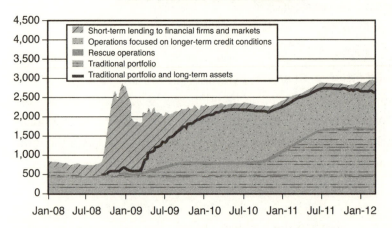

Figure 3.3 Composition of Federal Reserve's balance sheet, bil $.

Sources: Federal Reserve, Moody's Analytics

At the same time the Fed was flooding the financial system, so too were most of the central banks of the biggest developed economies. The Bank of England, the European Central Bank, and of course, the Bank of Japan pumped out trillions in pounds, euros, and yen. Relative to the size of their economies, their efforts were even more massive than the Fed's (see Figure 3.4). The world was awash in money.

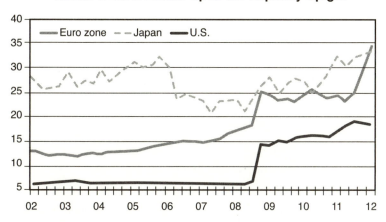

Global Central Banks Open the Liquidity Spigot

Figure 3.4 Central bank assets as a percentage of nominal GDP.

Sources: Fed, ECB, BoJ, IMF, Moody's Analytics

QE's most direct result was a significant reduction in long-term interest rates.[25] The rate on 10-year Treasury bonds ultimately sank below 1.5%, the lowest it had been since the 1950s. Fixed mortgage rates, which are closely tied to Treasury rates, fell to a record low below 3.5%. Businesses' long-term financing costs plunged; multinationals such as Microsoft, IBM, and General Electric could lock in funds for decades at nearly zero cost.

There was heated debate over how long QE would keep long-term interest rates low. One school of thought, made up mostly of bond traders, held that QE's impact on rates would last only as long as the Fed kept purchasing securities. The other view, held most forcefully by Fed policymakers, was that rates would remain low much longer, rising only when the Fed's holdings declined. Policymakers were proven right; long-term rates remained low for a long time.[26] Neither the bond market nor the economy floundered, even when the Fed decided not to expand its balance sheet further.

Arguably even more important for the economy was QE's salutary impact on the market for higher-risk financial securities, of the sort that had been shunned during the panic. Because investors were earning barely anything on cash and Treasury bonds, they had to take on more risk to even keep pace with inflation. QE thus made stocks and junk bonds, issued by smaller, less sturdy businesses, appear more attractive. Even a hint that the Fed was thinking of more QE caused financial markets to rally.

QE drew plenty of critics, however. The scariest accusation was that the Fed was monetizing the nation's debt—essentially printing money to pay for the government's obligations—and thus risking runaway inflation. Historically, such strategies had often destabilized prices, sometimes leading to epic hyperinflation. But this doesn't have to be the result if central banks manage the process well. A long causal chain separates the Fed's purchases of Treasury securities and inflation: Money created by the Fed (in the form of bank reserves) must first prompt new bank lending. Then the increased credit must fuel faster growth, lowering unemployment and raising capacity utilization. Only after that does inflation grow stronger. Given the U.S. banking system's troubles, the lack of business confidence and the high rates of unemployment that lingered after the Great Recession, the Fed had plenty of time to drain the money it had created before inflation became a problem. QE did cause inflation to stop falling, but this was by design, to ward off deflation. Although it would take years to know precisely how QE affected prices in the longer run, concerns about runaway inflation appeared off the mark.

Central bankers and finance ministers in emerging economies were nervous that much of the money created by the Fed and other developed-economy central banks would flow their way.[27] This could raise the value of emerging-market currencies and lead to speculation, bad lending, and overinvestment. Some emerging market central banks tightened their own monetary policy in response, while others imposed taxes and other controls to dissuade foreign investors. The protests grew so loud that there were fears a currency war might break out. Although emerging-market currencies did appreciate— which was appropriate given their strong economies and wide trade and current account surpluses—the currency war never materialized.

Other critics charged that the Fed was drifting into the realm of fiscal policy by buying mortgage securities as part of QE. Indeed, by working to directly lower mortgage rates, the Fed was subsidizing a particular sector of the economy, namely housing. It is important for the Fed to respect the line between monetary and fiscal policy, but arguing that QE took the central bank over the line was a stretch. The Fed plays a much larger role in housing and other markets when it influences the availability of credit via its regulatory functions. The Fed has particularly wide authority to determine mortgage lending standards.[28]

QE also unnerved bankers, whose profits depend on their ability to borrow short-term and lend long-term at higher rates. With short-term borrowing costs near zero, QE might weigh on bank profits if it forced them to lower lending rates. Yet if QE had an impact on bank profitability, it was difficult to discern, probably because most of the Fed's purchases were of bonds with maturities longer than 10 years. Most bank lending was for periods of 3 to 5 years.

Although criticism of QE was excessive, it wasn't completely misplaced. So with deflation risks fading in 2011, the Fed decided against another round of QE and instead engaged in what markets referred to as Operation Twist. This involved trading $400 billion in short-term Treasuries for the same amount of longer-term bonds, starting in October and ending in June 2012. The Fed subsequently extended its twist operation through the end of the year by several hundred billion dollars more. The process didn't create new money—the Fed's balance sheet held steady—but it lowered long-term rates even further. Operation Twist put some upward pressure on short-term rates, and it was limited by the Fed's quantity of short-term Treasury securities, but from the Fed's perspective, every little bit helped.

The other piece of Bernanke's plan involved making the Fed more open as an institution. Throughout its nearly 100-year history, the central bank's actions had been shrouded in secrecy. Few outside Washington and Wall Street even knew what the Fed did. Fed officials worried that politicians and unscrupulous investors might try to take advantage of greater transparency. This thinking began to change with Chairman Greenspan and was flipped on its head when Chairman Bernanke took over. As recently as the mid-1980s, the Fed's thinking about the economy and the direction of monetary policy had been completely opaque. By early 2012, the Fed was virtually an open book.

Bernanke's Fed laid out plainly what policymakers thought about the economy's performance, prospects, and implications for monetary policy. Each quarter, officials released a forecast for GDP, unemployment, inflation, and the federal funds rate. The forecasts extended beyond the next few years to the long run, when the economy was expected to be operating at full potential. The funds rate forecast wasn't a commitment by the Fed but a projection of what policymakers thought it would be given their forecasts for the economy and inflation.

Fed officials also broadcast their thinking about the economy and monetary policy with expansive policy statements after each FOMC meeting, with minutes released just a few weeks later and with regular public speeches by the Chairman and other board members. Chairman Bernanke even began giving regular press conferences, answering questions from the financial media directly and in public.

Transparency enables the Fed to quickly affect financial markets. In early 2012, when FOMC members provided their first funds rate forecasts, they projected that the rate would not rise until late 2014 (see Table 3.1). This surprised bond and stock investors; although markets anticipated rates would stay low for a while, few guessed it would be 3 years until the first hike. Long-term interest rates fell and stock prices rallied. The Fed had effectively eased monetary policy without having to provide either more QE or another Operation Twist.

Table 3.1 Target Federal Funds Rate at Year's End (*Number of Federal Reserve Members with Projected Targets, January 2012*)

	2012	2103	2014	Long-Run
0.25	14	11	6	
0.5	1	1	2	
0.75		2	1	
1	2	1	2	
1.25				
1.5			1	
1.75		1		
2		1	1	
2.25				
2.5			3	
2.75			1	
3				
3.25				
3.5				
3.75				1
4				7
4.25				3
4.5				6

Source: Federal Reserve Board, http://www.federalreserve.gov/monetarypolicy/ fomcprojtabl20120125.htm

That the Fed was no longer a black box also took some of the starch out of its harshest critics in Congress. Critics could still disagree with the Fed's monetary policy decisions, but now they could see precisely what was driving those decisions. In theory at least, this would make it more difficult for future Ron Pauls to credibly question the Fed's actions and motives.

The Bernanke Fed also made explicit what had always been an implicit inflation target.[29] The Fed said it wanted a 2% inflation rate and would set monetary policy to achieve that goal in the long run.[30] This was no surprise; 2% was about what inflation averaged during Bernanke's tenure as Fed Chairman, and policymakers had referred to it often in speeches and testimony. Nonetheless, the Fed sent a clear signal to investors that despite all the liquidity it had created via its zero-interest rate policy, QE, and Operation Twist, it would reverse those policies quickly if inflation threatened to exceed the 2% target. Being explicit cemented inflation expectations, and made it easier to actually hit the target.

Although the Fed didn't adopt an explicit target for unemployment—the other part of its dual mandate—its long-term forecast for the jobless rate provided a good sense of what policymakers thought their goal should be. A hard-and-fast target could be counterproductive because the unemployment rate consistent with a fully employed workforce changes with demographics and other factors. There is also no way to know precisely what the full-employment unemployment rate actually is.

Exit Strategy

By early 2012, the Federal Reserve had fully executed Bernanke's game plan. The federal funds rate was at the zero bound, and long-term interest rates were about as low as they had ever been. The Fed had injected trillions of dollars of new money to stimulate the economy.

The plan worked. Fears of deflation and economic depression vanished, inflation settled near the Fed's target, and the recovery was at least intact. Many threats remained—Europe was in disarray, millions of homeowners faced foreclosure, gasoline prices were near record highs, and fiscal austerity was dampening activity—but the Fed was on high alert and would remain so until these threats faded.

Ultimately, the Bernanke Fed would be judged by its ability to gracefully unwind its unprecedented actions. The chairman provided frequent strong assurances that the Fed could withdraw its monetary stimulus before inflation took off. The aggressive use of monetary policy to cushion the blow from the Great Recession was a significant achievement, but that achievement would be badly tarnished if it created another set of inflation problems down the road.

Bernanke had given significant thought to the problem, devising new policy tools to accomplish the task. Most important, he convinced Congress to give the Fed the authority to pay banks interest on their reserves.[31] This would let the Fed raise short-term interest rates even if the banking system were still awash in reserves and the federal funds rate were near zero. If the Fed were willing to pay a nonzero interest rate for banks' excess cash, then rates for all other borrowing and lending would rise as well.

To drain bank reserves more quickly, the Fed also created new financial instruments, including term deposits, which are much like certificates of deposit the Fed would sell to banks. Reverse repurchase agreements were another tool: The Fed would agree to exchange Treasury holdings for bank reserves. To ensure that these tools worked when needed, the Fed did several rounds of mock transactions with financial institutions. Policymakers were prepared to exit when the time was right.

The Fed flooded the financial system with extra money for several years, and it would take at least that long to drain it. Doing this without either undermining economic growth or igniting uncomfortably high inflation would be difficult. The Fed had the tools it needed, but knowing just when to use them was another matter. Inflation might still become a problem, but it would be a manageable one, and certainly much preferable to an economy sunk for decades in recession and deflation.

Future Fed chairmen would not have to apologize for the actions of the Bernanke Fed during the Great Recession.

Endnotes

1. This conversation took place at a hearing of the House Financial Services Committee on February 24, 2010. http://archives.financialservices.house.gov/Hearings/hearingDetails.aspx?NewsID=1104

2. A similar dark sentiment was expressed by Republican Presidential candidate Rick Perry in comments during his run in summer 2011. He said, "If this guy prints more money between now and the election, I dunno what y'all would do to him in Iowa but we would treat him pretty ugly down in Texas. Printing more money to play politics at this particular time in American history is almost treasonous in my opinion."

3. Federal Reserve Chairman Bernanke speech, "The Subprime Mortgage Market," was delivered on May 17, 2007 at the Federal Reserve Bank of Chicago's 43rd Annual Conference on Bank Structure and Competition, Chicago, Illinois. http://www.federalreserve.gov/newsevents/speech/bernanke20070517a.htm

4. I expressed my own frustration with the Fed's slow response to the deteriorating financial conditions in August, 2007. See "The Fed Has More Work to Do," *The Dismal Scientist*. http://www.economy.com/dismal/pro/article.asp?cid=76485

5. This is the so-called full employment unemployment rate—the rate estimated to be consistent with stable inflation.

6. The Greenspan Fed lowered the federal funds rate to 1% in summer 2003, where they stayed for a year due to deflation concerns.

7. The FOMC engaged in a detailed discussion of monetary policy options if the Federal Reserve were ever to hit the zero interest rate bound at the June 24–25 FOMC meeting. http://www.federalreserve.gov/fomc/minutes/20030625.htm

8. Bernanke did this in a speech before the National Economists Club in reference to a statement made by Milton Freidman. See "Deflation: Making Sure 'It' Doesn't Happen Here," November 21, 2002, Washington, D.C. http://www.federalreserve.gov/BOARDDOCS/SPEECHES/2002/20021121/default.htm

9. Congress explicitly gave the Federal Reserve its dual mandate of low and stable inflation and unemployment in 1977, when it amended the 1913 Federal Reserve Act.

10. The rule is named for its creator, Stanford University Prof. John Taylor. Taylor, John B. (1993) "Discretion Versus Policy Rules in Practice," *Carnegie-Rochester Conference Series on Public Policy*, 39. http://www.stanford.edu/~johntayl/Papers/Discretion.PDF

11. A put option on a stock gives an investor an option to sell that stock at a pre-set price, thus guarding against losses.

12. Federal Reserve "Semi-Annual Testimony Before Congress," testimony by Alan Greenspan before the House Committee on Banking and Financial Services,

July 22, 1999. http://www.federalreserve.gov/boarddocs/hh/1999/july/testimony.htm

13. "Monetary Policy and Economic Outlook," Alan Greenspan's testimony before the Joint Economic Committee, June 17, 1999. http://www.federalreserve.gov/boarddocs/testimony/1999/19990617.htm

14. According to the National Bureau of Economic Research, there was a recession in the mid-1920s that troughed in late 1927.

15. This narrative of the principal cause of the Great Depression was first put forward by Milton Friedman and Anna Schwartz in their seminal work "The Monetary History of the United States," 1963. Bernanke discussed their work in the context of his own views on the Great Depression in "On Milton Friedman's Ninetieth Birthday," Ben Bernanke speech at the Conference to Honor Milton Friedman, University of Chicago, Chicago, Illinois, November 8, 2002. http://www.federalreserve.gov/BOARDDOCS/SPEECHES/2002/20021108/default.htm

16. Fed officials subscribed to Treasury Secretary Andrew Mellon's infamous 'liquidationist' thesis, that weeding out weak banks was a harsh but necessary prerequisite to the recovery of the banking system.

17. This point is well articulated by Ben Bernanke in a speech before the National Economists Club, "Deflation: Making Sure 'It' Doesn't Happen Here," November 21, 2002. http://www.federalreserve.gov/boarddocs/speeches/2002/20021121/default.htm

18. Bernanke and other Fed officials preferred to call their massive purchases of Treasury bonds and other mortgage securities "large-scale asset purchases" and not "quantitative easing."

19. Technically, the Fed cannot purchase assets that are not issued or guaranteed by the federal government. In practice there are many ways for the Fed to bypass this constraint.

20. The broad trade-weighted U.S. dollar index was largely unchanged from the beginning to the end of the financial turmoil. The dollar did fall against some individual currencies during this period, such as the Canadian dollar and Chinese yuan, but it rose against others, such as the British pound and euro.

21. "Asset-Price 'Bubbles' and Monetary Policy," Ben Bernanke speech before the New York Chapter of the National Association for Business Economics, New York, New York, October 15, 2002. http://www.federalreserve.gov/boarddocs/speeches/2002/20021015/default.htm

22. The federal funds rate was actually reduced to 0.125%; enough above zero for money-market funds to cover their operating costs.

23. Inflation expectations are what households, businesses, and investors believe future inflation will be. This can be measured via surveys, financial markets, and other ways.

24. The Federal Reserve could actually simulate a negative interest rate by requiring banks to pay it interest on excess reserves. But this would be highly controversial and difficult to implement, and was not seriously considered.

25. For an account of how QE affected the economy, see speech by Brian Sachs, Executive Vice President of the Federal Reserve Bank of New York, "The Fed's Expanded Balance Sheet," given to the Money Marketeers of New York University, NYC, December 2, 2009. http://www.newyorkfed.org/newsevents/speeches/2009/sac091202.html

26. This was the flow-versus-stock debate. The stock argument rests on the portfolio balance channel theory of QE, in which the Fed's buying squeezes out private investors who require higher interest rates to buy long-term bonds given their more marginal tolerance for risk.

27. The loudest complaints came from Brazil's finance minister. The Brazilian currency had risen sharply, weakening Brazil's exports and overall growth.

28. Under the Home Ownership and Equity Protection Act (HOEPA) of 1994, the Federal Reserve has broad authority to regulate mortgage lending. The Fed is often appropriately criticized for not using this authority to stem the bad mortgage lending that took place during the mid-2000s housing bubble.

29. The Fed also came much closer to setting an explicit target for the unemployment rate.

30. The 2% inflation target is based on the inflation rate as measured by the core consumer expenditure deflator. The core deflator excludes volatile food and energy prices. Inflation as measured by the core consumer price index is generally a bit stronger than the deflator due to its somewhat different construction and composition.

31. The Fed was granted the authority to pay banks interest on their reserves as part of the TARP legislation in late 2008.

4

As GM Goes, So Goes the Economy

December 4, 2008 was a cold, beautifully clear morning in the nation's capital. As I walked up Capitol Hill from Union Station, I was unnerved to find a phalanx of camera crews just outside the Senate office building. The chief executives of the Big 3 Detroit automakers were there, talking to reporters, each standing next to one of his company's prized cars. At an earlier appearance before Congress seeking financial help, the executives had been publicly flogged for flying to Washington in their corporate jets. This time they made a show of driving to the capital.

I had been invited to offer a nonbiased view of whether taxpayers should bail out the automakers. I was viewed as a nonpartisan economist: I had worked as an unpaid advisor on the McCain 2008 Presidential campaign, but I also had a good relationship with economists in the Obama transition team. Both Republicans and Democrats felt I could provide an apolitical view. Many times before when I had testified in Congress, attendance was sparse. There may have been a few dozen observers and maybe a camera from C-SPAN. This time the entire nation would be watching, as news organizations from every corner of the country surrounded the automakers.

A long line had formed to get through security, and everyone seemed jittery, fearful this would make them late to the hearing. Just then a large group rushed by, trying to bypass security altogether. It was Chrysler CEO Robert Nardelli and what looked like an entourage of public-relations and financial types. They didn't get far. Guards told them to get back in line, which seemed to surprise Nardelli. He

71

was even more surprised when those at the head of the line wouldn't let his group duck ahead. He slinked to the back.

This small incident highlighted why the auto bailout was so politically difficult. Even with their industry careening toward financial oblivion, those in charge projected a sense of entitlement. They expected the public to help keep their companies afloat and didn't seem at all humbled by their request. Although lawmakers ultimately and appropriately helped the industry avoid calamity, it was a bitter pill for politicians and the public to swallow.

In theory, as well as in the minds of many voters, government ought to have let the industry go it alone. The automakers had clearly made their share of business mistakes over the years; now taxpayers were asked to shoulder some of the burden. The U.S. economy has been built on rewarding business success, not propping up failure. That is what bankruptcy is for; it enables businesses to clean up their messes in an organized and orderly way. Stakeholders present their case to a judge who finds the best way to balance the economic interests of all involved.

In practice, cutting the auto industry loose in the midst of the Great Recession would have been a grave error. By the time the automakers came to Congress, hats in hand, during the waning days of the Bush administration, the economy was already reeling. The recession had started a year earlier; more than 3.5 million jobs had vanished, and the unemployment rate was surging above previous peaks. The economy was in a tailspin, especially in the industrial Midwest where the Big 3 had most of their operations. Unemployment in Michigan was already in depression-like double digits.

Letting the automakers fail would also have dealt a blow to business and consumer confidence. The automobile has a special place in America's self-image, as well as in the world's largest and most productive economy. Auto companies have been key to the nation's technological prowess and acumen in management, marketing, and finance. In a real sense, the twentieth century had been the American

Century because of the automobile. Allowing the industry to collapse could both symbolize and literally trigger the economy's collapse.

There was also a strong economic argument for the government to step in. Bankruptcy works only when lenders are willing to carry a business through restructuring, providing what is called *debtor-in-possession* financing. Lenders charge a hefty interest rate for this and can seize a firm's assets if it doesn't repay the loan. Still, debtor financing is extraordinarily risky and not for the faint of heart.

In the aftermath of the financial panic, the credit spigot for debtor financing closed completely. Virtually no credit was available, let alone the tens of billions of dollars needed to keep the automakers operating in bankruptcy. Under those circumstances, a GM or Chrysler bankruptcy would not be a court-supervised reorganization, but a liquidation: Factories, offices, and research facilities would all be shuttered, and corporate assets sold off at rock-bottom prices. This in turn would begin a cavalcade of other bankruptcies and liquidations, as the automakers' suppliers went belly-up as well, followed by hundreds of auto dealerships across the country. With millions of jobs at stake, bankruptcy without some kind of government support simply wasn't an option.

Government backing was also needed to keep U.S. consumers buying vehicles from the Big 3. Americans' biggest purchase after a home is typically a car, and most households expect it to last at least several years. They need to have confidence in the manufacturers' warranties, to trust that someone can service it, and to believe the car will hold its value at resale or trade-in time. All this depends on the manufacturer being around. Few will buy from a carmaker that seems about to disappear, unless the government or some other entity credibly offers to stand behind the deal.

The Bush and Obama administrations put theory and philosophy aside to rescue the car industry. The federal government ultimately loaned GM and Chrysler, their finance units, and the auto supply industry a total of $82 billion. The initial loans were provided to keep

GM and Chrysler out of bankruptcy, but when it was clear that the automakers wouldn't obtain needed concessions from creditors, labor unions, and dealerships, the government forced them into Chapter 11. When they came out a few months later, Chrysler was effectively sold to the Italian automaker Fiat; GM went public with the U.S. Treasury as its largest shareholder. Both companies were smaller but with much lower cost structures that allowed them to earn profits with lesser sales.

The government's support for the auto industry went beyond financing. The U.S. Treasury established a fund to backstop automakers' warranties and restarted the asset-backed securities market that had supported auto lending to both consumers and dealerships. Then there was the much-criticized Cash for Clunkers program, which in summer 2009 provided rebates worth $3 billion to consumers who traded in gas-guzzling older vehicles for newer models. Cash for Clunkers did nothing more than entice trade-ins and new sales sooner, as consumers rushed to take advantage of the government rebate, but this was vital. It helped clear out inventories and gave production a lift at a critically important time when the automakers were exiting bankruptcy and the recovery was taking hold.

The auto industry rebounded smartly during the recovery and was instrumental in powering it as well. Auto sales, production, and employment improved steadily to the point where nearly one-fourth of the economy's growth in the 2 years after the Great Recession ended was tied to Detroit's revival. No other industry was as important to the post-recession rebound. And as the auto industry returned to profitability, the federal government began to unwind its intervention.

In contrast with Washington's bank bailout, aid to the automakers would have a net cost to taxpayers. How much would depend on when the government sold its remaining GM shares, but a reasonable estimate put the total bill at approximately $20 billion. There may also have been other costs that were harder to quantify. First, any industry bailout raises the specter of moral hazard: Would businesses and investors take on more risk than they should, thinking that Washington will catch them if they fall? Second, the government muscled ahead of other creditors in GM's and Chrysler's bankruptcies. Would this precedent discourage lenders from once again extending credit, raising its cost to future borrowers?

Finally, there was the threat of political interference in business decision making. Did labor unions receive an outsized ownership stake in the restructured automakers as a reward for backing Democrats? Would GM have the same commitment to its electric car, the Volt, if not for the administration's interest in green energy? Was GM picking its suppliers and dealerships based on which congressional district they were in? The auto bailout cost lots of money and created many questions. Still, the price tag would have been much larger and the questions much more difficult if the government had done nothing.

Headed for a Crash

The U.S. auto industry's troubles began long before the Great Recession. In the decade before that day in 2008 when their CEOs asked Congress for help, the Big 3 had seen sales plunge from more than 11 million vehicles annually to fewer than 6 million. The decline reflected a weaker global market for vehicles—sales had peaked in 2000—but also stiff competition from Japanese, German, and other foreign producers. For the first time since the automobile was invented, American car companies supplied less than one-half the vehicles purchased by U.S. households.

The Big 3 had been blindsided by a surge in gasoline prices. Buyers hadn't been concerned about gas mileage in the early 2000s, when a gallon of regular unleaded cost around $1. Big gas-guzzling sports utility vehicles and minivans had been all the rage and made big profits for the Big 3. But the strategy faltered as gas prices climbed through the 2000s, topping out above $4 per gallon in the summer of 2008 (see

Figure 4.1). Americans turned to smaller, more fuel-efficient cars, which were the specialty of foreign car companies. Gasoline prices fell as the recession intensified, but it didn't matter much because vehicle buyers' expectations were forever changed: They knew that although prices might move up and down, on average they would be a lot higher in the future. Consumers wanted different vehicles than the Big 3 were selling.

$4 Gasoline Sent the Auto Industry Crashing

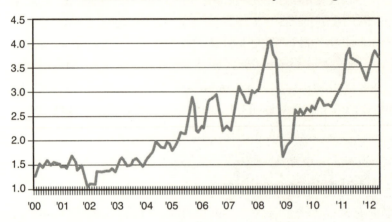

Figure 4.1 Cost of a gallon of regular unleaded, $ per gallon.

Sources: Federal Reserve, Bloomberg, Moody's Analytics

The Detroit automakers had also erred by offering increasingly aggressive price discounts and easier credit terms. Discounting had boosted sales as far back as the 1980s but became a vital strategy in 2001, when automakers offered 0% financing—free money—to anyone who purchased a vehicle in the month after the 9/11 terrorist attacks. It worked spectacularly; nearly 22 million vehicles (at an annualized rate) were sold that month (see Figure 4.2),[1] helping bring an early end to the downturn that had begun with the bursting tech stock bubble.[2]

Automakers Offer Big Discounts and Easy Terms

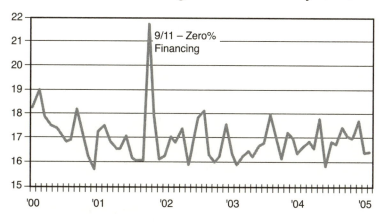

Figure 4.2 Vehicle sales, millions, annualized rate.

Sources: BEA, Moody's Analytics

But vehicle buyers became hooked on the sales promotions, putting off purchases until the next deal came around. By 2007 the average auto incentive package was worth more than $6,000, one-fourth of the average vehicle's list price. Incentives had roughly doubled in value since the start of the decade.

To sell more vehicles, the automakers turned to their financing units, GMAC and Chrysler Financial. These began pumping out loans and leases, lowering standards to increase volume. Subprime lending is generally associated with mortgages, but it was at least as big for autos. By the mid-2000s, nearly one-half of all auto loans were made to borrowers with weak credit scores.[3] Auto lenders stopped requiring down payments and extended loan maturities to reduce borrowers' monthly bills. The average vehicle loan grew in length by almost 1 year to more than 5 years during the early 2000s.

By early 2008, the Big 3's promotions had essentially brought forward millions of sales; that is, they had enticed buyers to act sooner than they would have otherwise. A family of four might have waited until they were five before buying a minivan but were persuaded not to wait by a big discount or easy credit. But this was unsustainable:

Demographic, wealth, and personal income trends supported at most 16 million vehicle sales per year. Discounts and easy financing had pushed sales above 17 million since the late 1990s. By early 2008, sales had exceeded fundamental demand by some 10 million vehicles. The entire industry would have had to shut down for almost 1 year to right the balance.[4]

Big 3 executives knew they were borrowing from future sales, though they undoubtedly underestimated the extent to which they were doing so. Still the executives stood by their strategy. Ford, GM, and Chrysler had high fixed costs, including pension and healthcare obligations to their unionized workers, the cost to maintain their dealer networks, and mounting debt obligations. Labor costs had been tamed somewhat—the United Auto Workers made consider-able wage and benefit concessions in 2007—but to cover their fixed costs and remain profitable, the industry needed to sell close to 17 million units annually. Detroit's Big 3 had to sell at least 10 million of those vehicles to hold their share of the market.[5] Without aggressive sales promotions, sales would slump and they would lose money.

This wasn't a winning long-term strategy even under good eco-nomic circumstances, and as the Great Recession intensified, it became disastrous. Not only did high unemployment sap vehicle demand, but the crippled financial system choked off auto lending and leasing. Even rental companies stopped purchasing new cars, and dealers couldn't raise the cash they needed to keep their lots filled.[6] By late 2008, both sales and production were in free fall, and the Big 3 were hemorrhaging money.[7]

The Rationale

The Senate hearing in which I participated in early December 2008 was held to determine what the federal government could do to help the Big 3 survive. Many congressional hearings are perfunctory, held so that legislators can put their views on the record. Most legislative decisions are made far from the microphones, in meetings between lawmakers, their staffs, and interested parties. This hearing was different. Because of the rapidly unfolding events and the high stakes involved, policy was being made in real time. The hearing lasted several hours with no breaks, at least not for me or the CEOs.[8]

The government's backstop of the financial system had historical precedent and a well-established rationale. That was less true here: Washington had little experience bailing out nonfinancial businesses such as Detroit's automakers. Chrysler and defense contractor Lockheed had received help during the 1970s after lawmakers argued that both were vital for the nation's defense. (Lockheed produced defense aircraft, and Chrysler was the nation's largest manufacturer of military tanks at the time.) But that aid had been limited to loan guarantees, and the sums were modest, at least compared with what the Big 3 wanted in 2008.[9] The assistance in the 1970s had nonetheless been highly controversial, barely squeaking through Congress. Bailing out the Big 3 this time would be a far harder sell.

This was as it should be. The U.S. economy works well because there is a bright line between the public sector and private business. Government sets and enforces the rules but does not determine which enterprises succeed or fail. That some fail is vital to the economy's success, as capital, labor, and other resources are freed for other, more productive endeavors. Bankruptcy makes this all happen with reasonable efficiency and fairness for all stakeholders. It is an uncomfortable process for everyone involved, but it creates a much stronger economy.

In rare instances, however, traversing that bright line is necessary. Exactly when is a matter of judgment, but as I told the senators that day, this was one of those times. The financial system was unraveling, the economy was sinking, and leaving the Big 3 without government help would risk chaos. The automakers would file to restructure under Chapter 11 of the bankruptcy code but would inevitably have to switch to Chapter 7: liquidation. The crippled financial system made it impossible to obtain debtor-in-possession financing, meaning the companies could not operate while they restructured. Even the bluest of blue-chip firms were having difficulty obtaining short-term loans; there was little chance the Big 3 could borrow another penny. They would have to shut factories and other operations and sell assets to repay creditors. For all the automakers' problems, they were still viable companies. Allowing them to vanish because the financial system was frozen made little sense.

Even if debtor financing had been available, it wasn't clear that the automakers could have survived long in bankruptcy without government help. Who would buy a new car from a company that might not be around next year? Who would provide service or supply parts after a few years? Who would honor the failed automaker's warranties? And what would be the resale value of such a car? These questions were already beginning to drag down the Big 3's sales. Their non-U.S. competitors weren't blatantly using these doubts to grab market share, but they didn't need to; American consumers were asking the questions themselves.

GM was in worse financial shape than Chrysler, which was in worse shape than Ford. GM was burning through cash at a rate that would have forced it to shut down in several weeks. Chrysler could have avoided bankruptcy longer, but given the slide in vehicle sales and its rapid loss of market share, not much longer. Ford had more financial latitude, but it too was at significant risk of bankruptcy if GM or Chrysler failed because of the resulting disruption to its suppliers, dealers, and creditors.

Liquidation of either GM or Chrysler would have meant worker layoffs in the hundreds of thousands—possibly in the millions—at just the wrong time. The Big 3 employed fewer than 250,000 people in the United States, but their broad links to the rest of the economy put closer to 2.5 million jobs at risk. For every job lost in auto assembly, another nine jobs would be lost at parts suppliers, auto dealers, steel and metal manufacturers, plastic and rubber companies, healthcare providers, trucking and freight operators, and others (see Table 4.1).

Table 4.1 The Auto Industry Means a Lot to the Rest of the Economy (*Change in Employment Due to a 1,000-Job Change in the Auto Assembly Industry*)

Total	9,100
Auto parts manufacturing	1,490
Auto maintenance & repair	940
Wholesale trade	840
Trucking	330
Warehousing	120
Machine shops	100
Foundaries	70
Plastics	70
Nuts & bolts	70
Machinery repair	60
Motor vehicle bodies	50
Glass	50
Steel mills	50
Tires	40
Other industries	4,820

Sources: Implan, Moody's Analytics

The fallout on the economy of the industrial Midwest would have been disastrous. Michigan and Ohio had already been in recession for a decade, and the collapse of the Big 3 would have undermined their economies for another one. Illinois, Indiana, and Wisconsin would also have been severely hurt. Worse, unemployed workers in the industrial Midwest would have had difficulty relocating to Alabama, Kentucky, Tennessee, or South Carolina, where Toyota, Volkswagen, and other non-U.S. car makers had plants. Midwestern house prices had fallen sharply, leaving many homeowners in that region owing far more than their homes were worth. To move they would have to either pay off their loans or default on their mortgages—a Hobson's choice.

The unraveling of the financial system made bankruptcy for the Big 3 even scarier. These companies carried big debts—approximately $400 billion including the obligations of their captive finance units—and had many investors and banks among their creditors. GM and Chrysler bonds had been rated below-investment-grade for some time; thus they were not held by pension funds or insurance companies but by investors specializing in distressed debt. Yet bankruptcy was still a step into the unknown.[10] Many regulators and analysts had misjudged the damage Lehman Brothers' failure would do to the financial system; the same could have been true if the automakers couldn't meet their financial obligations. The financial system's exposure to the Big 3 appeared manageable, but who knew for sure?

Another chilling imponderable was the effect on consumer and business confidence if the Big 3 vanished.[11] The auto industry has long been central to the American story symbolizing the nation's industrial might and innovative prowess. GM president Charles Wilson had famously said at his 1953 confirmation hearing to be secretary of defense: "For years I have thought that what was good for the country was good for General Motors, and vice versa." The sentiment was widely caricatured, but it couldn't be completely dismissed, even early in the 21st century.

The Bailout

The Senate rejected my advice, voting down a bailout for the automakers soon after the December 2008 hearing.[12] But it didn't matter. The lame-duck Bush administration intervened, dipping into the previously approved Troubled Asset Relief Program to lend the automakers $17.4 billion. Concerns about whether this was a proper use of the TARP were quickly set aside, given the risks of not acting. In return for the cash, GM and Chrysler were given 3 months to develop credible restructuring plans and prove they could return to profitability. Policymakers still held out hope the automakers could avoid bankruptcy.

When the TARP money ran out in March 2009, the new Obama administration extended more loans—but demanded in return that GM CEO Rick Wagoner resign and that Chrysler finalize a merger with the Italian automaker Fiat. Nearly $77 billion in TARP funds were ultimately given to the two companies and their finance units.[13]

Officials worked hard to keep the automakers out of bankruptcy, but ultimately there was no other option. The company's stakeholders—management, shareholders, debt holders, workers, suppliers, and dealers—could not come to terms without prodding from a bankruptcy judge. The process also sent an important signal to other industries hoping for taxpayer help in difficult times: The price of such help, if it were available at all, would be a painful trip through bankruptcy. The government directed the automakers to go into Chapter 11. Chrysler filed first, in April 2009, and GM followed in June.

With the government backstopping them, the companies quickly restructured, emerging from bankruptcy in only a couple of months. Management had been replaced, shareholders lost everything, bondholders received pennies on the dollar, the dealer network was streamlined, and the companies' U.S. workforces were about one-third of their previous size. As compensation, the government took a 60% stake in GM and an 8% stake in Chrysler.[14]

There was plenty of grumbling about the bankruptcy terms. Some secured debt holders, who had been first in line for repayment, felt particularly short-shifted. A number of the resulting lawsuits were still snaking through the courts nearly 3 years later.[15] Some auto dealerships closed by the automakers during the bankruptcy also sued. Although the courts would ultimately determine the merits of these cases, much more would have been lost had the government not intervened.

Legal challenges did not prevent the government from ending the Chrysler bailout in a reasonably graceful fashion. By spring 2010, Chrysler had repaid its loans, and Fiat bought the government's equity stake that summer. Fiat owned approximately 60% of the new Chrysler; the UAW took ownership of the rest as compensation for the pension benefits Chrysler owed its workers. The federal government had invested approximately $15 billion in the car company and lost a little more than $1 billion of that by the time it exited.

The exit from the GM bailout didn't go as well for the government, which invested more and ended up owning more than it did in Chrysler. The Treasury received partial repayment when GM went public in November 2010, reducing the government's stake from 60% to approximately one-third. By mid-2012, proceeds from the public offering and some debt repayment by GM had allowed the federal government to recover approximately one-half of the $62 billion it invested.

The ultimate cost to taxpayers would depend on the sales price for the government's remaining GM shares. The longer the government took to sell, the more likely it was to get its money back, but there were big potential costs to waiting. Most important was the risk of politicizing GM's business decisions. For example, the Obama administration had loudly touted the Chevrolet Volt extended-range electric car, but GM's CEO termed the Volt a "political football." Delays in selling the government's stake could also hurt the price of GM shares, moreover, as investors worried about government meddling in the company's business decisions. As a result, Washington was unlikely to hold on long enough to break even; it would likely lose approximately $15 billion on the GM bailout.[16]

The auto bailout went well beyond direct financial aid to GM and Chrysler. Auto suppliers received government guarantees that they would be paid.[17] New GM and Chrysler vehicles carried government-backed warranties to reassure buyers that they would obtain service if the companies disappeared.[18] Auto lending and leasing was revived by the Federal Reserve through the TALF fund, which provided cheap, nonrecourse loans to investors who bought highly rated securities backed by auto loans and other assets.[19] None of these programs were large, and they ultimately cost taxpayers nothing, but they were instrumental in restoring confidence in the U.S. auto industry.

Another small but highly effective effort to revive the auto industry was nicknamed Cash for Clunkers.[20] Congress put up $1 billion to fund rebates for anyone who traded in a gas-guzzler for a newer, more fuel efficient vehicle. The program began on July 1, 2009 and was so popular it ran out of money by the end of the month. Another $2 billion was exhausted by the end of August. Vehicle sales, which had collapsed during GM's and Chrysler's crisis, rebounded. From a dangerously slow pace of 10 million units per year in June 2008, they rose to well above 11 million in July and 14 million in August (see Figure 4.3). Vehicle inventories plunged as the number of units on dealers' lots fell.[21]

Cash for Clunkers Helped the Industry Climb Back

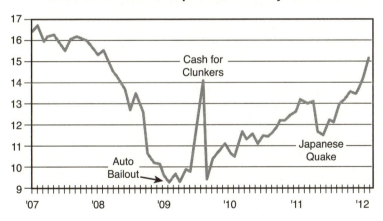

Figure 4.3 Vehicle sales, millions, annualized rate.

Sources: BEA, Moody's Analytics

Critics of the program argued that it simply shifted sales forward, stealing from the future. Rebates would do nothing to spark a long-term improvement in the U.S. auto industry or help the economy. The critics were correct, but most of the sales weren't brought forward by just 1 month or 1 quarter. Those who traded in vehicles were among America's most thrifty consumers; they likely would have kept their old cars for years until they were thoroughly worn out.[22] Cash for Clunkers was a compelling reason to buy at a time when vehicle makers desperately needed sales to restart their factories. The fortuitous timing gave sales a solid boost just as GM and Chrysler were coming out of bankruptcy. With bone-thin inventories, vehicle production quickly rebounded. It is no accident the Great Recession officially ended right when Cash for Clunkers kicked into gear.[23]

Auto-Led Recovery

The reviving auto industry was critical to the economic recovery. Vehicle sales rose steadily, from approximately 9 million per year at an annual rate in early 2009 to more than 14 million by mid-2012. This was still well below the 17-million unit pace seen before the recession, and below the 16 million trend sales that the fundamentals could support. But it was more than enough to convince automakers to increase existing workers hours and hire back many who had been laid off (see Figure 4.4).

More Auto Jobs and Lots of Hours

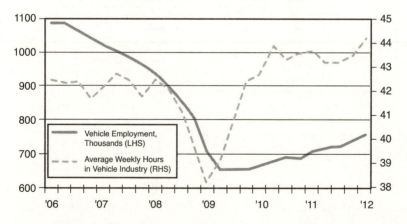

Figure 4.4 Motor vehicles and parts industry.

Source: Bureau of Labor Statistics

The nation's entire manufacturing base came back to life, pulled in significant part by the vehicle industry. Steel and fabricated metals, paint, electronics, carpets, glass, rubber, and machine tools all felt the boost. Although U.S. manufacturing is about much more than cars, much of the growth early in the recovery was a product of increased vehicle production. About one-half the growth in manufacturing during the first 2 years of the recovery reflected greater auto production, and one-half of the growth in real GDP was due to more manufacturing. Thus, one-fourth of the economy's growth during this period was solely attributable to the rebounding vehicle industry.

The economies of the industrial Midwest and South, where vehicle manufacturing is centered, began to brighten, most clearly in Michigan. That state's economy had cratered with GM and Chrysler, and it began to come back with the vehicle makers as well. Michigan's unemployment rate, which had peaked above 14% during the Great Recession, fell to near 8% by mid-2012. Although still high, Michigan's jobless rate was moving lower for the first time in a decade. Similar stories were evident in Alabama, Indiana, Kentucky, Ohio, and South Carolina.

Prospects for further gains in vehicle sales, production, and employment were good. Although much improved, sales remained well below trend levels. The 10 million vehicles in "spent-up demand" left from the automakers' aggressive promotions had been worked off and pent-up demand was developing. Consumers who had held off buying new cars, because they were worried about jobs or unable to find attractive financing, were getting closer to the point of purchase. As of mid-2012, such pent-up demand was likely worth nearly 2 million vehicles; whenever it was unleashed, sales were likely to experience an early-2000s-style boom, at least for a time.

All the vehicle makers, including the Big 3, were set to enjoy strong profits. With their significantly reduced costs, they stood to earn profits even if sales remained below 12 million units per year. Ford returned to profitability in 2009, GM in 2010, and Chrysler in 2012. There were sure to be missteps, but the vehicle industry was poised for solid growth in sales, production, earnings, and most important, in jobs.

Although the auto industry would likely have turned around eventually without government help, it would not have happened as quickly or as strongly. Without help, moreover, the industry would have emerged a shadow of what it had been. It is hard to imagine that GM could have ever recaptured its title as the world's largest vehicle producer without Washington. The recovery after the Great Recession wasn't as robust as anyone had hoped for, but it would have been much weaker without the auto bailout.

Endnotes

1. Vehicle sales are expressed at an annualized rate.

2. According to the National Bureau of Economic Research, this recession began in March 2001 and ended in November 2001.

3. This is based on data from credit bureau Equifax and includes auto loans originated by auto finance companies to borrowers with credit scores below 640. The average credit score across all American households is closer to 700. Auto lending by banks was of higher quality, with closer to one-fourth of loans made to borrowers with scores below 640.

4. In the year before the Cash for Clunkers program, the industry sold a little more than 10 million units. The estimated 16 million trend in annual vehicle sales was derived based on an error-correction model of vehicle sales.

5. Even before the UAW agreement, the industry had had some success in containing its labor costs. The industry's unit labor costs—labor compensation per unit of output—had actually declined during the late 1990s and early 2000s.

6. Dealers purchase vehicles from the manufacturers, generally financing the purchases by borrowing money in the asset-backed securities market, and repaying as they sell the cars and trucks.

7. Vehicle sales hit bottom in early 2009 at an annual pace just above 9 million units. This was the slowest rate since the recession of the early 1980s, when sales were similarly depressed by payback from a promotional effort.

8. This took a fair amount of physical stamina, and I contemplated asking for a break. I ultimately decided that if the CEOs could manage without one, so could I.

9. In 2011 dollars, the Lockheed loan guarantees amounted to approximately $1.5 billion. Chrysler's guarantees totaled less than $5 billion. In both instances, the government made money.

10. The credit-default swap market had also already priced in a high likelihood that the automakers would not make good on their debts.

11. According to the University of Michigan's survey, which began in 1952, consumer sentiment hit a record low in early 2009.

12. The House of Representatives did vote in favor of a $14 billion auto bailout.

13. In my Senate testimony I argued that the automakers would need between $75 and $125 billion to avoid bankruptcy. This was probably too little because it was based on a vehicle-sales outlook that turned out to be too optimistic.

14. When GM left bankruptcy, the U.S. government owned 60% of the company, the UAW owned 17%, the Canadian government owned 12%, and bondholders owned the rest. When Chrysler left bankruptcy, the UAW owned 55%, Fiat owned 20%, bondholders owned 15%, the U.S. government owned 8%, and the Canadian government owned 2%.

15. See http://www.indystar.com/article/20120422/NEWS05/204220368/Fighting-the-auto-bailout-was-turning-point-in-Richard-Mourdock-s-political-life?odyssey=tab%7Cmostpopular%7Ctext%7CFRONTPAGE

16. GM's stock price at its IPO was $33 but seldom traded as high as that afterward. To break even, the government needed to sell its remaining stake for approximately $44 per share.

17. The Automotive Supplier Support Program was established in March 2009.

18. The Warranty Commitment Program was established in March 2009.

19. The Term Asset Backed Securities Loan Facility was established in November 2008.

20. The program's formal name was the Car Allowance Rebate System. A number of developed economies implemented similar programs.

21. According to the Bureau of Economic Analysis, vehicle inventories in August 2009 hit a record low at approximately half the level prior to the Great Recession.

22. According to a survey conducted by the Department of Transportation, the average timeframe over which new car purchasers said they would have otherwise sold, traded in, or disposed of their old vehicle was nearly 3 years—far longer than the few months that the program's critics hypothesized.

23. Cash for Clunkers also provided environmental benefits. Trade-ins averaged less than 16 miles per gallon, but the new vehicles averaged more than 24 miles per gallon.

5

Stimulus Is Not a Dirty Word

The emails with the Obama transition team began only days after the November 2008 election. The economy was in free fall, and Obama's people were scrambling to respond. They were convinced, as were most economists, that a big fiscal stimulus plan was needed, and they were asking how big I thought it should be. What kinds of tax cuts and government spending increases should it include?[1] They also asked me to use my model of the U.S. economy to quantify the impact of various proposals on GDP, jobs, and unemployment.

Although I had been an economic advisor to the McCain campaign, I knew Obama's economic advisors well. Jason Furman, who had been a scholar at the Brookings Institution, a Democratic-leaning think tank, and later the National Economic Council, had asked me in January to be on a panel at Brookings to discuss the merits of fiscal stimulus.[2] Furman, former Treasury Secretary Larry Summers, and future CBO Director Doug Elmendorf were pushing the Bush administration to provide "temporary, targeted, and timely" fiscal support for the flagging economy.[3] Although we didn't know it at the time, the Great Recession had already begun.

The Bush administration had reluctantly accepted the idea, providing a round of temporary tax cuts in summer 2008. Although modest—totaling approximately $170 billion—the cuts seemed to help as the economy stabilized for a few months. But this was quickly undermined by fallout from the unraveling financial system. The Obama transition team knew that a much larger stimulus package was needed, including not only more tax cuts but also a temporary increase in government spending. But how big, and with what kinds of tax cuts and spending increases?

Initially, $400 billion was thought to be the right amount, with an equal mix of tax cuts—mainly in the form of a payroll tax holiday—and spending increases, mostly aid to unemployed workers and state and local governments, as well as infrastructure spending. But it didn't take long to realize that this wouldn't be enough, given the mounting economic damage from the financial panic. By Thanksgiving, the package had grown to $600 billion; by early December it was up to $800 billion. By Christmas, Christina Romer, who soon would take over the President's Council of Economic Advisors, had asked me to assess the economic impact of a $1 trillion stimulus package.

The Obama administration and Congress eventually came to terms, passing the American Recovery and Reinvestment Act in February 2009. The stimulus contained in the bill was valued at a little more than $700 billion.[4] Called ARRA or simply the Recovery Act, the legislation became synonymous with the government's response to the Great Recession and thus a lightning rod for the Obama administration's harshest critics. Some called the Recovery Act ineffectual and claimed that fiscal stimulus more generally leads to bigger government, bloated national deficits, and debt.[5] On the other side, some believed the Recovery Act was too small, given the downturn's severity, to revitalize the economy. There was also a scorched-earth faction that believed government should do nothing to stem the pain of recessions and let the economic chips fall where they may.

Those who argued the stimulus didn't work seized on the Obama administration's forecast that if the Recovery Act became law, the unemployment rate wouldn't rise above 8%.[6] In fact, the unemployment rate had already blown past 8% when that forecast was made, but Obama's economists didn't know it because the government's statistics badly lagged the economy's rapid deterioration. Forecasting the unemployment rate was a serious error by those marketing the merits of the Recovery Act, but in substance they were correct. The

Great Recession officially ended in June 2009, 4 months after the passage of the Recovery Act, and the point at which the stimulus was having its greatest effect. Without the stimulus, the recession would have been much longer and deeper, and unemployment much higher.

The administration's second marketing mistake was claiming to have "shovel-ready" projects lined up for the additional infrastructure spending included in the Recovery Act. Although spending on roads and bridges was a miniscule part of the stimulus package, it became a benchmark for the government's ability to pump stimulus money quickly into the economy. Though the administration had said the projects would be far enough in their planning to start up quickly, in many cases they weren't and didn't. The tax cuts, aid to unemployed workers, and money to strapped state and local governments helped immediately. But because of the infrastructure delays, the Recovery Act was tarred as too slow to help. Ironically, given the length and severity of the recession, the delay in infrastructure spending turned out to be a plus.

Critics who argued that any fiscal stimulus would only add to the nation's debt also had other, more substantive complaints. Some maintained that the more the government borrowed to finance tax cuts and spending increases, the more consumers and businesses would pull back. A drop in private spending, investment, and hiring would wash out any benefit from the government's actions. This might be a valid point if the government's borrowing drove up interest rates and crowded out consumer and business borrowing. It might also have some weight if households believed the government would eventually raise taxes and cut spending to pay for current borrowing, inducing people to save more in anticipation. Although conceivable, these theories did not accurately describe the U.S. economy in the early 21st century, a period characterized by low rates of interest and saving.

Critics also used the influential work of academic economists Carmen Reinhart and Kenneth Rogoff to argue that fiscal stimulus would fall flat because households, businesses, and banks were too burdened with debt to respond.[7] The economy was in a mess fundamentally because of out-of-control borrowing during the housing bubble; without a reduction in debt—known as deleveraging—consumer spending, investment, and lending would remain weak regardless of the stimulus. The stimulus might help modestly and for a short time, but after government help ended, the economy would still be in a rut, and the nation's debt load would be much larger. This is a plausible theory, but events belied it; the fiscal stimulus seemed actually to facilitate deleveraging. The government's aid gave the private sector enough financial breathing room to work debt down gracefully. In contrast with most of the countries examined by Reinhart and Rogoff, private-sector deleveraging in the U.S. occurred rapidly. By early 2012, it was largely over.

Across the spectrum from those who charged that fiscal stimulus didn't work were others who said it was too small; that government support worked well enough but much more was needed. This resonated with me.[8] The economy had lost more than 800,000 jobs in January 2009 as Congress debated the Recovery Act. The case for fiscal stimulus was even stronger, moreover, when considering that the other major option for cushioning the economy's plunge—help from the Federal Reserve—was nearly played out. The Fed's benchmark interest rate was already near zero, and the central bank had begun using an unprecedented tactic called quantitative easing (QE)—large-scale purchases of Treasury bonds and mortgage securities—to bring down long-term interest rates. With the Fed unable to do much more, the need for fiscal stimulus was all the greater.

I was thus disappointed when the House of Representatives scaled back the Recovery Act by more than $100 billion to get it through the Senate. Yet given the crumbling economy, getting the law passed quickly was even more important than its size. Many proponents also reasoned that if more help were needed later, lawmakers could be persuaded to provide it. Indeed, they did. As expiration neared for various parts of the Recovery Act, such as the emergency unemployment insurance program and accelerated depreciation of tax benefits for business investment, Congress agreed to extend them. Lawmakers also enacted other forms of stimulus, such as the payroll tax break for employers and the payroll tax holiday for workers.

Between 2008 and 2012, fiscal policymakers enacted more than $1.4 trillion in fiscal stimulus, a sum equal to almost 10% of GDP. This was the biggest federal stimulus since the New Deal in the 1930s, but it was proportional to the severity of the Great Recession. Fiscal stimulus has been used to respond to every downturn since the Depression, in amounts roughly equal to the gap between what the economy could produce and what it actually was producing when the recessions were deepest.[9] At the nadir of the Great Recession, that gap equaled just about 10% of GDP. Although the mix of tax cuts and spending increases wasn't what most economists would have prescribed unfettered by political constraints, it wasn't far off. Most measures included in the stimulus had big economic multipliers—that is, they produced a relatively large bang for the buck, or economic benefit per dollar cost to taxpayers.

A well-designed fiscal stimulus program also requires that temporary measures be withdrawn in a way that doesn't undermine growth. Early signs suggested the Recovery Act was on target here, as many of its provisions began to expire in 2011. But in mid-2012, the economy faced a potential major reversal; massive tax increases and government spending cuts were set to kick in early in 2013, threatening to undo much of the recovery's gains.[10] The effects of such sudden reversals in fiscal policy could be seen in Europe, where a number of economies had fallen back into recession. The United States was in much better shape, in large part because of successful fiscal and monetary stimulus programs. Still, U.S. policymakers needed to tread carefully to gracefully unwind the stimulus without damaging the recovery.[11]

The merits of fiscal stimulus inspire an almost theological debate. There is no way to wind the clock back to see how the economy would have performed without it. But economists have tools to simulate these counterfactual, "what-if" scenarios, and among those of us who run such experiments for a living, there is near universal agreement that without the fiscal stimulus, the Great Recession would have been much deeper and longer. The stimulus cost taxpayers a bundle, but if fiscal policymakers had done nothing, the costs to taxpayers brought on by a weaker economy would have been far greater.

Stimulus Logic

Within months of its passage, the Recovery Act had become deeply unpopular. Critics made it synonymous with all that was wrong with both the economy and with the government's response. Although the Great Recession had given way to recovery just months after the stimulus became law, growth was still tepid, and unemployment lingered near double digits. Stimulus was politically a dirty word.

Not surprisingly, the Recovery Act became a favorite target for the Obama administration's opponents, who asserted on talk shows not only that the stimulus had failed, but also that it was an un-American, unprecedented intrusion by government into the economy. They portrayed the stimulus as something only a socialist European government might try.

This demonization of the stimulus proved so politically potent that even lawmakers who had initially endorsed the Recovery Act began to run away from it. At a meeting I attended just prior to the 2010 election, Democratic congressmen were anticipating losing control of the House and blaming the stimulus for their party's coming defeat. They clearly had expected too much. Jump-starting the recovery wasn't enough; they evidently thought the stimulus should solve all the economy's ills. And judging by the 2010 election results, voters felt the same way.

Yet contrary to the critics' assertions, using fiscal stimulus to combat recessions isn't novel. It has been part of the policy response to most every recession since the 1930s. The logic is straightforward: When scared consumers and businesses pull back on spending and investment, government should fill the void, temporarily spending more and taxing less. The deeper the downturn, the bigger and more aggressive the government's response should be. And for the stimulus to be effective, it should give the most help to those struggling the most and do it quickly. Stimulus won't work if too many households and businesses are already in bankruptcy or foreclosure.

Another reason to use stimulus, particularly in serious downturns, is to avoid hysteresis. This sounds like a bad illness, and for an economy, it is the worst kind: The downturn is so bad it undermines the economy's capability to produce as much in the future. Workers unemployed for a long time may never return to work as their skills and marketability erode. What employer is going to hire someone who hasn't been able to find work for months or years?[12]

Both Democratic and Republican presidents have used fiscal stimulus. The Bush administration employed it not only in 2008, but also in 2001, 2002, and 2003 to cushion the stock market's technology bust and blunt the economic impact of the 9/11 terrorist attacks. In all, the Bush stimulus totaled 1.3 percentage points of GDP, about equal to the gap between actual and potential GDP at the worst point of the 2001 recession.[13]

Although the immediate objective of a fiscal stimulus is simply to end a recession and jump-start recovery, presidents from both parties have also used stimulus measures to achieve other policy objectives. The stimulus legislation in 2001 included lower personal marginal tax rates, which the Bush administration hoped would remain part of the tax code forever. (Whether they would was still a question in 2012. Originally scheduled to sunset in 2011, the lower Bush tax rates were extended until the start of 2013.) The Obama administration loaded the Recovery Act with funding for projects of various kinds, from road and bridge repairs to digitizing health records and research at the National Institute of Health.

The need for a fiscal stimulus was particularly acute in the Great Recession, which was so severe that it overwhelmed the federal budget's automatic stabilizers—spending and tax provisions designed to kick in when the economy struggles. Spending on unemployment insurance, for example, rises when more workers lose jobs, without Congress having to approve it. But unemployment insurance in most states provides only 26 weeks of benefits—sufficient for normal times or even a mild recession, but not for a time of nearly double-digit unemployment. It required a fiscal stimulus to extend UI benefits for as long as 99 weeks in some hard-hit states. This was ultimately the most costly part of the federal program.

Many nations rely more heavily than the United States does on automatic stabilizers and thus are less inclined to enact new stimulus during recessions. But given the severity of the Great Recession, fiscal stimulus was a part of nearly every nation's response. More than $5 trillion in global stimulus was fired at the Great Recession. China was particularly aggressive and successful, deploying a fiscal stimulus equal to almost 16% of its GDP, almost double the size of the U.S. response.[14]

The need for a fiscal stimulus was more urgent because of the Federal Reserve's plight. Normally, it is quicker and cheaper to combat recessions with monetary policy than with fiscal policy, which must endure a typically arduous political process. But monetary policy was all but played out by the time the Recovery Act reached Congress early in 2009. The Federal Reserve had cut its normal benchmark interest rates effectively to zero and turned to QE to help support the economy further. Although Fed Chairman Ben Bernanke argued the central bank still had monetary policy tools to battle the recession, in the next breath Bernanke beseeched the Obama administration and Congress to help out with a fiscal stimulus.[15]

Temporary Tax Cuts

After much brinkmanship, Washington's feuding lawmakers more or less came through. When all was said and done, policymakers agreed to $1.4 trillion worth of fiscal stimulus to fight the Great Recession. This was a massive response, equal to almost 10% of GDP (see Table 5.1). In the popular mind the stimulus remained synonymous with the Recovery Act, but it began in spring 2008, under President Bush, when the government mailed out tax rebate checks. A series of smaller stimulus measures followed, including the Cash for Clunkers auto rebates, tax credits for homebuyers, a payroll tax credit for employers who hired the unemployed, a payroll tax holiday for workers, and other programs.

Table 5.1 Fiscal Stimulus During the Great Recession (*Billions $*)

Total Fiscal Stimulus	1,433
Spending Increases	819
Tax Cuts	614
Economic Stimulus Act of 2008	170
American Recovery and Reinvestment Act of 2009	783
Infrastructure and Other Spending	147
Traditional Infrastructure	38
Nontraditional Infrastructure	109
Transfers to state and local governments	174
Medicaid	87
Education	87
Transfers to persons	271
Social Security	13
Unemployment Assistance	224
Food Stamps	10
Cobra Payments	24

Tax cuts	190
Businesses & other tax incentives	40
Making Work Pay	64
First-time homebuyer tax credit	14
Individuals excluding increase in AMT exemption	72
Cash for Appliances	0.3
Cash for Clunkers	3
HIRE Act (Job Tax Credit)	17
Worker, Homeownership, and Business Assistance Act of 2009	91
Extended unemployment insurance benefits Mar 16)	6
Extended unemployment insurance benefits (Apr 14)	12
Extended unemployment insurance benefits (May 27)	3
Extended unemployment insurance benefits (July 22)	34
Extended/expanded net operating loss provisions of ARRA°	33
Extension of homebuyer tax credit	3
Department of Defense Appropriations Act of 2010	>2
Extended guarantees and fee waivers for SBA loans	>1
Expanded COBRA premium subsidy	>1
Education Jobs and Medicaid Assistance Act of 2010	26
Tax Relief, unemployment insurance Reauthorization, and Job Creation Act of 2010	189
Temp extension of UI benefits (outlay)	56
Temp extension of investment incentives	22
Temp payroll tax holiday (change in revenue)	112
Temporary Payroll Tax Cut Continuation Act of 2011	29
Middle Class Tax Relief and Job Creation Act of 2012	125

Sources: CBO, Treasury, Recovery.gov, IRS, Department of Labor, Joint Committee on Taxation, Council of Economic Advisors, Moody's Analytics

The total effort was well apportioned between taxes and government spending, with more than 40% in tax cuts and less than 60% in spending increases. The tax cuts for individuals provided quick relief.

Lower- and middle-income households received rebate checks, had less taken out of their pay, and benefited from credits for purchasing homes and appliances. The tax cuts didn't pack as big an economic punch as an increase in government spending because some of the money was saved and some used to repay debt, rather than to fuel new spending that would stimulate further activity. On the other hand, tax cuts could be implemented quickly.

Critics such as Stanford University Professor John Taylor argued that because the stimulus tax cuts were temporary—in contrast with the kinds of cuts implemented by President Reagan in the early 1980s or President Bush in the early 2000s—they would do little to lift consumer spending.[16] But Taylor's concern was misplaced, as can be seen in the 2008 tax rebates. These payments significantly lifted after-tax income, but consumer spending did not immediately rise. One reason involved income caps: Higher-income households did not receive the tax rebates. At the time, stock and house prices were falling rapidly, prompting upper-income American families to trim spending and save significantly more. The saving rate for households in the top quintile of the income distribution surged from close to nothing in early 2007 to double digits by early 2008.[17] Lower- and middle-income households did spend a significant part of their tax rebates, but the sharp pullback by higher-income households significantly diluted the impact on overall spending.[18]

Businesses also received substantial tax breaks to increase investment, which had declined sharply during the recession.[19] Although such incentives have historically not been particularly effective as stimulus—they don't induce much extra near-term investment—they were more potent this time because of the financial system's near collapse and resulting credit crunch, which made businesses' cost of capital more of an impediment to investment.[20] The tax breaks also came at relatively modest cost to the budget because the revenue lost upfront would be largely paid back in subsequent years when businesses were making money again and had higher tax liabilities.

Emergency UI and the Multiplier

Fiscal stimulus included a potpourri of temporary government spending initiatives, the largest being the extension of unemployment insurance benefits beyond the regular 26 weeks states generally provide. Emergency UI is a tried-and-true form of stimulus, often used during recessions. It is also a humane thing to do when unemployment is high and long, as it was during the Great Recession. During the worst of it, well over half of all those unemployed were still out of work when their regular benefits expired.

Beyond meeting a pressing human need, however, unemployment insurance also constitutes one of the most potent forms of economic stimulus available. Most unemployed workers spend their benefits immediately; without such help, laid-off workers and their families have little choice but to slash spending. The loss of benefits is debilitating not only for unemployed workers, but also for their friends, family, and neighbors who may be providing financial help themselves. Emergency UI has one of the largest multipliers of any form of fiscal stimulus.[21]

Arguably the most hotly debated aspect of fiscal stimulus is the concept of the multiplier. Stimulus skeptics contend that multipliers don't exist, believing that temporary tax cuts or spending increases do not stimulate additional economic activity. Whatever the government does, they maintain, is washed out as consumers spend less and businesses cut back investment.[22] On the other side, I and other stimulus supporters argued that when unemployment is high, factories are running below capacity, and hotel rooms go unfilled, multipliers from government fiscal action can be large. Not only does the economy gain the value of additional spending or tax cuts, but those actions produce more consumer spending and business investment, multiplying their effectiveness.

It may seem odd that economists can't look at the historical record and settle this debate. Unfortunately, it is difficult to disentangle the data on government purchases to see whether changes stem from explicit policy decisions or result from other forces in the economy. Wartimes would seem to offer good case studies because defense outlays are clearly determined by policymakers, but even these are problematic. The war effort often requires that consumers defer spending, as they did in World War II. There was no rationing during the Vietnam War, but the private sector was running flat out. With unemployment low, increased defense spending crowded out consumer and business activity.[23]

This highlights an important point, namely that multipliers are not immutable; they vary depending on a range of factors, including the amount of slack in the economy. During the teeth of the recession, the multiplier on emergency UI was estimated to be more than 1.6. That is, for every $1 increase in emergency UI, GDP was $1.60 greater one year later (see Table 5.2).[24] By early 2012, the estimated multiplier was a much smaller 1.4. Unemployment was still high and factory utilization low, but conditions had improved, and there wasn't nearly as much slack in the economy.

Table 5.2 Fiscal Stimulus Multipliers (*As of the End of 2011*)

	Bang for the Buck
Tax Cuts	
Refundable Lump-Sum Tax Rebate	1.22
Non-refundable Lump-Sum Tax Rebate	1.01
Temporary Tax Cuts	
Child Tax Credit, ARRA Parameters	1.38
Payroll Tax Holiday for Employees	1.27
Earned Income Tax Credit, ARRA Parameters	1.24
Job Tax Credit	1.20
Making Work Pay	1.19
Payroll Tax Holiday for Employers	1.05
Across the Board Tax Cut	0.98
Housing Tax Credit	0.82
Accelerated Depreciation	0.29

	Bang for the Buck
Loss Carryback	0.25
Permanent Tax Cuts	
Extend Alternative Minimum Tax Patch	0.53
Make Dividend and Capital Gains Tax Cuts Permanent	0.39
Make Bush Income Tax Cuts Permanent	0.35
Cut in Corporate Tax Rate	0.32
Spending Increases	
Temporary Increase in Food Stamps	1.71
Temporary Federal Financing of Work-Share Programs	1.64
Extending Unemployment Insurance Benefits	1.55
Increase Defense Spending	1.53
Increase Infrastructure Spending	1.44
General Aid to State Governments	1.34
Low Income Home Energy Assistance Program (LIHEAP)	1.13

Note: The bang for the buck is estimated by the one year $ change in GDP for a given $ reduction in federal tax revenue or increase in spending.
Source: Moody's Analytics

Emergency UI isn't without problems. There are reasonable concerns that some recipients took advantage of the program, particularly since as many as 99 weeks of benefits were available in economically hard-hit states. Some unemployed workers could have delayed taking jobs, preferring to collect UI. Some older workers might also have delayed retirement until their benefits were exhausted. Anecdotal and statistical evidence pointed to such abuses; indeed, research suggested that the unemployment rate was approximately half a percentage point higher than it would have been without the disincentive effects of emergency UI.[25]

There were abuses, but the vast majority of UI beneficiaries needed the help. This could be seen most clearly in the ratio of unemployed workers per job opening. According to the Bureau of Labor Statistics, this ratio rose to about 6 to 1 during the worst of the recession and remained above the more normal 1 to 1 well into the recovery (see Figure 5.1). It also was wrong to assume that forcing the unemployed to take any job available was desirable. It may very well have been better for workers, employers, and the broader economy to let them search longer for appropriate jobs. Considering all the effects of the emergency UI program, including the disincentive effects and the benefits to aggregate demand, the program was a resounding success.

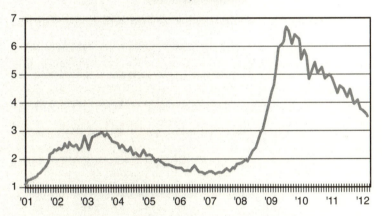

No Help Wanted

Figure 5.1 Number of unemployed for each job opening.

Sources: BLS, Moody's Analytics

Municipal Bailout

The fiscal stimulus also included a bailout of financially hard-pressed state and local governments. This too is typical in recessions. Because nearly all states are legally bound to balance their budgets, and because nearly all states face significant budget shortfalls during recessions, they would be forced to cut spending and raise taxes more sharply without federal aid, adding to the economy's weakness. Much of the federal help in the Recovery Act came via the Medicaid program, which states fund jointly with the federal government, and through support for schools, police, and firefighters.

State and local government aid is another especially potent form of stimulus with a large multiplier. But this is defensive stimulus; it prevents governments from having to make draconian cuts in services or raise taxes, which would weaken consumer spending. As was said in the debate over the fiscal stimulus, these measures *saved* jobs rather than *creating* them.

The principal rap against providing such aid is that it lets profligate state and local governments off the hook. They don't need to make the hard budget choices necessary to run efficiently. But this criticism rang hollow in the many states and municipalities that were forced to cut jobs and programs and raise taxes. State and local budget cutting was kept modest by federal aid early in the recession, but it intensified later when the federal money ran out. Most of the cutting was done by local governments in places where falling housing and commercial real estate prices reduced property tax revenues; eventually these governments laid off hundreds of thousands of teachers and other employees.[26] It was painful, but because of the federal aid, it was no longer lethal to the economic recovery.

This stands in striking contrast to the response to the recession in Europe. Instead of providing funds to help troubled nations such as Greece and Portugal survive the downturn, the European Union demanded that euro zone governments work harder to shrink their budget deficits. The resulting austerity only exacerbated Europe's downturn and added to national governments' budget problems.

Shovel Ready

Arguably the most visible and controversial part of the fiscal stimulus involved infrastructure spending. Although this was only a small part of the package, it became the litmus test of how quickly and effectively the stimulus affected the economy. This was a tough test. It generally takes time to get these projects going, which is not necessarily bad; rushing raises the risks of financing unproductive projects. Yet the time problem makes infrastructure spending an unwieldy form of fiscal stimulus. The last time it was tried was during the 1930s' Great Depression, when the federal government sponsored massive public works projects such as the Hoover Dam.

The Obama administration had argued that many of the projects it was funding were "shovel-ready," and thus ripe to begin boosting jobs and activity. The necessary design and engineering work was complete and the environmental impact studies done; all that was required was a check from the government. Although many of the projects did start in record time, there actually is no such thing as "shovel-ready," and as that became evident, criticism mounted of the entire stimulus package. The tax cuts and other spending were flowing into the economy quickly and on cue, but that didn't cut through the din of complaints over delays on the road and bridge projects. Moreover, although infrastructure delays were disappointing, they weren't that significant given the length and depth of the Great Recession. The infrastructure money ultimately proved welcome when it arrived as other stimulus activity began to fade.

Infrastructure spending has a sizable multiplier, providing a significant boost to the nation's depressed construction and manufacturing industries in areas with little else. The infrastructure projects were a hodgepodge, ranging from roads and bridges to electric power grids and medical records. But given the uncertain payoff of such projects, such diversification was probably a plus. Japan's experience with fiscal stimulus in the 1990s suggests large-scale traditional infrastructure spending offers diminishing returns. Overinvestment in bridges ulti-mately creates bridges to nowhere.

Although most projects were reasonably well vetted for their eco-nomic merits, not all were, and the process wasn't devoid of politics. Examples of questionable projects funded by stimulus money came to light, such as an airport renovation in thinly populated rural Pennsyl-vania or funding for aquatic farming in Minnesota. And concern that some lawmakers would try to turn temporary stimulus spending into permanent spending was, I can testify, legitimate. But on the whole, given how much money flowed from government to the private sector in such a short period of time, it is surprising that there weren't many more stories of politics trumping economics.

Strong Evidence

To conclusively prove that the fiscal stimulus worked would require a time machine; we would effectively need to rerun history without the stimulus to see if things turned out as well. But although proof may not come neatly packaged in ways that meet the standards of physical science, the circumstantial evidence is as strong as any in economics. Moreover, economists' historical models of the economy, which act something like time machines, can be simulated to gauge what stimulus actually accomplished.

Such evidence argues strongly that fiscal stimulus worked: It short-circuited the negative cycle of the Great Recession and pro-vided a catalyst for recovery. The stimulus was never intended to be a source of long-term economic growth, only to calm scared consum-ers and businesses to help them get back on their feet. The timing of events was more than coincidence: The Recovery Act was passed in February 2009. The Great Recession officially ended in June, and job growth resumed a year later in February 2010. America's epic slide ended just when the fiscal stimulus was providing its maximum boost to the economy.

What matters for economic growth is the pace of the change in taxes and government outlays created by the stimulus. There was no stimulus working at the end of 2008, but by the second and third quarters of 2009, the stimulus had pumped more than $100 billion into the economy (see Figure 5.2). This massive, rapid change was why the economy went from free fall to recovery in just a few months.

Surging Fiscal Stimulus Ended the Great Recession

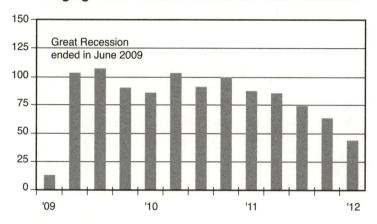

Figure 5.2 Fiscal stimulus spendout, bil $.

Source: Moody's Analytics

Based on the stimulus' size and its estimated multipliers, the government's effort added almost 4 percentage points to real GDP growth in the third quarter of 2009, when the recovery began. Without the stimulus, the recession would have continued.[27] Even if the multipliers are smaller than my estimates, it is a big stretch to suggest the recession ended when it did for reasons that had nothing to do with the stimulus.

A more involved multiplier analysis uses economic models to measure the stimulus' impact. Models are quantitative representations of the economy based on historical data and information. Economists apply various statistical techniques to data collected as far back as the Great Depression to capture the workings of the economy. It's not unlike a model of an office building, used by architects to assess how it would fare in an earthquake or terrorist attack.

Not surprisingly, there are nearly as many models of the economy as there are economists. Surprisingly, most concluded that the fiscal stimulus was a plus for the economy. There were a few dissenters, but they focused on narrow aspects of the stimulus package.[28] The Congressional Budget Office—the nonpartisan federal government agency established by Congress to assess the economic impact of government policy—determined that the stimulus provided a meaningful boost to the economy (see Table 5.3). According to the CBO, if there had been no Recovery Act, there would have been between 1.3 and 2.8 million fewer jobs by the first quarter of 2010 when job growth resumed. My own estimate was 1.9 million jobs.[29]

Table 5.3 Estimated Macroeconomic Impact of the Recovery Act (*Change Attributable to American Recovery and Reinvestment Act*)

	Real GDP		**Unemployment Rate**	
	Low Estimate	**High Estimate**	**Low Estimate**	**High Estimate**
2009	0.9	1.9	-0.3	-0.5
2010	1.5	4.2	-0.7	-1.8
2011	0.8	2.3	-0.5	-1.4
2012	0.3	0.8	-0.2	-0.6
	Employment (Millions)		**Employment, FTE (Millions)**	
	Low Estimate	**High Estimate**	**Low Estimate**	**High Estimate**
2009	0.5	0.9	0.7	1.3
2010	1.3	3.3	1.9	4.8
2011	0.9	2.7	1.2	3.7
2012	0.4	1.1	0.4	1.3

Notes:

FTE is a year of full-time-equivalent employment, which is equal to 40 hours of employment per week for one year.

CBO determined a range of economic impacts derived from different models of the economy; the low and high estimates in the range are shown in this table.

The results are for calendar years.

Source: Congressional Budget Office, http://www.cbo.gov/sites/default/files/cbofiles/attachments/08-24-ARRA.pdf

More jobs means a lower unemployment rate. According to the CBO, the Recovery Act lowered the jobless rate as much as 2 percentage points by late 2010 when unemployment was peaking at 10%. That is, without the Recovery Act, unemployment would likely have topped out near 12%. This was close to what I projected in my January 2009 testimony before the House Budget Committee when I argued that even more stimulus was needed, given how high unemployment would be even with the Recovery Act.[30]

The Obama administration also expected the Recovery Act to lower unemployment by a couple of percentage points, but they erred badly when they forecast that the jobless rate would peak around 8% if the bill were passed. This made little sense, given that the day before it released its forecast in early January, the Bureau of Labor Statistics had reported that unemployment jumped one-half percentage point to 7.8%. The mistake handed the administration's opponents a political tool, which they used inappropriately but effectively to undermine the merits of the stimulus. The narrative regarding the stimulus was set: Economists could claim it had worked as it was supposed to, but that didn't resonate with the public.

As more data became available, economists used other techniques to isolate the impact of the fiscal stimulus. One particularly fruitful approach was to examine how different state economies responded.[31] Aid to state and local governments and some infrastructure spending were allocated to states based on fixed formulas, independent of how the state's economy was doing. States that received more of these funds as part of the Recovery Act did measurably better, pretty much as the models had predicted.

It's unfortunate that the question of how much the fiscal stimulus has helped cannot be settled through an accounting exercise. Washington's bean counters cannot canvas the country and pick out which jobs were created or saved by the stimulus. The best tools available involve statistical analysis, which is subject to a range of uncertainties. But although the exact number of jobs that would have been lost without the fiscal stimulus will never be known for sure, it is clear that number is significant. Based on my research and that of others, I'm confident that if not for the stimulus, the Great Recession would have been much longer and deeper and the cost to taxpayers much greater.

Exit Strategy

A fiscal stimulus should be judged not only by how effective it is in ending recessions, but how gracefully it is removed. Tax cuts and spending increases are meant to be temporary, lasting until the economy is healed but no longer, lest they inappropriately add to the nation's deficits. Managing this transition can be tricky. It is never entirely clear when the economy is solid enough to do without the help of the stimulus.

Proof of how difficult this can be could be seen in Europe, where the transition was badly misjudged. European policymakers were eager to withdraw both monetary and fiscal stimulus that had been in effect during the Great Recession, and acted to end support as quickly as possible. By early 2011, the European Central Bank was tightening monetary policy and national government budgets were swinging sharply from stimulus to austerity. Some of this stemmed from a concern, which was acute in Germany, that stimulus would cause inflation to flare up. There was also a view that fiscal austerity would reestablish investor confidence, which had been shaken by mounting national budget deficits. The theory was that austerity would lead to lower long-term interest rates, whose economic benefit would offset any drag from cuts in government spending and higher taxes.[32] This was a serious misjudgment. European austerity was so severe it pushed the euro zone back into recession, making it all the more difficult for governments to bring their budgets back in order.

The ECB was forced to reverse course by late 2011. It then began cutting interest rates, buying the debt of troubled European sovereigns, and providing trillions of cheap euros to the banking system to head off bank failures and a financial crisis. The ECB's actions quickly dwarfed those of the Federal Reserve and even the Bank of Japan, which had been struggling to jump-start its economy for decades.[33] European fiscal policymakers were slower to change course, but as livid voters threw out governments across the continent in the spring of 2012, sentiment swung away from fiscal austerity and toward policies that would promote growth.

U.S. policymakers took a different course. Despite intense debate and brinkmanship, which peaked in the August 2011 showdown over the Treasury's debt ceiling, monetary and fiscal stimulus were withdrawn much more slowly. The Federal Reserve held firmly to its zero-interest rate policy and remained clearly willing to provide more quantitative easing if it was needed. Congress and the Obama administration also allowed the fiscal stimulus to fade away gradually; they came to terms on additional payroll tax cuts, more emergency unemployment insurance and temporary extensions of the Bush-era tax cuts.

The stimulus went from adding almost 3 percentage points to real GDP growth at its peak in 2009 to adding modestly to growth in 2010 (see Figure 5.3). Fiscal policy turned into a slight drag in 2011, and became a bigger drag in 2012. U.S. policymakers arguably had more room to maneuver than did those in Europe; the U.S. was the global economy's safe haven and benefited from a persistent flight to quality that kept interest rates low and supported stock prices. But the stronger U.S. economy also helped, in no small part because of the aggressive use of stimulus during the recession and its judicious withdrawal during the recovery. There was much more work to do to make the federal budget sustainable, but policymakers seemed to realize that this would take time. Washington may have been politically dysfunctional, but somehow managed to get it roughly right.

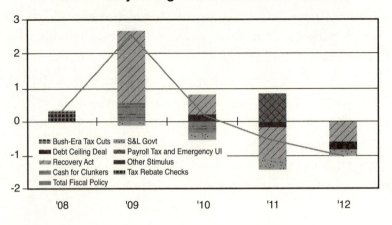

Figure 5.3 Contribution to real GDP growth under current law, %.

Source: Moody's Analytics

Endnotes

1. Many other economists were also surveyed by the Obama economic team for their opinions.

2. Being on a panel with former Treasury Secretary Robert Rubin, Harvard Professor Martin Feldstein, and former CBO Director and Federal Reserve Vice Chairman Alice Rivlin thrust me into the economic policy debate. A transcript of the Brookings event on fiscal stimulus is available at http://www.brookings.edu/events/2008/01/10-fiscalstimulus.

3. For a good explanation of the Three T's principle behind fiscal stimulus, see http://www.brookings.edu/research/opinions/2008/01/26-economic-stimulus-furman

4. The Recovery Act officially totaled $783 billion, but $72 billion of this was an extension of the inflation patch to the Alternative Minimum Tax that is routinely extended by Congress and thus did not represent additional stimulus.

5. Stanford University Professor John Taylor was among the strongest proponents of the view that fiscal stimulus does little if anything to support economic growth. See "An Empirical Analysis of the Revival of Fiscal Activism in the 2000s," *Journal of Economic Literature*, 2011. http://www.stanford.edu/~johntayl/JEL_Taylor_Final%20Pages.pdf

6. See "The Job Impact of the American Recovery and Reinvestment Act," Christina Romer and Jared Bernstein. January 9, 2009. http://www.economy.com/mark-zandi/documents/The_Job_Impact_of_the_American_Recovery_and_Reinvestment_Plan.pdf

7. The Reinhart-Rogoff book *This Time Is Different* analyzes financial crises through the ages and around the world to draw parallels with the Great Recession. The authors argue the economic and fiscal fallout from financial crises lasts for many years. See http://press.princeton.edu/titles/8973.html

8. I made the case for additional stimulus as part of the Recovery Act in testimony to the House Budget Committee in January 2009. See http://www.economy.com/mark-zandi/documents/House%20Budget%20Committee%20012709.pdf

9. The difference between actual GDP and what the economy can produce or its potential GDP is known as the output gap. The Congressional Budget Office provides an estimate of potential GDP and the output gap http://www.cbo.gov/publication/42912

10. To end the standoff over raising the Treasury debt ceiling in August 2011, the Obama administration and Congress agreed to cut $2 trillion in government spending over the following decade. Those cuts were slated to begin in 2013.

11. A vocal group represented by Nobel laureate and *New York Times* columnist Paul Krugman argued that even more government spending was needed. Krugman noted that unemployment and underemployment remained unacceptably high and would likely take years to return to normal levels. He also rebutted worries that the federal government was borrowing too much and that interest rates would rise significantly. See "End This Depression Now" http://books.wwnorton.com/books/978-0-393-08877-9/

12. The role of hysteresis in determining appropriate fiscal policy is well laid out in "Fiscal Policy in a Depressed Economy," Delong and Summers, Brookings Papers on Economic Activity, Spring 2012. http://www.brookings.edu/~/media/Files/Programs/ES/BPEA/2012_spring_bpea_papers/2012_spring_BPEA_delongsummers.pdf

13. This includes only the cost of the tax cuts from 2001 to 2003. The tax cuts instituted in this period were largely due to expire at the end of 2012.

14. The Chinese stimulus also included increased bank lending, which might also be thought of as a form of monetary policy.

15. See Chairman Bernanke's testimony before the House Budget Committee on January 17, 2008. http://www.federalreserve.gov/newsevents/testimony/bernanke20080117a.htm "There are limits to what can be achieved by the central bank alone," Bernanke said in November 2010. "A fiscal program that combines near-term measures to enhance growth with strong confidence-inducing steps to reduce longer-term structural [budget] deficits would be an important complement to the policies of the Federal Reserve."

16. See "Why Permanent Tax Cuts are the Best Stimulus," *The Wall Street Journal* op-ed, John Taylor, November 25, 2008. http://online.wsj.com/article/SB122757149157954723.html

17. Saving rates by income quintile is calculated based on data from the Consumer Finance Survey and Consumer Expenditure Survey.

18. Strong evidence of the benefit of the tax rebates on consumer spending is provided in "Consumer Spending and the Economic Stimulus Payments of 2008," Parker, Souleles, et al., December 2009. http://finance.wharton.upenn.edu/~souleles/research/papers/ESP2008_v7b_results.pdf

19. These included accelerated depreciation benefits and net-operating-loss rebates.

20. See Cohen, D. and Cummins, J. "A Retrospective Evaluation of the Effects of Temporary Partial Expensing," Federal Reserve Board, Finance and Economics Discussion Series Working Paper No. 2006-19 (April 2006). Also see House C. and Shapiro, M. "Temporary Investment Tax Incentives: Theory with Evidence from Bonus Depreciation," NBER Working Paper 12514, September 2006.

21. The fiscal stimulus also provided help to financially pressed families in forms that carry large multipliers, including food stamps, payments to allow unemployed workers to keep health coverage, and Social Security.

22. Harvard Professor Robert Barro strongly argues this view in "Government Spending Is No Free Lunch, *The Wall Street Journal* op-ed, January 22, 2009. http://online.wsj.com/article/SB123258618204604599.html

23. A good analysis of the impact of defense spending on economic activity that controls for some of these problems is found in Nakamura and Steinsson. 2011. "Fiscal Stimulus in a Monetary Union: Evidence from U.S. Regions." Unpublished paper, Columbia University. http://www.columbia.edu/~en2198/papers/fiscal.pdf

24. The multipliers in Table 5.2 are calculated based on simulations of the Moody's Analytics macroeconomic model of the U.S. economy.

25. See Mazumder, "How Did Unemployment Insurance Extensions Affect the Unemployment Rate in 2008–10," Federal Reserve Bank of Chicago, Essays on Issues No. 285, April 2011. http://www.chicagofed.org/webpages/publications/chicago_fed_letter/2011/april_285.cfm and Valletta and Kuang, "Extended Unemployment and UI Benefits," Federal Reserve Bank of San Francisco Economic Letter 2010–12, April 19, 2010. http://www.frbsf.org/publications/economics/letter/2010/el2010-12.html

26. By mid-2012, it seemed possible for state and local governments to ultimately shed as many as one million jobs.

27. Real GDP grew at an annualized pace of 1.7% in the third quarter of 2009. Without the stimulus, this analysis suggests it would have instead declined 2.3%.

28. Representative of this work is "New Keynesian Versus Old Keynesian Government Multipliers," John F. Cogan, Tobias Cwik, John B. Taylor, Volker Wieland, Journal of Economic Dynamics and Control, 2009. http://www.volkerwieland. com/docs/CCTW_100113.pdf

29. See "Estimated Impact of the American Recovery and Reinvestment Act on Employment and Output," Congressional Budget Report, August 2011. http://www. cbo.gov/sites/default/files/cbofiles/attachments/08-24-ARRA.pdf. A broader set of estimates of the economic impact can be found in "The Economic Impact of the American Recovery and Reinvestment Act of 2009," Council of Economic Advisors, July 2011. http://www.whitehouse.gov/sites/default/files/cea_7th_arra_ report.pdf

30. See Table 3 of that testimony.

31. Former CEA head Christina Romer provides a good description of this work in "What Do We Know About the Effects of Fiscal Policy? Separating Evidence from Ideology," speech at Hamilton College, November 7, 2011. http:// elsa.berkeley.edu/~cromer/Written%20Version%20of%20Effects%20of% 20Fiscal%20Policy.pdf

32. This perspective had its intellectual underpinnings in work by Alesina, Alberto, and Silvia Ardagna. 2010. "Large Changes in Fiscal Policy: Taxes Versus Spending." Tax Policy and the Economy 24: 35–68. http://www.nber.org/papers/ w15438

33. The shift in ECB policy was facilitated by a change in leadership during summer 2011. Italian Mario Draghi took over as president of the central bank, and within a few months the ECB's balance sheet was bigger than that of Bank of Japan, and almost twice that of the U.S. Federal Reserve, relative to each economy's GDP.

6

The Foreclosure Fiasco

The call with Bob Steele wasn't going well. He was curt and growing increasingly annoyed as I laid out a plan to stem the accelerating housing crash. It was summer 2008, and it was clear that housing was the core of the economy's problem, although it wasn't yet clear that the problem was catastrophic.

Moody's executives had arranged the call. They knew the Under Secretary for Domestic Finance in the Bush Treasury Department from his years working at Goldman Sachs. Two years earlier, Moody's had purchased Economy.com, the firm I had cofounded in 1990, and I had gained some credibility within the credit rating agency by arguing that housing was a bubble and that Moody's highly profitable mortgage securitization business was severely threatened. The executives hoped that a more aggressive government response to housing's crisis might salvage some part of the securitization market.

My proposal was unorthodox, and it quickly became apparent that it was much too much for the Under Secretary.[1] I argued that to stem the housing collapse, the government needed a program of principal reduction for mortgages. With house prices in free fall, millions of homeowners were being pushed underwater—their homes were worth less than the debt they owed. Homeowners in this precarious situation were more likely to stop paying on their mortgages and foreclosures would soar. Only a plan to reduce the debts of these stressed homeowners would stop this nightmare quickly. To discourage homeowners from defaulting simply to cut their mortgage debt— a form of what economists call moral hazard—I proposed that eligible

119

homeowners share any future house price appreciation with their mortgage lenders.[2]

Bob Steele wasn't having any of it. He didn't seem to think housing's problem was that big, and certainly not big enough to demand that taxpayers help reduce homeowners' mortgage debts. Not only was this likely to be costly and laden with moral hazard, he argued, but it also wasn't fair to those homeowners who struggled successfully to pay their mortgages, and thus wouldn't receive a reduction. Urban legend has it that the Tea Party was borne out of the anger that greeted even the chance that government would go in this direction.[3] I agreed that it would be costly and that some would benefit more than others, but I argued that without policies along these lines, taxpayers would pay much more, and that everyone would be measurably worse off.

I suppose it wasn't realistic to think the Bush administration would deviate radically from its incremental approach to the housing problem. The administration had done a few positive things, such as working with the mortgage industry to establish Hope Now—a consortium of mortgage-related companies working to establish standards and facilitate mortgage loan modifications. The White House also supported efforts to temporarily eliminate the tax liability on mortgage debt forgiven in a short sale—a sale for less than the amount owed on a mortgage. Such taxes had been a significant impediment to resolving underwater mortgages and putting properties back on the market. So that Fannie Mae, Freddie Mac, and the Federal Housing Administration would increase lending as private lenders pulled back, President Bush included higher conforming loan limits—caps on the size of mortgage loans these lenders could make—as part of his fiscal stimulus plan. But compared with these policy steps, my proposal appeared quite radical. The call with Steele ended abruptly, but the debate over how to end the foreclosure crisis raged on.

Aside from the fiscal stimulus, no issue was more important than housing for President Obama's new economic team. The Great Recession wouldn't end unless the housing market stabilized. A key early decision for the incoming Obama team was whether to support an effort to allow homeowners to have their mortgages reduced in bankruptcy. Historically, bankruptcy judges had significant discretion in restructuring a troubled borrower's debts but could not touch first mortgages. This was to encourage lenders to offer lower mortgage rates and easier terms to prospective borrowers. Now a change was being proposed that would retroactively affect mortgages made during the housing bubble. Proponents argued that because these loans had been poorly made in the first place, it was permissible for the government to change the rules after the fact.[4]

Candidate Obama endorsed the idea, but President Obama demurred. It could serve as a big stick to get lenders to work with borrowers, but for the government to change the terms of a mortgage—a private contract between a lender and a borrower—felt like an assault on the rule of law. If government could alter the rules after the fact, lenders in the future would demand compensation for the risk of such changes occurring again. This would mean higher lending rates, tougher terms, and less credit for future borrowers. The administration decided to use carrots instead to address the foreclosure crisis.

It seemed clear that avoiding foreclosure was in everyone's interest. Foreclosure is extraordinarily costly. Homeowners likely to lose their homes have little incentive to keep them up and may take out their frustration by removing plumbing fixtures, copper wires, or anything else of value. The legal and maintenance costs are enormous, and vacant properties quickly fall apart, as vandals and varmints damage structures. The broader economic costs are also significant; homes in foreclosure sell at big price discounts, driving market prices down for everyone and pushing more homeowners underwater, which leads to more defaults and further house price declines. Logic strongly suggests that everyone—lenders, homeowners, and taxpayers—should share the cost helping homeowners avoid foreclosure.

The administration's attempt to implement this logic was the Making Home Affordable Program, announced by President Obama in February 2009, and in effect by that summer.[5] The plan offered a plethora of clever incentives to get mortgage lenders to modify loans and reduce monthly payments for struggling homeowners. It also encouraged Fannie Mae and Freddie Mac to make use of the lower mortgage rates engineered by the Federal Reserve to refinance homeowners who had little or no equity. Such borrowers hadn't been able to refinance at reasonable rates. The program's goals were ambitious—two to three million mortgage loan modifications and four to five million refinancings.

The mortgage market's issues were much too complex for the administration's goals to be realized, at least quickly. The Making Home Affordable Program helped, but there were numerous problems. Many of the troubled mortgage loans had been used to back mortgage securities, whose owners—investors from all over the globe—had different incentives. Some weren't enthusiastic about loan modifications; they preferred to push the loans through foreclosure quickly. The big banks servicing the loans were also unsure that modification and refinancing made economic sense for them. The process was further slowed by lawsuits and countersuits over the cost of the defaults and foreclosures. It took months, and then years, for the various parties to understand the program. The administration made numerous changes, and by 2012 it was working better, but even then the program seemed unlikely to achieve its stated goals.

Some aspects of the policy response to the housing crash worked surprisingly well. Most notable was the role played by the Federal Housing Administration. The FHA, which had been all but dormant during the housing bubble, sprang back to life during the bust, accounting for about one-third of all mortgage loans at the height of the credit crunch. During this period, when banks were making few loans of any kind, mortgage borrowers could still obtain credit because of the FHA. This was precisely what the agency's New Deal-era designers had had in mind when they set it up in the 1930s. Without a steady flow of credit from the FHA, the housing market would have completely shut down, taking the economy with it. The agency's extraordinary efforts took a toll on its finances, but the FHA seemed likely to navigate this without having to turn to taxpayers for help.[6]

Three successive temporary tax credits for homebuyers were much criticized at the time, but proved surprisingly effective. Each break lasted only a few months, giving buyers compelling reasons to act rather than wait for prices to fall further. The tax savings were enough to more than compensate buyers for any additional expected price declines. Home sales gyrated as the credits were extended, withdrawn, then extended again, but the free fall in sales and prices stopped. Government policy succeeded in breaking a vicious deflationary psychology that had gripped the housing market.

The government's effort to shore up housing was well timed. By mid-2009, house prices had already fallen by about a third nationwide. In the hardest hit markets, such as Las Vegas, Miami, and the Central Valley of California, prices were down more than 60%. Combined with low and falling mortgage rates, this made single-family housing affordable again—as affordable as homes had ever had been, at least by some measures.[7] It also was no longer clear that renting was a better bargain than owning for many households. Critics argued that government housing policy was keeping prices artificially high, but these concerns were misplaced. Although prices wouldn't rise on a consistent basis for several more years, the price declines and housing crash were largely over. Policy had prevented housing from falling to levels that would have rekindled financial panic and renewed the Great Recession.

Criticism that policymakers were inappropriately slowing down the foreclosure process also seemed misplaced, at least through much of the crisis. As the robo-signing scandal that broke in late 2010 had made clear, it was important to ensure homeowners were treated fairly in foreclosures.[8] The slower process also prevented too many distressed properties hitting the market at once, which would have caused prices to spiral lower. The policy's critics had a better case after the mortgage companies had agreed to change foreclosure procedures and house prices had stabilized. Millions of troubled loans remained to be resolved before housing could truly find its footing. This required the court system to work through its backlog of cases and for state and municipal governments to reevaluate the complex mediation efforts many had put in place. By mid-2012 it was time to move on.

How the response to the housing crash would ultimately be judged also depended on how gracefully the government unwound its involvement in the housing and mortgage markets. As the Obama administration prepared to face the voters again, Fannie Mae and Freddie Mac remained firmly in government control, and the FHA remained an outsized part of the mortgage market. Private lenders were still hobbled, and the mortgage securitization market was still broken. There was widespread agreement that this wasn't desirable or sustainable, but there was no clear vision of what mortgage finance would look like in the future.

There was also no consensus about whether government should continue to subsidize homeownership as it had long done. The mortgage interest tax deduction, favorable capital gains treatment, access to credit created by the FHA, and lower mortgage rates afforded by Fannie Mae and Freddie Mac all cost taxpayers a bundle. It was difficult to see how this largesse could continue at a time when policymakers were scouring the federal budget for savings. And although it had long been conventional wisdom that homeownership was good for both households and their communities, the millions of foreclosed homes showed clearly that not everyone could afford to own.

Housing Boom and Bust

No industry reaches deeper into the economy than housing, and the boom and bust of the 2000s took the economy for a wild and scary ride. The Great Recession could not end until housing hit bottom, and the recovery could not take hold until housing was on the rise again. Policymakers rightly focused on addressing the foreclosure crisis.

Selling and building homes is big business, and in many U.S. towns during the boom it seemed like the only business. When the housing market was at its most crazed in the mid-2000s, nearly 8.5 million homes, or about one-tenth of the entire housing stock, were turning over annually (see Figure 6.1).[9] House flippers, who bought and sold homes quickly using little if any of their own money, had overrun places like Florida, Nevada, Arizona, and California. Real-estate speculation was rampant in many markets, and prices soared.

House Flipping Surged During the Bubble

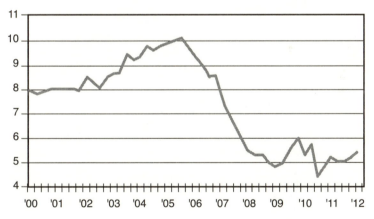

Figure 6.1 Ratio of home sales to single-family housing stock, %.

Sources: Bureau of Census, National Association of Realtors, Moody's Analytics

Rapidly rising house prices emboldened buyers to ramp up borrowing, and lenders to offer them cheap and easy credit. Low- and no-down payment mortgages became the norm; cash-out refinancing, in which homeowners borrowed more than the current mortgage balance, was all the rage. Hundreds of billions of dollars were pulled out of homeowners' equity in this period. Some of it went to pay for sensible things such as tuition or business start-ups, but more of it went for questionable things such as new cars, vacations, or dinners out. The total amount of mortgage debt rose even faster than house prices. In the decade before the bubble burst, national house prices doubled and outstanding mortgage debt tripled.

The private mortgage securities market was responsible for much of this. In the mid-1990s, before the lending boom, there were only a couple hundred thousand subprime, alt-A, and option-ARM loans outstanding. By the mid-2000s, there were more than 8 million of these loans, accounting for an enormous one-fifth of all mortgage debt outstanding (see Figure 6.2).

Private Mortgage Securities Market Soars

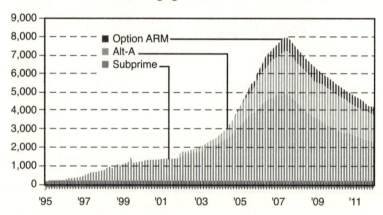

Figure 6.2 First mortgages outstanding, millions.

Source: Moody's Analytics

Homebuilders suspected they were selling many of their new homes to flippers, but they couldn't resist. Builders built like there was no tomorrow, adding more than a couple of million homes each year during the boom—more than could be absorbed by new households, used as second homes, or to replace obsolete structures.[10] By the mid-2000s when the bubble was fully inflated, housing was vastly unaffordable, overvalued, and overbuilt.

The housing boom was dizzying, and the bust was harrowing. When the flippers figured out they were flipping mostly to each other, the game was up. Speculators began defaulting on their mortgages, shocking the financial institutions that had lent to them. Flippers went from making timely loan payments straight through delinquency and into foreclosure. They had made bum investments, and by returning the keys to lenders, they were washing their hands of the problem.

Lenders and investors in residential mortgages suffered massive losses, undermining their solvency and driving the global financial system to its knees. Between 2006 when the housing bust began and 2011, financial institutions realized more than $900 billion in losses on mortgage lending (see Table 6.1). Not surprisingly, nearly half were on loans funded by the private mortgage securities market. The old banking adage proved true: "If it's growing like a weed, it probably is one." Only a government bailout saved the financial system and forestalled a more severe credit crunch. Yet losses continued to mount, and it would take years of legal wrangling to sort out who would bear the costs.

Table 6.1 Residential Mortgage Loan Realized Losses (*Billions* $)

	2006	2007	2008	2009	2010	2011	2006-2011	Share of Losses,%
Total	17.3	45.4	181.8	305	198.8	167.4	915.7	100
Government Backed	7.4	13.9	55	113.8	57.9	53.1	301.2	32.9
Fannie Mae & Freddie Mac	1.1	8.1	47.3	103.4	43.8	38.2	241.9	26.4
Fannie Mae	0.8	5	29.8	73.5	26.6	27.5	163.3	17.8
Freddie Mac	0.3	3.1	17.5	29.8	17.2	10.7	78.6	8.6
Federal Housing Administration	6.3	5.9	7.6	10.5	14.1	14.9	59.3	6.5
Privately Backed	9.9	31.5	126.8	191.1	140.9	114.3	614.5	67.1
Depository Institutions	2.7	7.3	35	54.9	48.2	35.3	183.4	20
Private Label Mortgage Securities	7.2	24.2	91.8	136.2	92.7	79	431.1	47.1
Subprime	5.6	15.4	55.9	71.5	38.9	34.7	222.1	24.3
Alt-A	0.2	0.9	10.8	27.5	23.8	20.3	83.4	9.1
Option ARMs	0	0.2	5.1	17.8	17.4	14.5	55	6
HELOC	0.2	1.5	5.1	5.1	3.4	2.1	17.4	1.9
Jumbo	0	0	0.3	1.9	3.1	3.7	9.1	1

Note: Total of private label mortgage securities includes securities not in components shown in the table.
Sources: Fannie Mae, Freddie Mac, HUD, FDIC, Federal Reserve Board, Moody's Analytics

The housing bust wiped out the net worth of millions of home-owners, for whom a house was the most important asset. Well over $7 trillion in homeowners' equity, half of all existing equity at the peak, was lost in the housing crash. Middle-income households were hit especially hard; unlike their wealthier neighbors they didn't have stocks or other investments to cushion the blow. With their balance sheets in tatters, these families had no choice but to curtail spending.[11]

Shaky house prices also made it difficult for small-business own-ers to use their homes for seed money or loan collateral. When I started my company in the early 1990s, I used my home as collateral for a loan to pay the company's first employee. I would not have been able to do that if my home's value had not held up. The housing crash caused bank lending to dry up to small businesses, and because small businesses are a key part of job creation, this was a significant impedi-ment to a better job market.

Strapped local governments also struggled with the impact of falling house prices on property tax revenues. Despite rising millage rates in many parts of the country, property tax revenues declined for the first time on record. Local governments thus had little choice but to cut budgets and lay off teachers, firefighters, and police, ulti-mately cutting more than half a million jobs. And considering the lag between house price changes and tax assessments, local government revenues and jobs weren't likely to bounce back quickly.

The most worrisome development was the vicious cycle that took hold in housing by fall 2007. Falling house prices pushed more and more homeowners underwater, producing more defaults, foreclo-sures, and short sales—and because these distress sales involved large discounts, still lower house prices. There were fewer than 2 million underwater homeowners in 2005, most with only slightly negative equity. By late 2007, 6.5 million owed more than their homes were worth on the market, and by early 2009 at the peak, 16 million were in this uncomfortable position. For more than half of those households, mortgage debt exceeded the home's value by more than 30% (see Figure 6.3).

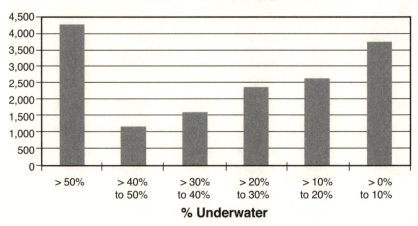

Figure 6.3 Number of underwater homeowners, thousands, 2009q1.

Sources: Equifax, Moody's Analytics

Threatening to send this vicious cycle into hyper-drive were surging defaults by subprime borrowers, whose mortgage payments were rising suddenly. Most subprime mortgages were of the type known as "2-28" loans, with payments fixed for 2 years, and adjusted after that based on 6-month Libor rates. Subprime loans made during the height of the housing bubble were first reset in 2007. At that point the Federal Reserve had yet to push interest rates very low, so the average subprime borrower's monthly mortgage payment jumped from $1,200 to an unmanageable $1,550.[12]

Dazed and Confused

Pressure mounted on the Bush administration to act, but the White House had little appetite for an aggressive response. Officials tended to believe that private lenders and homebuilders had gotten themselves into trouble and should figure a way out of it. There was also wide confusion about what government could do to help.

The administration's first response was to have the FHA refinance subprime homeowners whose mortgage payments were being reset at much higher levels. To qualify for what was dubbed an FHA Secure loan, homeowners had to stay current on their payments prior to the payment reset, make at least a 2.5% down payment, and have sufficient income and a stable job. The program fell flat because those who needed it most also faced job insecurity and had trouble coming up with even small down payments.

FHA Secure was followed by Hope Now, a voluntary consortium of the nation's largest mortgage companies, credit counselors, Fannie Mae, and Freddie Mac.[13] The group was charged with finding ways to head off the tsunami of foreclosures threatening to wash out the housing market.[14] No one had ever anticipated that many millions of mortgage loans might go bad at once, and the system wasn't up to the task. Companies that serviced mortgage loans were profitable when most borrowers paid on time, but they lost money when forced to work through problems with borrowers who weren't paying at all. This was a labor-intensive and costly process, and the servicers weren't being compensated for it.

Further complicating matters was mortgage loan securitization, which combined the most troubled subprime loans into pools. Servicers collected payments on the loans in the pools and forwarded them to investors. Little thought had been given to the scenario that was now unfolding, in which lots of borrowers stopped paying all at once. Servicers had little guidance from investors, and investors couldn't agree how to proceed.

"Tranche warfare" broke out among investors. Tranches were layers of mortgages, arranged in the securities so that some would suffer first and others later if borrowers began to default. Investors who owned the riskiest layers now began to feud with those who owned the safer parts. The first group wanted servicers to cut the borrowers a break and modify their loans; for these investors, a lower monthly payment was better than nothing. But investors in the safer tranches favored letting the weakest borrowers default. These investors weren't immediately at risk, and modifying loans would add to the costs and raise the odds of more problems later. The mortgage servicers froze, afraid of the legal crossfire.

Also mucking up the modification process were second liens. About half of those homeowners whose first mortgages were in trouble also owed money on home equity loans or other second mortgages.[15] The owners of those second mortgages had to agree to any modification of a first mortgage before it could take place. This isn't that complicated in theory, but the mortgage industry's poor recordkeeping often made it painfully difficult to determine who held a borrower's second lien. Even when they could be identified, some second-lien owners would withhold consent unless they were paid. This infuriated first-mortgage owners, who felt they were being shaken down, and drove many loans into foreclosure.

Hope Now succeeded in bringing the players together, and it also opened lines of communication between stretched homeowners and mortgage servicers. But the program couldn't overcome the economic and legal barriers to modification. Lenders were also putting most troubled homeowners into repayment plans, which provided little relief; the plans simply let delinquent homeowners resume paying their mortgages with no change in terms. Borrowers still had to make up missed payments and pay associated penalties. Monthly payments actually rose under many repayment plans. Hope Now couldn't keep enough distressed homeowners out of foreclosure.[16]

Bold and Foolhardy

The foreclosure crisis metastasized in 2008. It no longer was just about a few million subprime borrowers who had overreached with the help of overly aggressive lenders. The crisis now involved nearly all U.S. homeowners with mortgages—some 55 million households—and two of the nation's blue-chip companies, Fannie Mae and Freddie Mac, whose stock and debt were owned by hundreds of millions of investors across the globe.

Fannie and Freddie, also called government-sponsored enterprises or GSEs, are mammoth financial institutions vital to the nation's housing market. In 2008, they either owned or insured some $5 trillion in residential mortgage debt; not quite half of all the mortgage debt outstanding. For context, this was approximately equal to the amount of U.S. Treasury debt then held by the public. Moreover, the collapse in private mortgage lending had made the GSEs much more important; aside from the FHA, no one else was making mortgage loans.

Cracks in the GSEs' financial façade had become obvious by spring 2008. Mortgage defaults were up everywhere—not just in California and Florida, where Fannie and Freddie had historically made fewer loans, but also in places such as Minneapolis and Dallas, where the GSEs were the principal sources of mortgage credit. Although GSE loans performed better than others, they were still losing money, and the losses were washing away the institutions' capital cushions. Those cushions were thin, relative to Fannie's and Freddie's size. Commercial banks at the time generally held assets equal to 10 times their capital; for investment banks the limit was 30 times. Fannie's and Freddie's assets were closer to 70 times their capital.[17] As the situation deteriorated, this lack of a cushion spooked investors, and they sold the GSEs' stocks and bonds. The run became self-fulfilling, as other potential investors were scared away and other institutions grew afraid to do business with Fannie and Freddie.

Confidence continued to erode during the summer, compelling Bush Treasury Secretary Henry Paulson to ask Congress for what he called a "bazooka" to deal with it. In late July, Congress granted the government authority to add capital to the GSEs and to take them over if necessary.[18] To dispel concerns that the GSEs might have trouble raising cash, they were given access to the Fed's discount window and a larger credit line to the Treasury. In testimony to Congress, Secretary Paulson said

> If you've got a squirt gun in your pocket, you may have to take it out. If you've got a bazooka and people know you've got it, you may not have to take it out.

Yet the bazooka did come out, and only a few weeks later. The GSEs' new regulator, the Federal Housing Finance Administration, put them into conservatorship on September 6, 2008. Shareholders in Fannie Mae and Freddie Mac were wiped out as the U.S. government took full ownership. Bondholders were made whole, and with the full faith and credit of the Treasury backstopping Fannie and Freddie, bond investors no longer had any concern about getting their money back. The GSEs' borrowing cost thus declined. The government was now the nation's mortgage lender; thus mortgage credit would continue to flow regardless of bottom-line profits.

It was an incredibly bold move, and many would argue a brave one, but it wasn't clear that it was necessary. The consequences, moreover, would last years or even decades. The government could have guaranteed the GSEs' borrowings, much as the FDIC did with bank debt in the middle of the financial panic just a few weeks later. Any liquidity concerns would have been quickly dispelled. The government could have taken an equity position in the GSEs without wiping out shareholders, just as the TARP funds were used to recapitalize the nation's big banks. The GSEs needed capital, not an unlimited pipeline to the Treasury. Instead of extending a helping hand, the government put the GSEs in a death hug.

This exacerbated the financial panic, setting off a cascade of bank failures in the days after the takeover. Stock- and bondholders in financial institutions no longer knew where the government stood. If owning a stake in the two biggest financial institutions on the planet wasn't safe, what was? Certainly not Lehman Brothers, which collapsed a week later.

The government takeover of Fannie and Freddie also severely complicated the reconstruction of the mortgage finance system. Few thought the federal government should forever remain the nation's dominant mortgage lender, but reprivatizing Fannie and Freddie would be extraordinarily difficult. In whatever form they were reincarnated, their relationship with the government would be different than it had been before the financial panic. Their focus on providing mortgage credit to disadvantaged groups with lower homeownership rates might diminish, for one thing, making it politically hard for Congress to set the firms free.

Quelling the Chaos

When the Obama economic team took over in early 2009, the nation's housing and mortgage markets were in chaos. House prices were spiraling lower, pushing millions of homeowners underwater. Unemployment was rising rapidly, and foreclosures surged. Housing and the broader economy were inextricably intertwined, and unless the free fall in housing was stemmed, the Great Recession would only intensify.

Knowing this, policymakers threw everything they had at the housing crash. The Federal Reserve began buying mortgage securities backed by Fannie and Freddie in January and kept buying them for more than a year. The Fed became the largest investor in GSE securities, with some $1.25 trillion on its balance sheet. Mortgage rates moved steadily lower, reaching record lows. A few legislators complained that the Fed had wandered into Congress' domain of fiscal policy, but although this was a reasonable concern, the lower borrowing costs were instrumental in keeping housing from unraveling completely.

To ensure that the credit crunch didn't cripple the housing market, Congress extended higher conforming loan limits for Fannie, Freddie, and FHA loans as part of the Obama administration's stimulus legislation, the American Recovery and Reinvestment Act of 2009.[19] Mortgage credit remained tight, but below certain limits, homebuyers with jobs and solid credit scores continued to find loans. Indeed, government-backed mortgages were about the only loans being made during the panic and credit crunch.

Congress also lobbed several rounds of tax credits at housing. The first, included as part of the Bush stimulus, was small; only lower-income, first-time homebuyers qualified. Although they received some cash up front to make down payments, they had to repay with higher taxes in the future.[20] The Recovery Act included a much larger tax credit for first-time buyers that was theirs to keep. Home sales surged as that second credit neared expiration in fall 2009. A last, larger homebuyers' tax credit went into effect a few months later, and sales popped again, although not as much as the previous time.

The tax credits didn't spark additional home sales so much as pull sales forward from the future; sales weakened sharply as soon as the credits expired. The credits also were expensive, costing the Treasury tens of billions of dollars, and much of the benefit went to homebuyers who would have purchased homes anyway. But the credits were instrumental in breaking a deflationary, self-reinforcing cycle that had taken hold in the market. Prospective buyers were sitting on the sidelines, waiting for prices to stop falling before acting—and their reluctance caused prices to drop still more. The tax benefit gave buyers a reason to stop waiting, and the free fall in house prices abated (see Figure 6.4).[21]

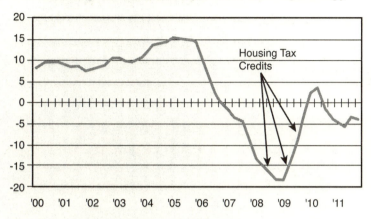

Housing Tax Credits Dispel Deflation Psychology

Figure 6.4 House price growth, percent change year ago.

Source: Fiserv Case Shiller

Emptying the Pipeline

Reducing the number of homes in the foreclosure pipeline was another key to stabilizing housing. By early 2009, the pipeline included more than 3.5 million homes and was growing rapidly (see Figure 6.5).[22] These included loans somewhere in the foreclosure process and those more than 3 months past due. In normal times, approximately half a million loans fall into these categories at any one time. The increase put significant pressure on all U.S. house prices because they foreshadowed a huge rise in the number of distressed properties that would eventually be put back on the market at large discounts.[23] House prices wouldn't rise again until the foreclosure pipeline shrank.

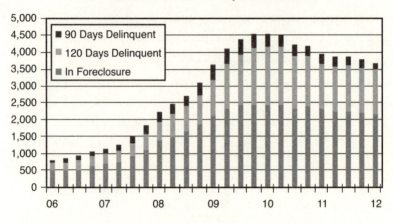

Figure 6.5 First mortgage loans, thousands.

Sources: Equifax, Moody's Analytics

The Making Home Affordable Program was the Obama administration's attempt to work the pipeline down. It was a potpourri of initiatives that offered incentives and set standards and guidelines for mortgage servicers, lenders, and investors to modify first and second home loans, refinance mortgages, and facilitate short sales and deeds-in-lieu.[24] Given the extraordinary complexity of getting the various interest groups to work together, the programs had to evolve continually.

HAMP was the flagship effort.[25] Like Hope Now, HAMP was voluntary, but once a mortgage company agreed to participate, it was required to follow HAMP rules.[26] Most critically, each troubled loan considered for a modification had to be run through a calculator to determine its net present value after modification. That value was compared with the price it would likely fetch in a distress sale. If the modification had a higher NPV than the foreclosure, the loan was modified, most often, by having the interest rate reduced or the term extended to reduce the homeowners' monthly payment. The goal was to get the payment down to 31% of the homeowner's income; a ratio thought to be affordable. To tip the scales of the NPV calculation in favor of modification, HAMP provided mortgage servicers and owners a cash incentive if they modified.

With so many moving parts, it wasn't surprising that HAMP got off to a messy start. Troubled homeowners were quickly put into HAMP modifications without the necessary information on employment, debt, or loan-to-value ratios being collected to determine whether the process would actually help them avoid foreclosure. HAMP modifications required a 3-month trial, in which the homeowner had to remain current on the new loan before it was made permanent. Many failed to make it.

HAMP kicked into higher gear over the next couple of years, but never lived up to expectations. President Obama was hoping for between 2 million and 3 million HAMP modifications when he unveiled the program in summer 2009, but as his first term wound down, closer to 1 million homeowners had been helped.[27] Efforts to promote principal reductions through HAMP also failed. The President went so far as to triple the monetary incentives to Fannie Mae and Freddie Mac for principal reduction mods, but the GSEs' regulator, the FHFA, was reluctant to go down this path.[28] The FHFA's objections to principal reduction were the same ones that Under Treasury Secretary Bob Steele had expressed on the phone to me 4 years earlier.

HARP, the mortgage refinancing plan, also had trouble getting off the ground.[29] The program's working assumption was that refinancing as many homeowners as possible into mortgages with lower interest rates would help them and aid the economy as well. Lower monthly payments would ease financial pressure on households, enabling many to stay current on their loans and stay out of the foreclosure pipeline. With mortgage rates at record lows, this seemed like a slam-dunk idea.

The problem was that millions of underwater or nearly underwater homeowners couldn't refinance. The mortgage rates they were offered were so far above the going rate for borrowers with equity that it didn't make economic sense to refinance. Fannie Mae and Freddie Mac were adding interest-rate surcharges, arguing that underwater borrowers were at greater risk of defaulting. Other lenders were charging more to compensate for put-back risk, the chance that if they made a loan and sold it, it would come back to them after a default. Lenders were especially sensitive to this, worrying that they would be forced to buy back loans found to have been originated improperly.[30] Hundreds of billions of dollars in loans made during the housing boom were being put back; lenders weren't going to make the same mistake by refinancing underwater borrowers.

After a couple of years of lackluster HARP refinancing amid low mortgage rates, a number of key changes were made. Most important, Fannie and Freddie agreed to lower their interest-rate surcharges when refinancing their own loans and to ease off on putting back refinanced loans to lenders. Because Fannie and Freddie would suffer anyway if the loans they owned defaulted, it made sense for them to refinance homeowners regardless of how much equity they had. And because the loans had been originated at least a couple of years earlier, the agencies already had a good idea how well the loan was originated.[31] With fixed mortgage rates falling below 4% in early 2012, HARP refinancing picked up, but remained below expectations. HARP was supposed to produce 3 million to 4 million refinancings, but unless there were more changes, and unless rates remained extraordinarily low a lot longer, this seemed unlikely.

HAMP, HARP, and the rest of the Making Home Affordable Program didn't live up to its goals. The programs were nevertheless instrumental in ensuring that the foreclosure pipeline didn't burst. This was all the more impressive given the blizzard of scandals and lawsuits that engulfed nearly all parts of the housing and mortgage markets, slowing the foreclosure process to a crawl. Most important, as the end of President Obama's first term approached, the foreclosure crisis was fading and no longer a mortal threat to the broader economy.

Endnotes

1. The idea that principal reduction was necessary was ultimately adopted by a range of economists including Harvard Professor Martin Feldstein (http://www.nytimes.com/2011/10/13/opinion/how-to-stop-the-drop-in-home-values.html), Harvard Professor Kenneth Rogoff (http://www.theatlantic.com/business/archive/2011/10/wisdom-on-housing-from-rogoff-and-blinder/247066/), and even Federal Reserve Chairman Ben Bernanke (http://www.federalreserve.gov/newsevents/speech/bernanke20080304a.htm).

2. My proposal for shared-appreciation mortgages is described in the "Home Appreciation Mortgage Plan," May 2008. http://www.economy.com/mark-zandi/documents/Home-Appreciation-Mortgage-Plan.pdf I made a similar proposal in the "Homeownership Vesting Plan," December 2008. http://www.economy.com/mark-zandi/documents/Homeownership_Vesting_Plan.pdf

3. In a February 19, 2009 broadcast on CNBC, editor Rick Santelli ranted about the Obama administration's plan, announced the day before, to help stressed homeowners modify and refinance their loans. Santelli denounced the plan as "promoting bad behavior" by "subsidizing losers' mortgages" and raised the possibility of putting together a "Chicago Tea Party in July."

4. I was one of those proponents. My views are detailed in testimony before the House Judiciary Subcommittee on Commercial and Administrative Law, January 29, 2008. http://judiciary.house.gov/hearings/printers/110th/40455.PDF

5. The Obama administration's loan modification and refinancing plan is described in detail at http://www.treasury.gov/initiatives/financial-stability/programs/housing-programs/mha/Pages/default.aspx

6. The FHA suffered large losses on its mortgage loans, as did every financial institution exposed to the housing and mortgage markets. The FHA's capital was substantially depleted and even as the housing crash came to an end in 2012, it was unclear whether the FHA would need help from taxpayers to remain solvent.

7. The National Association of Realtors' housing affordability index, which gauges the ability of median-income households to purchase median-priced homes at prevailing mortgage rates, rose to a record high in 2012.

8. The robo-signing scandal involved the revelation that many mortgage servicers were not completing the necessary legal paperwork in states where foreclosures went through the courts. State attorneys general banded together to sue the big mortgage service companies. They settled the case in February 2012.

9. This included both new and existing homes. In a well-functioning U.S. housing market, there should be closer to 6 million home sales annually.

10. This includes single family homes, multifamily homes, and manufactured housing. A well-functioning U.S. housing market would see closer to 1.75 million homes built each year to meet demand from new households, to serve as replacement structures, and to provide second homes.

11. This is known as the wealth effect. A decline in household wealth reduces consumer spending as less wealthy households save more, spend less, and curtail borrowing.

12. Adding to the concern at that time were the large payment resets due to hit option ARMs. Most of these mortgages featured 5 years of fixed payments and rates pegged to Libor after that. Option ARMs issued at the peak of the housing bubble in 2005 and 2006 were thus due to reset for the first time in 2010 and 2011. Yet this never became a crisis because of the Federal Reserve's zero-interest rate policy and various loan mitigation efforts.

13. Various agencies also initiated their own loan modification efforts. The FDIC worked with homeowners who had borrowed from institutions later placed in federal receivership. Fannie Mae and Freddie Mac had their own programs, as did mortgage lenders and servicers such as Bank of America, Citigroup, and JPMorgan Chase. But although laudable, these efforts did not reach the most troubled homeowners.

14. Hope Now was formally established in October 2007. At its inception the consortium included lenders representing 60% of outstanding mortgages, counseling services, trade organizations, and a group representing investors in mortgage-backed securities http://www.hopenow.com/

15. During the housing boom, home equity lines of credit (HELOC) were a popular way for homeowners to raise cash, and a way for homebuyers to avoid more costly mortgage insurance. In so-called "piggy-back seconds," a homebuyer would take out a first mortgage with an 80% loan-to-value ratio, and thus not require insurance; then also take out a HELOC to cover the rest of the home's purchase price.

16. Hope Now ultimately played a constructive role in the foreclosure mitigation effort. Modifications involving interest rate reductions and term extensions increasingly became the norm.

17. The GSEs' regulator, the Office of Federal Housing Enterprise Oversight, permitted such high leverage on the theory that Fannie's and Freddie's assets were traditionally low-risk, fixed-rate mortgage loans to prime borrowers. Those loans they owned or insured that had down payments of less than 20% also were backstopped by private mortgage insurance. Even these loans were in trouble, but for Fannie and Freddie, the bigger problem was in their below-prime, alt-A loans. Meanwhile, the firms that wrote private mortgage insurance contracts were struggling even more than Fannie and Freddie, creating doubts about their ability to meet their own obligations.

18. The Housing and Economic Recovery Act of 2008 was passed on July 30, 2008. http://www.gpo.gov/fdsys/pkg/PLAW-110publ289/pdf/PLAW-110publ289.pdf

19. The loan limits for single-family residences were increased to the lesser of $729,750 or 125% of the median home value within a given metropolitan statistical area.

20. The Bush housing tax credit was much like a zero-interest rate loan to first-time homebuyers to help with a down payment.

21. The third tax credit made it clear that repeating this tactic would be counterproductive. Homebuyers were becoming conditioned to wait for the next tax break to buy. Realtors and others in the housing industry thus did not ask for a fourth temporary tax break.

22. This was also called the shadow inventory.

23. At the height of the distress sales, homes sold in foreclosure for nearly 25% less than comparable homes sold conventionally.

24. The incentives in the Making Home Affordable Program were funded by money appropriated as part of the Troubled Assed Repurchase Program.

25. HAMP—the Home Affordable Modification Plan—was fashioned off a proposal made by then FDIC Chairwoman Sheila Bair. The FDIC had engaged in similar modifications for mortgage loans of banks that it had taken over during the financial panic.

26. Mortgage company participation in HAMP and HARP was high. This made economic sense for the companies, but there was also substantial pressure to participate from regulators and policymakers.

27. This likely understates HAMP's benefit; it helped streamline the modification process and facilitated more than four million additional modifications done by lenders outside of the HAMP process.

28. In early 2012, the Obama administration proposed tripling monetary incentives to Fannie and Freddie under HAMP for principal reductions. For every dollar Fannie and Freddie took off a home mortgage, taxpayers would pay up to 63 cents, using money from the $700 billion TARP fund originally appropriated to help struggling financial institutions.

29. HARP is the Housing Affordable Refinancing Plan.

30. Fannie, Freddie, and private mortgage insurers were aggressive in putting back loans to lenders if they violated standards, also known as representations and warranties.

31. To receive a HARP refinancing, the loan had to be originated prior to June 2009.

7

Fixing the Financial Plumbing

The Treasury Department building, next door to the White House in the middle of Washington DC, projects all that the U.S. financial system would like to be: solid, confident, well appointed but not especially ornate. It is fitting that a statue of Alexander Hamilton stands watch outside. The first U.S. Treasury Secretary knew that his young nation's economic success depended on repaying the debts it had run up to finance the Revolutionary War.

When I visited the Treasury in spring 2010, the financial system seemed to be falling well short of the aspirations embodied in that building. I was having lunch with Michael Barr, the Assistant Treasury Secretary for Financial Institutions, who was working feverishly on legislation to fix a system that was badly broken. The legislation came to be known as Dodd-Frank, after Connecticut Senator Chris Dodd and Massachusetts Congressman Barney Frank, the Democrats who shepherded the reforms through an extraordinarily contentious Congress.

The principal subject of the lunch was the Consumer Financial Protection Bureau. Dodd-Frank would establish this new regulatory agency to make sure the products and services that banks, brokerages, and insurance companies sold were suitable for American consumers. Supporters believed the financial crisis had been brought on in part by badly designed loans, particularly mortgage loans, that many borrowers did not understand. A growing body of evidence suggested this lack of understanding lay behind many bad borrowing decisions made during the boom.

145

Indeed, it was hard even for a financially sophisticated mind to get around the blizzard of available loan products: Adjustable-rate mortgages (ARMs) based on esoteric indexes such as Libor and the Eleventh District cost of funds; or option-pay ARMs that could grow rather than shrink over time, leaving households deeper in debt than when they bought their homes. The Federal Reserve was supposed to make sure households knew what they were getting from lenders, but it appeared to have given this task short shrift, focusing on other, weightier responsibilities.

Before it could even begin to address this problem, however, the Consumer Financial Protection Bureau had become a lightning rod for everything the financial industry disliked about Dodd-Frank. Banks and other financial institutions were fearful that the CFPB would stifle the creation of new products and raise the cost of existing ones. Bankers thought the paperwork and other compliance costs would be overwhelming. Most finance industry people hated Dodd-Frank in its entirety, but the CFPB was taking the brunt of the criticism.

At lunch that day, Assistant Secretary Barr tried to marshal my support for the new agency. He didn't have to try hard. Although I was sympathetic to the bankers' concerns about overregulation, their objections seemed to ignore the profligate lending that had inflated the housing bubble. I thought the CFPB could be for financial products what the Food and Drug Administration was for pharmaceuticals. Like the FDA, the CFPB would get it wrong some of the time, but like the FDA, it would help ensure that consumers understood what they were being sold, and got what they paid for.[1]

Although the debate over the CFPB was important, it was a bit perplexing to see it dominate the larger debate over Dodd-Frank. Other parts of the reform legislation reached much farther into the U.S. financial system. Regulators had been told to identify and address threats to the system, an ambitious goal by itself. The Federal Reserve had long denied that it was responsible for keeping bubbles from forming in markets, like technology stocks or housing. Other regulatory agencies were even more reticent to look for threats outside their own narrow oversight groups. Dodd-Frank demanded that they try.

Regulators were also told to make sure that one troubled financial institution couldn't drive the entire financial system into insolvency. The crisis that began in early 2007 turned into a panic by late 2008, largely because the Treasury, Federal Reserve, and other regulators created chaos by the apparently ad-hoc way they handled failing banks and brokerages. They folded Bear Stearns into JPMorgan Chase, leaving Bear Stearns' creditors with almost nothing. When the Treasury put Fannie Mae and Freddie Mac into conservatorship, shareholders were effectively wiped out but bondholders were left whole. Lehman Brothers creditors were put through a wrenching bankruptcy process. After that it was unclear what regulators were prepared to do to end the crisis. When unnerved investors dumped financial stocks and bonds, the system veered close to collapse, leaving the government no choice but to bail it out at great cost to taxpayers. Dodd-Frank aimed to make sure that this would never be repeated.

One way to do that was to prevent individual financial institutions from becoming big enough to bring down the broader financial system—in other words, too big to fail. In an ideal world the government wouldn't need to worry if a bank or brokerage failed; the costs of such a failure would fall on the institution's own creditors, not on taxpayers. Dodd-Frank hoped to get there by spelling out in advance the process under which troubled institutions would be liquidated, merged, or otherwise resolved. This, it was hoped, would make it more difficult for institutions to become too big to fail. If creditors knew up front that there was no possibility of a government rescue, they would demand that the institutions better manage risk or take less of it. The reform legislation also designated certain "systemically important financial institutions"—SIFIs—for tougher oversight, holding those that posed risks to the system to higher standards.

The crisis had also made it clear that some of the biggest risks facing the financial system originated outside traditional banks, from a network of institutions and markets called the "shadow banking system." These included hedge funds, private-equity firms, and other institutions that originated, funded, and traded a dizzying array of loans, securities, and derivatives. Understanding conventional depository institutions is difficult enough; getting a grip on the opaque, lightly regulated shadow banking system is all but impossible. Dodd-Frank tried to shine a light on this part of the financial system by requiring that firms register, disclose their operations, and trade on open exchanges. The reform legislation also required that those who package loans into securities take at least a small ownership stake in those securities, to encourage more prudent lending. Many of the most egregious subprime mortgage loans were created and funded by institutions in the shadow banking system with no such skin in the game.

Dodd-Frank became law in summer 2010, after a long and bruising political battle. Bankers and congressional Republicans steadfastly opposed much of the legislation. To try to muster support, President Obama first wooed, then cajoled, then attacked the bankers, unnerving the financial community.[2] Bankers were also upset that many of Dodd-Frank's provisions weren't fully spelled out in the legislation, and would not be for years. The delays were due in part to the bankers' own objections; lawmakers had also left many details up to regulators, who moved slowly. Regulators struggled to balance the lawmakers' intent with the realities of how financial institutions and markets work, and tried not to make matters worse.

The political vitriol surrounding the passage of Dodd-Frank and the considerable uncertainty created by its changes slowed decision making by regulators and stunted the financial system's revival. Credit, which had been choked off during the financial panic, began to flow again in the recovery, but painfully slowly. Small businesses and potential homebuyers complained that banks weren't making loans. There were many reasons credit was tight, but one of them was Dodd-Frank.

The reform legislation overreached in some ways and fell short in others. For example, the Volker rule, which barred large financial institutions from trading solely to generate profits rather than for clients or to hedge risks, would prove impractical and counterproductive. When JPMorgan Chase reported a multibillion dollar loss from trading in spring 2012, some claimed this as proof that the Volker rule was important. To the contrary, Morgan's loss highlighted how difficult it was to determine what kinds of trading should be allowed so that large multinational banking institutions could hedge their risks.

Dodd-Frank was also largely silent on the future of mortgage finance. By 2012 there was widespread agreement that letting the government do most of the lending, via Fannie Mae, Freddie Mac, and the FHA, was unsustainable.[3] The Obama administration outlined potential ways to approach mortgage finance reform, but this was outside Dodd-Frank and was not seriously pursued with Congress.[4] The administration's caution may have been excusable given the lack of political or intellectual consensus on the issue, and the more immediate challenges of ending the housing crash. Still it was increasingly evident that the housing market would never fully revive until the mortgage finance system was reformed.[5]

Dodd-Frank was a massive undertaking. There were considerable political and economic costs involved in its passage and implementation. But given that our financial system had been driven to its knees and required two big helping hands from government to stand again, significant reform was inevitable. Although Dodd-Frank wouldn't prevent future financial crises, it promised to make them less frequent and less likely to lethally threaten the economy.

Systemwide Failure

The most direct cause of the Great Recession was the bad lending, involving trillions of dollars, that occurred during the mid-2000s. The U.S. financial system extended too much credit to too many households and to a fair number of businesses that would be unable to repay after suffering even the mildest of financial setbacks. And there were plenty of setbacks, resulting in a flood of losses that undermined the financial system's capital base. This choked off credit even to creditworthy borrowers. The closing credit spigot in turn halted economic activity, causing millions to lose their jobs and profits to plunge; this caused even more loans to go bad, deepened the losses and created an even larger capital shortfall for the banks. This adverse self-reinforcing cycle was at the center of the worst economic and financial crisis since the Great Depression.

Evidence of the system's failure is clear in the credit statistics. During the worst of the financial crisis in early 2009, an astonishing 62 million consumer accounts, involving more than $1.1 trillion in liabilities, were delinquent or in default.[6] Some 10% of all liabilities were affected, involving everything from first mortgage loans to credit cards. Commercial and industrial loans, corporate bonds, and commercial real estate debt didn't perform much better.

The cost of all this bad lending added up to $2.6 trillion (see Table 7.1), or more than 10% of the approximately $24 trillion in U.S. credit outstanding at the time.[7] Of these expected losses, $1.2 trillion was suffered by depository institutions; nearly $950 billion by pension funds, insurance companies, hedge funds, and mutual funds; and $350 billion by government-sponsored enterprises such as Fannie Mae, Freddie Mac, and the FHA. One-half of the financial loss was borne by U.S.-based institutions and the rest by those based overseas, mostly in Europe. Europe's subsequent economic problems thus owe significantly to the U.S. financial crisis.

Table 7.1 Financial System Losses on Unsecuritized Loans and Securities (*Billions $*)

	Face Value	Realized Losses	Loss Rate, %
Residential Mortgages	10,856	1,339	12.3
Consumer Credit	2,025	262	12.9
Commercial Real Estate	3,425	471	13.8
Corporate	7,835	491	6.3
Total	24,141	2,563	10.6

Realized Losses				
	Banks	Insurance	Pension Funds	GSEs and Government	Hedge Funds and Mutual Funds
Residential Mortgages	550	205	145	321	118
Consumer Credit	167	38	16	-	41
Commercial Real Estate	250	74	59	30	58
Corporate	284	79	61	-	67
Total	1,251	396	281	351	284

Note: GSEs are government sponsored enterprises, the largest being Fannie Mae and Freddie Mac
Source: Moody's Analytics

There was plenty of blame to go around for the bad lending, including both market and regulatory failures. Someone had to provide the credit; that role was filled by global investors flush with cash. Emerging economies such as China and Russia piled up a surfeit of dollars from their lopsided trade with the United States. These countries invested initially in risk-free U.S. Treasuries but eventually sought greater returns in riskier securities, including mortgage-backed bonds and derivatives. With hundreds of billions to invest and little time, emerging-market investors did little or no research on their own.

The U.S. financial system funneled the money from global investors into loans to U.S. households and businesses via the process of securitization. But this process was fundamentally broken: No one involved—from the mortgage firms that originated the loans to the investment banks that packaged them into securities, to the rating agencies that graded those securities to the investors who bought them—made sure the loans were good. Everyone in this complex process thought someone else was watching, but no one was. Securitization was guided by a crazy salad of laws, regulations, and accounting rules supposedly designed to prevent bad lending, but the tide of investor dollars overwhelmed the process. There was too much money to track, and for a time the profits were too good to cause anyone to worry.

A great deal of faith had been placed in the market's ability to regulate itself, with self-interested global investors making sure their securities were built on good loans. This didn't work out. As financial instruments grew more complex, fewer investors were willing or able to pay what it cost to evaluate those securities. They relied instead on the rating agencies, many of whose evaluations later proved inaccurate.

Regulators could have intervened but did not.[8] The mid-2000s marked the apex of a quarter- century of deregulation, dating back to the Reagan administration. Deregulation had been desirable in the early 1980s; at the time, credit was costly or unobtainable for many households and firms. But as the 21st century unfolded, deregulatory fervor went much too far. Even the Federal Reserve, the nation's key banking regulator, believed self-interested global investors could police the markets, and that regulators would do little more than muck up an efficient lending process. This view was misplaced as lending became increasingly egregious. The byzantine regulatory framework didn't help either; an alphabet soup of federal and state agencies all vied for relevance among the institutions they oversaw. At a time when the financial system was globalizing and changing rapidly, even the savviest regulators would have had trouble keeping up.

Out-of-control hubris fueled runaway lending. House flippers were empowered by lenders' belief that house prices would never fall. Lenders, investment banks, and rating agencies thought their data and models were sophisticated enough to prevent major mistakes. Investors thought wild business-cycle swings were things of the past. Central bankers believed that even if things didn't go as planned, they could step in and limit any economic fallout. Overconfidence bred greater and greater risk-taking, leading to trillions in losses and a crippled financial system.

Systemic Risk

Prior to the financial panic, no one was explicitly charged with seeing if the system in its entirety was taking on too much risk. Each regulator, and there were many, focused on its own small piece of the system and zealously guarded its turf. No one considered how the moving parts worked together.

The explosion in subprime mortgage lending that fueled the housing bubble was a good case in point. It seems difficult to believe in hindsight, but during the height of the housing craze, the information available on such lending was astonishingly spotty. Even what constituted a subprime mortgage was unclear. Credit rating agencies collected data on loans backing the mortgage securities they reviewed, but the data wasn't well organized and not publicly available. Even lenders didn't have a good grip on what was going on, and regulators appeared to be flying close to blind. I remember making a presentation to Federal Reserve governors in early 2005 on the subprime threat, and it was clear that even my incomplete data was better than theirs.

This sort of thing wasn't exceptional, moreover, but more the rule. The economic mess created by subprime lending was one for the history books, but the dearth of information on financial products and markets is commonplace. There always is great confusion in the fast-moving financial system, and regulators have always had a difficult time keeping up. It wasn't until late 2006, for example, that regulators agreed to issue rules limiting nontraditional mortgage lending, and it was mid-2007 before they seriously began to address subprime lending. This was well after the financial crisis had erupted.[9]

To address this yawning gap in regulation, Dodd-Frank established the Financial Stability Oversight Council. It was to be the supreme regulator, a panel that included the Treasury Secretary and the heads of both the Federal Reserve Board and the Federal Deposit Insurance Corporation. The FSOC was to find threats to the financial system and nip them in the bud. The key was FSOC's responsibility for identifying "systemically important financial institutions." By definition, SIFIs included all banks with assets of more than $50 billion, but the designation could apply to any financial institution with broad links into the financial system, including hedge funds and insurance companies. Some light would shine on the shadow banking system.

To give the FSOC the information it needed, Dodd-Frank established the Office of Financial Research. The OFR was set up to ensure that Fed officials would never again need people like me to tell them things they didn't know about subprime mortgage lending. Of course, even the best data doesn't preclude bad judgment. The board members at my 2005 meeting seemed relatively sanguine about the boom in mortgage lending. The only serious questions came from Ned Gramlich, by then a well-known skeptic of the housing boom. I'm not sure that anyone's minds would have been swayed by my presentation even if my data and logic had been foolproof.

Resolution Authority

The financial system is enormously complex; even the most insightful regulators, armed with expanded Dodd-Frank authority and additional resources, would eventually miss something. Major U.S. financial institutions have failed regularly ever since Alexander Hamilton set the system up. Taking on risk is a vital part of any market economy; there will be times when institutions take on too much, and aren't stopped until too late.

How to deal with financial failures has always been a problem, moreover. Bankruptcy works for nonfinancial businesses but isn't well suited for financial firms. Bankruptcy is designed to be deliberate; dividing the assets and liabilities of a failing firm among creditors takes time.[10] Financial failures, by contrast, happen fast. Depositors withdraw their cash and counterparties stop doing business, sending shaky institutions into a rapid death spiral. The FDIC was established in the 1930s to deal with bank runs, but it was never equipped to handle large, complex financial institutions with lines of business across the globe.[11] By the early 21st century it still wasn't clear who was.

The problem became glaringly obvious in the financial panic of 2008, as one institution after another ran aground. With no well-defined roadmap for resolving troubled institutions, regulators took many different routes, creating confusion and ultimately chaos. Creditors fled, institutions collapsed, and the government was forced to bail out the system. Dodd-Frank, although not a perfect plan for managing failing, systemically important financial institutions, was a big improvement.

Under Dodd-Frank, the power to take over a major institution that was careening toward insolvency resided with the U.S. Treasury Secretary, in consultation with the president. The regulatory agencies also had a strong voice: Two-thirds of the members of the Federal Reserve Board of Governors had to vote to invoke the process, and the Fed also needed the support of either the FDIC, the Securities and Exchange Commission, or the new federal insurance regulator (also established by Dodd-Frank), depending on the type of institution in trouble. The U.S. District Court in Washington could review the Treasury Secretary's decision if requested by the failing institution's board of directors; although it was not clear how significant a check this would be. The DC court wasn't known for its experience with insolvency law, and a board under extreme pressure would likely go along with regulators and not request judicial review.

Dodd-Frank defined the SIFI resolution procedure reasonably well, but when it was to be applied remained a matter of judgment and thus somewhat arbitrary. The resolution power was to be used in times of "systemic" crisis, but how regulators would decide when such a crisis was occurring was impossible to know. Nothing in Dodd-Frank, moreover, prevented regulators from using these powers in less dire circumstances. Although hard and fast rules would have been nice, the complexities and the idiosyncratic character of financial crises mean that any resolution process, even bankruptcy, required a big dollop of judgment.

The FDIC was an instrumental player in the Dodd-Frank resolution plan. The agency was charged with the nuts and bolts of dealing with failing SIFIs, much as it had done with smaller institutions since the 1930s.[12] The FDIC determines whether institutions can be fixed or must enter receivership—the official term for a government takeover—and be dismantled. To do this without disturbing the financial system, the FDIC must enter the picture long before an institution is on the brink of failure. Regulators must work with a bank's managers, pressing them to address problems. If that proved impossible, the FDIC had to provide enough support to maintain the institution's key assets and operations while figuring out how to sell it all off. The FDIC could draw funds from the Treasury if needed, repaying the government eventually through an assessment on other large financial firms.

This is much easier said than done, particularly when financial markets are in turmoil, but the FDIC handled itself well during the financial panic. At the height of the mayhem, the agency shut down Washington Mutual, the nation's largest savings and loan, after it was mortally wounded by mortgage losses and a depositor run.[13] WaMu's shareholders and bondholders were wiped out, and what was left was quickly sold to JPMorgan Chase.

Wachovia, the nation's fourth largest bank, had a much messier end a few days later. Wachovia's problems were similar to WaMu's, and the FDIC was inclined to follow the same script. But Treasury officials objected, correctly noting that Wachovia was systemically important: Wiping out its creditors could have further unhinged the financial system. The notion that some institutions are systemically important predated Dodd-Frank; Congress had asserted as much in legislation passed after the savings and loan crisis of the early 1990s.[14] The FDIC quickly recognized the merits of this approach and provided assistance to Wachovia before auctioning it off to Wells Fargo.[15]

How the FDIC would handle a troubled financial institution that was not technically a bank was impossible to know, as it had never done so. However, the agency did produce a fascinating study, explaining how it would have handled the failure of investment bank Lehman Brothers.[16] Regulators' decision not to save Lehman from bankruptcy helped trigger the financial tsunami in fall 2008. The FDIC says it would have begun much earlier to address Lehman's capital and liquidity shortfalls. The study describes steps the agency would have taken to sell Lehman's assets while committing funds to lessen the risks for buyers as well as for Lehman's shareholders and creditors. The FDIC asserts it would have handled Lehman's liquidation, if it had come to that, in a way that would have been less costly to the financial system and better for creditors, who ultimately received pennies on the dollar.

Although the FDIC's assertions are impossible to verify, Dodd-Frank at least left regulators with a detailed plan for resolving complex, troubled financial institutions.

Too Big to Fail

Dodd-Frank also took a crack at the too-big-to-fail problem, which put government in the uncomfortable and highly unpopular position of having to bail out large financial institutions. There was wide agreement that saving creditors, such as Citicorp's shareholders or bondholders in Fannie Mae or Freddie Mac, from trouble created moral hazard. Knowing the government would bail them out encouraged these institutions to take greater risks and to grow as big as possible to ensure the government's backing.

The financial panic had made it clear that Fannie and Freddie were not the only institutions too big to fail; so was Citigroup, the insurer AIG, Bank of America, and many others. The Bush administration had tried unsuccessfully to draw a line in the sand with Lehman Brothers, but that merely showed how acute the too-big-to-fail problem had become. And the financial system's consolidation during the panic—with JPMorgan gobbling up Bear Stearns and Washington Mutual, and Bank of America acquiring Merrill Lynch and Countrywide Mortgage—indicated it was getting worse.

Identifying systemically important institutions is key to addressing the too-big-to-fail issue. Such institutions need stiffer capital standards and liquidity requirements and much greater regulatory oversight to ensure they can withstand greater financial stress. Dodd-Frank made annual stress tests a part of this oversight to make sure the SIFIs had enough capital and sufficient liquidity to survive whatever appeared likely to threaten the system. The stress tests conducted in early 2012, for example, were based on a hypothetical collapse in the euro zone.[17] Dodd-Frank also required large institutions to prepare so-called "living wills"—plans to wind themselves down if they stumbled and became insolvent.

A number of other issues continued to dog regulators. The decision to label an institution systemically important could be made arbitrarily or under political influence. Publicly naming a SIFI (systemically important financial institution) could also be counterproductive to the goal of eliminating too-big-to-fail because investors could reward such institutions by lowering their cost of capital. This was why, when the subject came up at a House Financial Services Committee hearing in which I testified in late 2009, Chairman Barney Frank voiced strong opposition to the idea.[18] But devising a formula to determine which institutions needed tougher standards and more oversight turned out to be impractical. Institutions also lobbied hard not to be labeled SIFIs, suggesting the regulatory costs of the designation were greater than the benefits.

Defining the resolution process for SIFIs would help ease the too-big-to-fail problem by persuading creditors of big institutions that in a crisis there was a good chance they wouldn't be rescued. The FDIC would instead take over, sharply reducing or wiping out their investments. In theory, investors would therefore lower their bids for the institutions' securities and demand that they behave more prudently. Big institutions wouldn't be as large or as vulnerable if something went wrong.

There was some evidence in 2012 that this had already begun to happen. Credit rating agencies had historically given higher grades to firms likely to be backstopped by the government. That meant a higher probability that bond investors would not lose money if the institution ran into trouble. Investors paid more for this, which lowered the institution's borrowing costs. After Dodd-Frank, however, the ratings boost diminished meaningfully. It still existed, meaning there still were institutions perceived as too big to fail, but to a lesser degree than before the financial reform act passed.

The financial system's near-collapse and government bailout amplified calls to reform the system by forcing big institutions to break up, or limiting their growth so they could not be too big to fail. This was an understandable reaction—but ultimately a futile and counter-productive one. Forcing the financial system's biggest institutions to shrink sufficiently to eliminate the too-big-to-fail problem would be too arbitrary and wrenching. It is impractical to think regulators could impose such restrictions reasonably and cost-effectively.

That isn't to say that there isn't plenty of room for smaller institutions. Although large banks were likely to dominate the financial landscape, smaller players catered to the idiosyncratic needs of America's Main Street businesses. There are few economies of scale to small-business loans, which require close knowledge of a firm and its owners. Small-business owners also prefer to work with smaller banks, which are more likely to stay with them in tough times. It is a notable strength of the U.S. financial system that so many small institutions nurture the entrepreneurship vital for innovation and long-term growth.

But trying to purge institutions that are too big to fail would put the U.S. financial system at a distinct competitive disadvantage vis-à-vis its global competition. Large Canadian and Australian banks weathered the financial crisis well, for example, and made rapid inroads into U.S. banking markets. Banks from China and other emerging economies would not be far behind. Small U.S. banks would simply be taken over, shifting the too-big-to-fail risk overseas, outside the control of U.S. regulators.

Large financial institutions were also needed to finance and back-stop the shadow banking system. Much of the short-term cash that supports trading activity and fuels the securitization machine comes from large institutions. Moreover, it is more efficient and practical for regulators to intently watch over a few large institutions and, by extension, the rest of the financial system. This is roughly how things were supposed to work before the financial crisis.

Out of the Shadows

Taming the shadow banking system was a crucial goal of Dodd-Frank. Within this world were investment banks, hedge funds, private equity firms, mortgage companies, securitization vehicles, asset-backed commercial paper conduits, and money market mutual funds. Arcane markets for repurchase agreements, credit default swaps, and other derivatives were also part of the shadow system.[19] Collectively, they performed much the same function as the traditional bank system, namely investing savings and making loans. The difference was that shadow banking before Dodd-Frank was almost completely unregulated, and there was little information available about who was doing what.

Yet shadow banking provided a valuable service, dispersing the risks of lending to nearly every corner of the world. By matching investors and borrowers with different plans and appetites for risk, the shadow system enabled more lending at lower cost. The system not only funded lots of new homes and cars, but also businesses with promising technologies and new ideas that might otherwise not have obtained credit. It all worked well for a while, and shadow banking became a major part of the financial system. At its peak in the mid-2000s, it was briefly bigger than the traditional banking system (see Figure 7.1).

The Rise and Fall of the Shadow Banking System

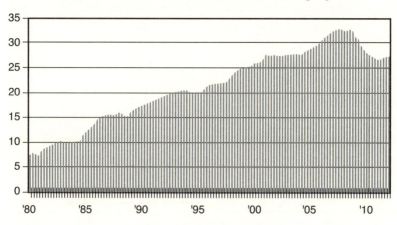

Figure 7.1 Shadow banking share of credit market debt outstanding, %.

Source: Federal Reserve Board Flow of Funds

But with so much money to be made and hubris running high, shadow banking ultimately spun out of control. This brought down not only Bear Stearns and Lehman Brothers, but also the insurance giant American International Group. This blue-chip financial firm for decades provided nothing but plain-vanilla insurance products before the lure of vast profits led it into the shadows. Before AIG went down in September 2008, costing taxpayers tens of billions of dollars, it was one of the largest players in the highly risky derivatives market, insuring mortgage-backed bonds using credit default swaps.

The financial crisis also proved that shadow banking institutions are just as susceptible to runs as traditional banks. Unlike traditional banks, however, there is no FDIC deposit insurance in the shadow world. Scared investors bailed out of money-market mutual funds after the Lehman collapse, forcing one of the largest and oldest, the Primary Reserve Fund, to "break the buck"—letting its per-share net asset value fall below $1. Money funds fueled activity throughout the shadow banking system, and when the cash dried up, the system shuddered.[20] The repurchase or repo market, where institutions make short-term deals swapping securities for cash, also came under severe strain. As traders grew worried about their counterparties, they did less and less business.[21]

Dodd-Frank attempted to force the shadow banking system out of the shadows, in the belief that transparency is vital. To this end, the financial reform required hedge funds to register with the SEC, collected more information on the insurance industry, and asked money-market funds for more disclosure so that regulators could better understand that industry's fault lines. Because all these institutions played some role in the financial crisis, it was critical for regulators to know more about them.

More substantively, Dodd-Frank required that derivatives trading take place on open central clearing platforms, rather than over the counter. This would both give traders a better idea of who they dealt with and enable regulators to know whether speculators were playing in the market. Speculation isn't inherently bad—it makes markets more liquid and prices more accurate—but not knowing the degree to which markets are driven by speculation can be a problem, especially in a crisis.

The reform also required that issuers of securities backed by mortgage loans, credit cards, and other loans enable investors to evaluate the creditworthiness of the loans underlying their securities. Issuers of stocks and corporate bonds had always provided extensive information to investors, but this was not the case for asset-backed securities. Dodd-Frank made it much more difficult for mortgage loans based on false employment information or sketchy appraisals to find their way into mortgage security pools. An independent third party would vet the information to ensure its accuracy and timeliness, which should help ensure better lending and re-establish investor confidence in securitization.

Dodd-Frank's creators also hoped to buoy investor confidence by requiring producers of asset-backed securities to have skin in the game. Investment banks and others who packaged loans into bonds would have to own some of those bonds, retaining some of the same risk that other investors were taking. With no such requirement in place before the crisis, loan packagers had nothing at stake, so they paid little attention to how the loans backing the securities were underwritten. Lots of bad loans were originated, so lots of bad securities were sold. Barney Frank told me soon after Dodd-Frank's passage that he thought risk retention was one of its most important contributions.[22]

What If?

If Dodd-Frank had been in place before the financial crisis, would it have been averted? Would the crisis have been as cataclysmic? There is no way to know for sure, but I believe that although Dodd-Frank would not have forestalled the financial crisis, the damage to the financial system and economy would not have been nearly as great if the reforms had been there to begin with.

Even a perfect regulatory structure would have been unable to stop the global flood of cash that poured into the U.S. in the 2000s, fueling the lending boom that created the crisis. Emerging economies such as China and Russia accumulated trillions in surplus dollars from trade with the U.S. Central banks, and private investors from these countries initially bought risk-free Treasury securities but gradually moved into riskier financial products in a quest for greater returns, doing little due research about what they bought. Nothing in Dodd-Frank would have successfully dammed off the U.S. financial system from the flood of liquidity generated by this global macroeconomic imbalance.

If the Financial Stability Oversight Council had existed, it likely would have raised alarms about soaring speculation and leverage, although it is doubtful that such a body would have done much to stop it. Regulators, particularly at the Federal Reserve, had publicly expressed skepticism about risk-taking at Fannie Mae and Freddie Mac but did not require these institutions to make changes. Doing so would have been politically difficult. It is also unlikely that a pre-crisis FSOC would have been willing to require investment banks such as Bear Stearns and Lehman to raise more capital and reduce leverage; indeed, regulators were allowing many of these institutions to increase leverage, assuming the banks had the acumen to manage their risks. Regulators also displayed little interest in demanding more disclosure or curbing risk-taking by hedge funds.

But had Dodd-Frank been in place, securitization might not have grown as dysfunctional. Everyone involved, from investment banks to credit rating agencies to investors, would have had more complete and accurate information about the loans backing the securities. If issuers of asset-backed securities had been required to retain some of the risk, it may also have curbed some of the worst lending. The bad lending that led to the crisis occurred in part because no one had sufficient incentive to make sure the underlying loans were sound.

Risk-taking in the derivatives markets would likely also have been less wild with Dodd-Frank in place. AIG failed largely because it took on too much risk in credit default swaps. Had there been greater disclosure required, it would have been more difficult for the giant insurance firm to become such a large player in that market without someone noticing. AIG would have also received scrutiny from the FSOC and other regulators, a big difference from the cursory oversight it was actually given by the now-defunct Office of Thrift Supervision.[23]

Households might not have borrowed as aggressively during the housing boom if they had fully understood the loans they were taking on. Federal Reserve surveys show a sizable proportion of sub-prime mortgage borrowers were unaware that their payments were likely to balloon 2 years or less after they signed the loan. The Consumer Financial Protection Bureau probably would have helped with that. Although the CFPB might not have banned subprime lending outright, it almost certainly would have made it more difficult. Option-ARM loans likely would not have grown so popular.

Perhaps most important, Dodd-Frank would have allowed a more orderly resolution of troubled institutions. Important financial players such as Fannie and Freddie, Bear Stearns, Lehman Brothers, and AIG were not under the purview of regulators when they fell, as they would have been under Dodd-Frank. Regulators botched these resolutions, igniting the financial panic, in large part because they lacked clear authority. They were making it up as they went along, losing precious time and losing the confidence of creditors. Dodd-Frank may not have crossed all its t's, but at least it provided a detailed outline.

It would not have been politically easy for the Treasury to invoke its special resolution authority under Dodd-Frank; given the kind of crisis that was developing, however, the Treasury surely would have done so. The FDIC would have had trouble carrying out its responsibilities, particularly given the complexities of dealing with overseas regulators, but its handling of the crisis would still have been an improvement over what actually happened. No matter how skilled the regulators were, Lehman's collapse would have created some ripples, perhaps even a few waves. But it is likely we would have escaped the tidal wave that washed over the global financial system.

Road to Redemption

Odd as it may sound given what we have been through, the U.S. financial system remains one of America's biggest global comparative advantages. The Italians make great sunglasses, the Russians make excellent vodka, but Americans make the best financial products. Not always, as the financial meltdown has made clear, but in most times our financial system has worked admirably to take what little saving we do and using it to finance the investment needed to power the most productive economy on the planet.

Despite its past failures and current problems, the U.S. financial system can be redeemed. It must be, as credit is the mother's milk of growth; without credit the economy cannot flourish. And credit can't flow freely without a well-functioning financial system. To revive the system, however, trust needs to be restored. Unless both those who lend and those who borrow believe they are getting a fair shake, credit won't flow, at least not at reasonable cost. Trust is particularly important to keep global investors buying U.S. bonds, stocks, and other financial products. With so many Treasury bonds to sell to fill the gaping federal budget deficit, we need global investors to have full faith in our system.

The Dodd-Frank reforms are as large as any since the 1930s. Given the complexity of the problems, the legislation amounts to an admirable effort. The reforms will ensure a more steadfast, albeit slower-paced, financial system. Although there will be future financial crises, they will be less severe. Dodd-Frank has many moving parts, and not all will work as intended, but the legislation put our financial system on the road to redemption and on the path back to being the envy of the world.

Endnotes

1. In a prophetic comment at lunch, Assistant Secretary Barr noted that those opposed to the creation of the CFPB would someday be sorry that the bureau would have a single director rather than a board like many other agencies, and that it would be housed in the Federal Reserve, protecting its budget from a potentially hostile Congress.

2. President Obama spoke directly to Wall Street executives on financial regulatory reform on April 23, 2010. He chided them for their "reckless behavior" and implored them to "join us instead of fighting us." http://www.nytimes.com/2010/04/23/business/economy/23prexy-text.html?pagewanted=all

3. I participated in a Treasury Department conference on the future of housing finance considering these issues as early as August 17, 2010. http://www.c-span-video.org/program/295074-1

4. The Obama administration produced a whitepaper on mortgage finance reform that provided a good framework for understanding the options but took no position on which was most appropriate. http://www.treasury.gov/initiatives/documents/reforming%20america's%20housing%20finance%20market.pdf

5. Dodd-Frank also missed an opportunity to reform the alphabet-soup of federal and state regulators. The one substantive change was eliminating the thrift charter and combining the Office of Thrift Supervision with the agency regulating commercial banks. Regulatory arbitrage would be more difficult under the proposed structure but would remain a significant problem.

6. This is according to credit file data from credit bureau Equifax.

7. The projection is based on a range of other forecasts, including expected peak-to-trough declines near 35% in house prices, and a peak unemployment rate of 10%.

8. I argued in a November 1, 2005 article "Where Are the Regulators?" that regulators needed to take a stronger stance against the decline in mortgage underwriting standards. http://www.economy.com/dismal/pro/article.asp?cid=18664

9. This guidance issued in October 2006 limited nontraditional mortgage products, which primarily included alt-A lending. http://www.fdic.gov/news/news/financial/2006/fil06089.html. Guidance restricting subprime lending didn't come out until June 2007. http://www.fdic.gov/news/news/press/2007/pr07055a.html

10. This is a matter of substantial debate. House Republicans, who were in the minority when Dodd-Frank was debated, proposed an alternative resolution plan that would have adapted bankruptcy rules to accommodate multinational, multi-subsidiary financial firms.

11. The FDIC and its authorities were established in the Federal Deposit Insurance Act of 1933.

12. Broker-dealers remain partly outside this new process, but insurance companies are under the authority of state regulators.

13. Washington Mutual was seized by the Office of Thrift Supervision, the saving and loan industry's regulator at the time, and put into receivership by the FDIC on September 25, 2008.

14. This was part of the Federal Deposit Insurance Corporation Improvement Act of 1991. A good explanation of the regulatory and legislative response to SIFIs can be found in "Systemically Important or 'Too Big to Fail' Financial Institutions," Congressional Research Service, January 12, 2012. https://www.hsdl.org/?view&did=707303

15. The auction wasn't particularly smooth either. Citigroup and Wells Fargo were both suitors for Wachovia, and the FDIC initially chose Citigroup. But one day later, Wells Fargo made a counteroffer that the FDIC accepted. Four days after the Citigroup-Wachovia announcement, a new deal was struck between Wells Fargo and Wachovia. Although the new deal was better for the FDIC, the action caused problems for Citi and added to the uncertainty about resolutions.

16. The Orderly Liquidation of Lehman Brothers Holdings under the Dodd-Frank Act, *FDIC Quarterly*, 2011, Volume 5, No.2 http://www.fdic.gov/regulations/reform/lehman.html

17. The Federal Reserve, which manages the stress tests, doesn't provide an explicit narrative describing the scenario, but details of its economic projections, such as European GDP, were consistent with a break-up of the euro zone.

18. This occurred at a hearing of the House Financial Services Committee, "Experts' Perspectives on Systemic Risk and Resolution Issues," September 24, 2009. http://www.economy.com/mark-zandi/documents/House-Financial-Services-Financial-System-Regulatory-Reform-Written-Testimony-092409-FINAL.pdf

19. An insightful discussion of the role of the shadow banking system in the financial crisis can be found in the following speech by Federal Reserve Chairman Ben Bernanke, "Some Reflections on the Crisis and the Policy Response" April 13, 2012. http://www.federalreserve.gov/newsevents/speech/bernanke20120413a.htm

20. The flight of money fund investors also became an aggravating factor during Europe's debt crisis in 2011 and 2012. Money funds were big investors in the IOUs of European banks; when the funds stopped buying, the banks were pressured to fill the void by borrowing from the European Central Bank.

21. The Federal Reserve was particularly focused on the tri-party repo market, after taking extraordinary actions during the crisis to avert a collapse of confidence in this market.

22. I was skeptical that the skin-in-the-game rules in Dodd-Frank would revive the private mortgage securities market. See "Reworking Risk Retention," Zandi and DeRitis. Moody's Analytics Special Report, June 2011. http://www.economy.com/mark-zandi/documents/Reworking-Risk-Retention-062011.pdf

23. Dodd-Frank folded the OTS, which oversaw savings and loan companies, into the FDIC. The OTS not only misread the crisis at AIG, but it also failed to keep the nation's largest S&L, Washington Mutual, from falling into receivership during the crisis.

8

The Fallout

When my son turned 11, I opened a Schwab brokerage account for him. This was in the midst of the technology bust; stock prices had fallen far below their bubble peaks, so it seemed like a good time to buy. More important, it seemed a good way for him to learn about investing, the economy, and the world around him. We didn't catch the market's bottom—9/11 hit a few months later—but we did pretty well over the next several years. I taught him about the merits of long-term investing and diversification; staples in our portfolio included blue-chip companies such as JPMorgan Chase, IBM, ExxonMobil, and Boeing.

A decade later when he turned 21, the Schwab account became his, and to send him on his way, I put some cash into the account. It was summer 2011 and the market was anxious again—about the European debt crisis, Congress' battle over the Treasury debt ceiling, and the U.S. debt downgrade by Standard & Poor's. I suggested that it might again be a good time to buy, and a couple of months later I asked my son what he had purchased; the stock market had rallied by then, and I was feeling pretty good about my advice. After some hemming and hawing, it was clear he hadn't taken it; the cash was still sitting in his account.

I blurted out something about at least helping his old man out and buying some Moody's stock, but he stood his ground. He pointed out that in the decade we had been buying and selling stocks together, our portfolio had gone nowhere. Equity prices had risen and fallen, but in the end we hadn't gained a cent. It was true. In my son's investing life, the stock market had swung wildly, but on net returned nothing to investors. From his vantage point cash, which was yielding close to nothing because of the Fed's zero-interest rate policy, was a better choice than a wrenching ride in the stock market.

My son's reluctance to take a chance on American companies was telling. He had been fortunate not to personally feel the devastating impact of the Great Recession, although it was obvious that the downturn had wrecked the financial lives of tens of millions of American households. Still, the experience had demonstrably changed his thinking. He was in his early 20s, a prime age for risk-taking (at least it had been for me), yet he was skittish about taking any risk at all. This wouldn't mean much if it were just his personality, but it struck me that his perspective was symptomatic of a widespread nervousness, even pessimism, regarding our nation's economic prospects. The Great Recession had done significant damage to the national psyche.

Confidence and risk-taking are what make our economy tick. Entrepreneurship distinguishes the U.S. economy from all others, but it faded in the downturn. Why isn't a mystery: The collapse in the financial system made it all but impossible for a startup to find credit or seed money. Those were scary times, but even well into the recovery, the pace of new business formation remained depressed. This would have been understandable if it were limited to hard-hit industries such as construction and financial services, but it was the case across all industries.

Business managers who panicked during the downturn remained fearful during the recovery. They eventually stopped laying off workers, and by the time the recovery began, the layoff rate had fallen to near a record low. But the pace of hiring fell as well, and picked up painfully slowly. With firms so on edge, almost any shock—such as the Greek bailout, the Japanese tsunami or the threat to shut down the U.S. government—would cause growth plans to be delayed or canceled. Shocks aren't unusual even in normal times, but they don't cause broad economic damage when firms take them in stride. These times, however, weren't normal.

Workers too felt besieged and acted that way. The quit rate—the share of workers who leave a job each year, with or without other offers of employment—plummeted. Even unhappy workers weren't about to take a chance and leave their jobs. Many had home mortgages that were underwater—the debt exceeded the homes' market value—making it financially difficult to pack up for greener pastures even if they wanted to.

The Great Recession did much more than take away Americans' swagger. It also became a political and economic inflection point. For one thing, it suddenly was no longer possible for U.S. consumers to drive global economic growth. From the early 1980s to the mid-2000s, Americans were the world's most sought-after buyers; our seemingly bottomless demand for goods was responsible for pulling China and other emerging economies out of their dark ages. Lower- and middle-income U.S. households borrowed to spend well beyond their incomes, whereas those with higher incomes cut back saving, believing their inflated stock portfolios and home values made them rich. The Great Recession put a quick end to all this, shutting down the borrowing binge and making the affluent fear for their net worth.

The country's single-minded quest to increase homeownership also halted, at least temporarily. Since the 1930s, policymakers of all stripes had wholeheartedly supported efforts to increase the share of Americans who owned their homes, with great success. It was universally believed that people with financial stakes in their communities were more likely to act like responsible citizens. This was good for the economy as well, so big tax breaks and other subsidies were extended, making homeownership an integral part of the American Dream. But many such dreams turned into nightmares during the housing bubble as millions of households found themselves in homes they couldn't afford, even with the government's help. Attitudes toward homeownership eventually began to change: Households questioned whether a home was a good investment, banks grew more cautious about handing out mortgages, and policymakers grappled with the actual cost of subsidizing single-family housing.

It became starkly evident during the Great Recession that there were two Americas. The gap between haves and have-nots had been widening for decades, but now it became a gulf. The mortgage brokers, real estate salespeople, carpenters, and others who lost jobs in the housing bust were smart and industrious, but their skills were obsolete. Until they could retool, jobs were going to be hard to land. And even if aging, out-of-work baby boomers were up to the task, chances were small that they would ever see another paycheck as large as those they had lost. The boomers' kids were also at a disadvantage, looking for first jobs at a time when few businesses were hiring. Even if they found work, it often wasn't what they had been hoping or studying for while running up big student debts in college.

The economic slide that began in the United States quickly reverberated across the globe, opening up fault lines that ultimately threatened to shake apart Europe's decade-old experiment with a single currency. The euro zone was an incomplete union at its inception; disparate nations agreed to a common monetary policy under the European Central Bank, but they made no arrangements to coordinate other key decisions, such as government spending and taxation. The severe stresses of the Great Recession made it clear that too many European nations had borrowed too much when times were good, and that their antiquated economies weren't prepared to carry those debts in the bad times. The euro zone could either come to a catastrophic end or unite more fully, which would also require significant economic sacrifice.

In the fast-changing emerging world, countries such as China were also forced to rethink their models for growth. If U.S. and European consumers couldn't buy as much of their output, demand would have to grow at home. But this would require big changes: Stronger currencies to make goods and services more affordable; a social safety net to provide for health and retirement needs so that consumers didn't feel pressed to save so much, and a modern financial system to make credit accessible. Emerging nations built stockpiles of cash when sales to the United States and Europe were booming; now they needed to spend it to help rebalance the global economy.

In the United States, the Great Recession also laid bare deep political fissures regarding the role of government in the economy. Government action had forestalled another depression, but that meant nothing to the unemployed and the have-nots. To millions of Americans, whatever policymakers had done wasn't enough—or perhaps it was too much—and regardless, it had helped the wrong people. Why should bankers receive assistance, while distressed homeowners were left hanging? At best the government was incompetent; at worst it was corrupt. The Tea Party and Occupy Wall Street became outlets for a deep and wide well of frustration.

It was not hyperbole to say that fallout from the Great Recession would shape economics and politics for generations.

Buying Binge to Bust

In the United States, the Great Recession put a stop to a quarter-century long buying binge. In the early 1980s, approximately two-thirds of the economy's output—a.k.a. gross domestic product or GDP—went to meeting consumer demand. It had been this way since soon after World War II. But by the mid-2000s, with the housing bubble at its height, consumer demand was soaking up more than three-quarters of GDP.[1] More critically, household spending was increasing much faster than incomes, whereas the saving rate—the percentage of after-tax income that consumers didn't spend—fell sharply, from almost 10% to practically zero.

Everyone saved less, regardless of income, age, education level, or whether they owned a home.[2] The biggest decline occurred among middle- and upper-middle-income households in their 30s and 40s who owned homes and had at least some college education (see Figure 8.1).[3] Among this group, saving didn't merely decline; at the peak of the buying frenzy, it vanished and became *dis-saving*—people were borrowing and spending more than they earned. They were using their homes as piggy banks, taking out home-equity loans or refinancing first mortgages, enlarging their loans and taking out the difference in cash. With house prices surging, interest rates low, and lenders falling over themselves to extend more credit, this was easy and seemed to make financial sense. The withdrawal of homeowners' equity peaked in 2007 when households pulled out an astonishing $800 billion, equal to 8% of their after-tax income.

From Saving to Dis-saving

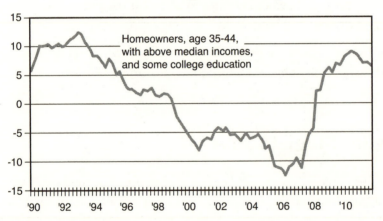

Figure 8.1 Personal saving rate, %.

Sources: Federal Reserve, Moody's Analytics

Lower-income households were mainly renters and never had saved much—it is hard to put anything aside when cash is always tight—but they too became dis-savers during this period.[4] Despite their low incomes and often low or nonexistent credit scores, lenders offered credit cards, auto loans, or consumer financing for appliances or furniture. Lower-income borrowers avidly drew down the new credit.

Higher-income households saved a lot less, too, thinking that rising stock and house prices made frugality unnecessary.[5] They had enough in their checking accounts, pensions, and other assets to pay for their children's college educations and their own retirements. They briefly became dis-savers when stock prices soared during the late-90s tech bubble. Because this group earns a lot of money, changes in their saving rate had an outsized impact on overall consumer spending and saving.

The emerging world, led by China, benefitted enormously from America's avid spending. The flow of goods into the United States swelled at a double-digit pace, doubling as a share of GDP between 1980 and the mid-2000s. China had sold almost nothing to the United States as recently as the early 1980s; by the mid-2000s, it was sending more than $300 billion in goods each year, almost one-fourth of everything the United States imported.[6] China's dramatic growth and that of many other emerging countries was powered by U.S. consumers.

By the time the Great Recession hit, many American households were living on the financial edge. Their debt burdens were setting records, and they were collectively dis-saving. Many would have had difficulty even if stock and housing values had remained high, but their finances were devastated when prices collapsed. Lower- and middle-income households had no choice but to stop spending aggressively and start saving again. Financial institutions stopped lending altogether; homeowners' piggy banks had been shattered. Credit would eventually flow again as the financial system was repaired, but never as freely, at least not for many years. Lenders were chastened and more tightly bound by Dodd-Frank and other regulations. Lower- and middle-income households had no choice but to pace their spending with their incomes more closely.

High-income households also realized they weren't that wealthy after all. Indeed, given the wild swings in stock and house prices, they had no idea what they were worth. This was particularly nerve-wracking for the large number of baby-boomer households in their

50s and early 60s who were quickly approaching retirement. They couldn't comfortably retire without a better fix on their own wealth. Hedonistic boomers began to save in a serious way, many for the first time in their lives (see Figure 8.2). As millions of boomers headed toward retirement, it was unlikely they would ever spend as freely as they once had.

Boomers Save for the First Time in Earnest

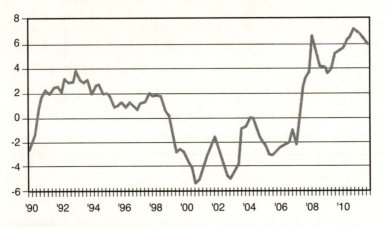

Figure 8.2 Personal saving rate, %.

Sources: Federal Reserve, Moody's Analytics

Indeed, life would probably never be the same for most American consumers after the Great Recession. Still reluctant savers at heart, they wouldn't be as free with their money as they had been. Consumer spending would increase at rates roughly consistent with the growth in incomes, but it would no longer be the engine powering the United States or global economies.

Homeownership Overreach

Ever since the troops came home from World War II, owning a home had been a cornerstone of the American dream. Homeownership was thought to be the best way for middle-class families to build wealth, and more homeowners meant more stable communities, with households psychologically as well as financially invested in safe, well-kept neighborhoods. Homeowners were more reliable employees, more likely to pay their taxes, more civic-minded citizens. Higher homeownership was not only good economics but also good politics: After Franklin Roosevelt it became a goal of both Democratic and Republican presidents.[7] But the Great Recession upended conventional wisdom on the merits of homeownership.

The percentage of U.S. households who own their homes rose quickly after World War II, from approximately 40%—where it had been since 1900—to almost 70% in the mid-2000s (see Figure 8.3). The rise had been driven by the Federal Housing Administration, a creation of the New Deal, and by the introduction of the 30-year fixed rate mortgage loan. Most mortgages before the Depression took the form of 3- to 5-year "bullet" loans, which did not amortize and were due in full at maturity. Such loans could be rolled over easily when credit was ample, but when panicked depositors pulled money out of the banks during the Depression, millions of households lost homes. The FHA invented the 30-year fixed-rate mortgage to shelter homeowners from the business cycle and attract Depression-scarred households back to the housing market.

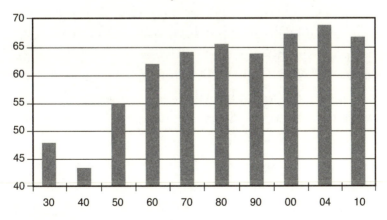

Homeownership Soars After World War II

Figure 8.3 Homeownership rate, %.

Source: Bureau of Census

The 30-year fixed rate loan received another boost from the Federal National Mortgage Association, known as Fannie Mae, another Depression-era creation. As it evolved, Fannie Mae bought the mortgage loans that private lenders made, packaged the loans into securities that it guaranteed in case of default, and sold those securities to investors. The Federal Mortgage Loan Corporation, or Freddie Mac, was created by Congress in the early 1970s to do the same thing in competition with Fannie Mae.[8]

Without the FHA, Fannie Mae, and Freddie Mac, the 30-year fixed-rate mortgage rate loan would be as rare in the United States as it is in the rest of the world. Homeownership rates in many countries that don't have 30-year fixed-rate mortgages are comparable to those in the United States, but in most cases took longer to catch up. The fixed-rate mortgage is now a mainstay of the U.S. housing market, but its existence depends on the government backstop provided by these institutions.[9]

Freddie, Fannie, and the FHA support homeownership in many other ways as well. The FHA makes loans available to lower-income and first-time homebuyers who can't make large down payments by requiring only 2.5% of the mortgage amount up front. The Veterans Administration does the same thing for military personnel. The FHA, Fannie, and Freddie have also pushed private lenders to end discrimination in mortgage lending and provide credit to disadvantaged households. And the FHA stands as a ready source of mortgage loans when private mortgage lenders pull back, as they did during the Great Recession.[10] Without the FHA, mortgage lending would have dried up, and the housing crash would have been measurably more severe. More households would have lost homes to foreclosure, and homeownership would have fallen even more.

The U.S. tax code provides big subsidies to homeowners. Homebuyers deduct the upfront fees and points they pay mortgage lenders and pay no federal taxes on the first $500,000 realized in the sale of their principal residences (provided they've lived there for at least 2 of the past 5 years). And homeowners can deduct the interest on a first mortgage. This is a boon to tens of millions of generally higher-income taxpayers who itemize deductions on their tax returns. The U.S. Treasury gives up more than $100 billion a year in tax revenue for these breaks.[11] Whether this largesse actually raises the homeownership rate is questionable, but that certainly has been the intent.[12]

With so much seemingly going housing's way in the mid-2000s, households bought into the idea that a home was a fantastic investment. Indeed, renting seemed to be for suckers. Those who worried about a bubble were told again and again that U.S. house prices had never fallen across the country all at once since the Great Depression—and of course the economy would never suffer anything like that again. Besides, where else could you put your money? Stocks were less alluring after the tech bust, and interest rates were so low that it seemed to make little sense to invest in Treasury bonds or certificates of deposit. As the housing bubble inflated, most American households were financially and psychologically all in.

When the bubble burst, the financial and psychological damage was incalculable. Attitudes about homeownership were flipped on their head. My grandfather had rightly seen his home as an important part of his retirement savings. My father and I hadn't hoped for the same thing, but we did expect our homes to at least hold their value after inflation. My son holds no such thoughts. To him a home is a place to live and nothing more; not an investment, and certainly not a good one. I suspect his thinking will change as the nightmare of the housing bust fades and he starts a family, but he will always think of owning a home through the prism of the bust.

Policymakers also rethought their long-held views on housing. With millions of homes stuck in the foreclosure morass, and many of those vacant, whole neighborhoods fell into disrepair. Some households in the process of losing their homes took out their anger on the properties, ripping out anything of value as they left. Banks that had taken decrepit properties in repossession were not prepared to spend what it took to keep lawns cut, pools clear, and vandals out. It turned out that homeownership was only good for communities if people could afford the homes they lived in.

With the nation's fiscal problems mounting, policymakers also questioned the subsidies given to homeowners in the tax code. Not only were these costly for the Treasury, but it also wasn't clear they made economic sense. Was it actually true that renters were less valuable as employees or neighbors? Moreover, with the government effectively making nearly all the nation's mortgage loans via the FHA, Fannie, and Freddie, the only way to get private lenders back into the business would be to raise the cost of borrowing from the government.[13] Private lenders couldn't compete with the government unless government charged more to borrowers. Cutting tax benefits to homeowners was still extraordinarily difficult politically, but the Great Recession created a chance for policymakers to finally take a hard look at the system they created.

The decades-long quest for greater homeownership was over. As housing began to finally recover from the crash, the homeownership rate was back to where it was in the mid-1990s, prior to the boom. It probably wouldn't fall much further, but it wasn't likely to rise again soon.

Two Americas

"We are the 99 percent!" This was the chant of the Occupy Wall Street movement, a short-lived but angry protest that began in New York City and spread through much of the country in winter 2011. The protesters were a motley group, but they shared the sense that their economic fortunes were flagging for reasons that seemed out of their control. Moreover, they knew that "the 1 percent" was doing fabulously well and was sure to do even better in the future. Particularly aggravating to the protesters was that many of this 1 percent worked on Wall Street, where the financial crash and the Great Recession had begun. The gap between American haves and have-nots—now rebranded the 1 percent and 99 percent—had existed for a long time, but before the Great Recession it was of concern mainly to academics. Shopping malls were full, and it was easy to get a mortgage loan or a credit card. With hard work and a bit of luck, moreover, it had seemed almost anyone could hope to join the 1 percent. The recession seemed to change all that.

There have always been rich and poor Americans. The gap between haves and have-nots has waxed and waned, but even during the 1960s, when the gap was about as small as it has ever been, households on the top 20% of the income ladder took home more than 40% of all income. The lowest-earning 40% of the population received no more than 15%. But this gap grew steadily in the decades that followed, and by the time the Great Recession hit, more than one-half of all U.S. income was going to the top 20%. The shares of the rest had declined proportionally (see Figure 8.4).[14, 15]

Top 20% Take Home 50% of the Income

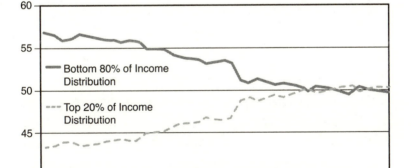

Figure 8.4 Share of income, %.

Source: Bureau of Census

Inexorable forces have widened the gap. Of these, globalization and technological change are the two most powerful. Global economic integration pitted U.S. workers with lesser skills and education against lower-cost workers from China and the rest of the emerging world, at the same time as it gave U.S. workers with more skills and education access to new markets. Those with unique talents, such as basketball player LeBron James or pop-star Lady Gaga, could grow unimaginably rich, with paying fans from Tokyo to Moscow to Nairobi. And rapidly changing technologies such as the Internet, the mobile phone, and the transoceanic container ship upended whole industries and occupations. Newspapers and recorded music had supported hundreds of thousands of jobs as recently as the late 1990s; a decade later both industries were in tatters. Their former workers typically lacked the skills needed by the firms that had made them obsolete, such as Google or Apple.

For a time it seemed that lower-income households were keeping up despite the changes. Their incomes lagged those of the rich, but they could keep spending as long as they could borrow. Credit cards, auto loans, and mortgages were easy to get, even without a good credit score, substantive collateral, or proof of employment. Borrowing also became much cheaper; interest rates had been falling since the early 1980s, and surging house prices gave lower- and middle-income homeowners more equity to tap.

School was also a way up the income ladder. College wasn't cheap, but loans and public aid made it affordable at some level for most families. The payoff was clear, moreover; the average college graduate earned more than twice as much as someone who did not finish high school (see Figure 8.5). Those with post-college degrees earned more than three times as much. Poverty was not assumed to be permanent; with discipline and gumption, it was believed, anyone could move up.

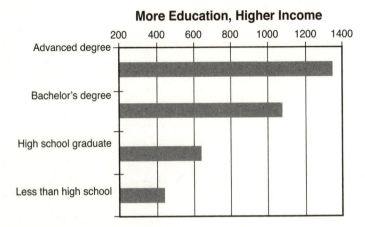

Figure 8.5 Median weekly earnings, $, 2011q4.

Source: BLS, Moody's Analytics

The Great Recession was hard on everyone, but for lower- and middle-income people it was overwhelming. With so many unemployed and for so long, millions more fell into this hard-pressed group. At the worst of the recession, one in six workers were either unemployed or underemployed, not counting those so discouraged that they had stopped seeking work altogether.[16] Even several years after the economy had begun to grow again, about one-half of all unemployed workers had been in that condition longer than 6 months. For many, skills and marketability had eroded to the point where it was all but impossible to land another job without more school or training (see Figure 8.6).[17]

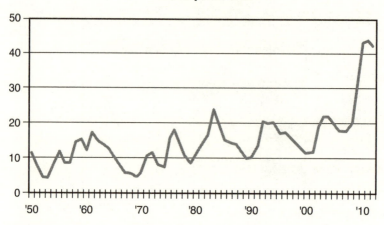

No Help Wanted

Figure 8.6 Share of unemployed out of work more than 6 months, %.

Sources: Bureau of Labor Statistics, Moody's Analytics

Indeed, many of the jobless would likely never work again in their previous professions. There was no place for many former construction workers, real estate agents, mortgage brokers, or school teachers: The downsizing of their fields was permanent. This was especially hard on people in their 50s and early 60s, who were the least likely to be rehired by businesses faced with rising bills for employees' healthcare. It also made less sense for these older workers to spend time and money on retraining. Many took unemployment insurance benefits as long as those lasted and then retired. Others obtained disability benefits, at least for a while.[18]

Young people entering the workforce for the first time were also sorely disappointed. Not only were older workers keeping jobs longer to try to replenish their nest eggs, but many young people also lacked sufficient education; either they had left school too soon, or the schools they had attended had let them down. At the worst of the recession, close to one-fifth of those in their late teens and early 20s who were looking for work couldn't find it, and among those who hadn't graduated high school, one-third were unemployed. There is strong evidence that a starting salary foreshadows lifetime earnings.

People who start out in a bad economy are likely to earn much less over their careers.

Many prudently chose to return to school; enrollment surged in universities, colleges, and vocational and technical schools. But school was expensive. College tuitions had doubled over the previous decade, and with the collapse in house prices, families could no longer borrow against their homes to pay the bills. For many the only other option was to borrow more, and student lending took off. Households soon owed more on school loans than on their credit cards and auto loans combined.[19] This became especially onerous when kids failed to graduate, a not-uncommon outcome, particularly at many for-profit institutions of higher education. With no degree but big debts that couldn't be discharged in bankruptcy, a family faced a bleak situation.[20] What was supposed to have been a way up the income ladder turned out to be a way down.

Making matters worse, the credit spigot closed during the recession. Almost overnight it became close to impossible for lower- and middle-income households to obtain credit cards, auto loans, or mortgages. With the added pressure of earlier debts, millions of consumers had no choice but to spend less. They could no longer keep up with the more affluent. People of modest means now had to live like it. Wealthier households weren't immune to the same problems, but for most, the pain of unemployment was relatively short, and they had plenty to tide themselves over. As a result, the top 20% of income earners accounted for 60% of all household spending, up from just over one-half a couple of decades earlier (see Figure 8.7). Even more dramatically, one-third of all spending was done by households in the top 5%.

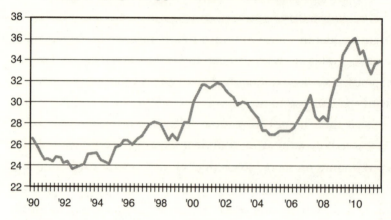

Consuming a Bigger Piece of the Economic Pie

Figure 8.7 Share of personal outlays by those in the top 5%.

Sources: Federal Reserve, Moody's Analytics

There always will be winners and losers in our economy; it wouldn't be as strong and dynamic if there weren't. Winners are rewarded for hard work, ingenuity, and yes, luck. But this system works only if the losers have a real opportunity to pick themselves up and try again. If they don't see such a chance, society begins to break down. Movements such as Occupy Wall Street and the Tea Party reflect the angry belief that the losers aren't receiving a fair shake, and that the winners have rigged the game so that they never will. Unaddressed, this anger can boil over, and unruly protests are just the beginning. The more serious threat is that anger captures the political process and undermines the things that make our economy successful. Globalization and technological change, for example, are big positives, yet unless everyone has a full opportunity to enjoy their benefits, they may not be permitted to continue.

The Great Recession didn't create the two Americas, but it deepened the divides and put them into clear relief. A problem that had received only cursory attention now was front and center.

European Existentialism

The Great Recession didn't cause the European debt crisis, but the downturn exposed fundamental flaws in the way the euro zone had been put together, and threatened to fracture it.[21] Although the recession had its beginnings in the United States, it quickly hit Europe's financial system and economy even more seriously. Europe's banks were hip deep in U.S. mortgage-backed securities and other investments—Britain's HSBC and France's BNP Paribas had reported problems with them even before their U.S. counterparts had. European policymakers, meanwhile, had been much more timid in their responses to the economic hurricane than those in the United States.[22]

Europe's first cracks became visible in spring 2010, when a new Greek government revealed that the country had a much larger budget deficit than the previous government had reported—and that Greece might have trouble making its debt payments on schedule. Investors in Greek debt, mostly European banks and other financial institutions, panicked, dumping the country's bonds and refusing to buy more. The Greek government couldn't raise the cash it needed to pay its employees and the military, its pension and health care bills, and the rest of its obligations. It needed financial help.

The European Union—the principal pan-European governing body—and the International Monetary Fund—a global financial institution that helps countries in financial trouble—bailed Greece out.[23, 24] The EU and IMF would provide Greece with low-cost loans if Greece would make the changes in its budget and economy needed to convince global investors to come back and buy its bonds. Yet instead of regaining confidence, investors turned on other European nations with problems similar to Greece, including Portugal, Ireland, Italy, and Spain. Borrowing costs rose sharply.

By mid-2011 it became painfully clear that Europe's problems ran deep. The euro zone nations shared a common currency and monetary policy but not much else. Nations had agreed to keep their government deficits and debt loads within limits when the currency union was formed, but none stuck to the agreement, not even France and Germany, the euro zone's largest economies.[25] Joining the euro zone created a boom in the countries on the periphery of Europe but set them up for a huge fall. Their historically high interest rates plunged near to the low levels that prevailed in Germany, as investors wrongly assumed that being in the currency union meant that Greeks, the Irish, and Spaniards would behave like Germans.

Instead, the low rates ignited an un-German borrowing binge. Some of the borrowed money funded generous pensions and salaries for government workers. Some financed housing bubbles that dwarfed even those in the United States. Little went to financing the kinds of investments that make economies more productive and competitive. Germany was a big beneficiary; its economy had come through the reunification of East and West in the 1990s tougher and healthier. Germany produced a lot of what the periphery bought, and Germany's trade surplus grew while the periphery descended deeper into debt. By the time the Greek government made its surprising announcement in 2010, Greece's economy could not compete with Germany or anyone else (see Figure 8.8).[26] By mid-2012, Ireland, Portugal, and Spain had also come, hats in hand, to the European Union for help.

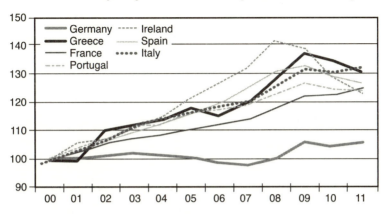

Figure 8.8 Unit labor costs, 2000=100.

Sources: EU Commission

In the past, the typical solution for this kind of economic trouble had been for a nation to cut interest rates and devalue its currency, after obtaining help from the IMF. A weaker currency makes everyone in the country poorer, as the cost of imported goods surges while incomes decline. Eventually, however, the currency falls enough to make whatever the country exports a bargain in the rest of the world, spurring sales and growth. In most cases, the nation continues to pay its debts, but not always; Iceland repudiated its obligations in the Great Recession, and Argentina did the same a decade earlier. A painful recession always follows, but the economy generally settles down and begins to expand again after a few years.[27]

But currency devaluation wasn't an option for nations that wanted to remain in the euro zone. Germany, which was putting up most of the money to help its troubled neighbors through bailout funds called the European Financial Stability Facility and the European Stability Mechanism, would not allow the euro to be debased. The German economy was humming, and a weaker euro would only fuel inflation, a major fear in Germany since the hyperinflation of the 1920s. The German prescription for troubled nations on the euro zone periphery was austerity. Greece and the others had to put their fiscal houses in order and force their populations to cut wages and benefits sufficiently to restore their economies' competitiveness.

The austerity was excessive and counterproductive. So much was cut so quickly that much of Europe returned to recession. Greece, where the unemployment rate approached 25%, entered a depression. Economies shrank so fast that tax revenue evaporated, making government budgets sicker instead of healthier. Greeks seriously debated whether to leave the euro zone, restore the drachma, their currency before the euro, and follow Argentina's path. The Greeks' unhappiness was echoed throughout Europe as governments were toppled and replaced by parties that advocated less austerity.

Europe prepared for a possible crackup of the euro zone. A key to containing the fallout if any country did leave the currency union was insulating and hardening the banking system. German, French, and British banks had made lots of loans over the years to periphery-nation governments, businesses, households, and banks. With losses on these loans mounting on top of the losses already suffered during the Great Recession, banks' capital cushions were depleted, putting the system at risk of insolvency if there were another shock. A major bank failure could send the entire system crashing down. It appeared that might actually happen in summer 2011, but the prospect stirred the previously reluctant European Central Bank to action. The ECB cut interest rates and banks' reserve requirements, bought the debt of troubled periphery countries and, most important, loaned the banks more than €1 trillion at low interest rates for more than 3 years, with the banks allowed to put up almost anything, including Greek sovereign debt, as collateral.[28] There would be no major bank failures.

Still, Europe was doomed to at best muddle through unless its nations could forge a much stronger fiscal and political union. How such an entity would look was a ripe topic for speculation. Most likely, some sort of pan-European institution, perhaps an EU with much greater clout, would be given the final authority to approve national budgets. In exchange for giving up a consequential amount of sovereignty, each nation's debt would be backed by all of Europe's countries collectively. Because the region as a single entity ran deficits and debt that appeared manageable, investors would be soothed, interest rates would decline, and the crisis would be over.

The rub was that Germany would dominate any pan-European institution charged with overseeing national budgets. Only the Germans had the financial resources to backstop all of Europe and would do so only if the rest of Europe were willing to enforce German-style budget discipline. But no politicians ever want to cede power, and given European history, asking European nations to effectively give over their budgetary authority to Germany would be politically difficult, to say the least. Under the most sanguine scenarios, the process would take years, and it likely would require many more rounds of financial turmoil before European nations were convinced there was no better option.

The global economy would ultimately hang on the Europeans' ability to thread this needle. The Great Recession was the catalyst for the European debt crisis, but Europe's existential struggles quickly became the most serious near-term threat to world prosperity.

Dark Pessimism

As a newly minted economist many years ago, I believed that everything about the economy could be measured accurately by data, assessed with statistical and mathematical tools and represented with precision by equations that relate one part of the economy to another. Although I still rely heavily on data and models, as I've grown older, I've come to realize that there is much more to an economy than a collection of formulas. The collective psyche matters a lot, too, particularly at times such as the start of a recession or a recovery. The relationships represented by formulas are not immutable and change significantly when people are wildly euphoric, as they were in the

Internet craze of the late 1990s, or abjectly pessimistic, as they were after the Great Recession.

Of all the fallout from the Great Recession, the most difficult to gauge, and thus arguably the most serious, is in the general mood. For the first time in my professional lifetime, intelligent, well-informed people are beginning to ask if something is fundamentally wrong with our economy. Businesses are wondering whether they should invest and hire; households wonder if their kids will ever find jobs that will support them, and policymakers are questioning whether they did the right things to get the economy out of its morass. Will we ever get our groove back?

Endnotes

1. More accurately, this is the ratio of the sum of consumer spending and residential investment to GDP. It is also a bit of an overstatement to say that consumer demand accounted for three-fourths of economic output because a significant and rising share of consumer spending goes to imported goods produced elsewhere.

2. This analysis is based on data from the Federal Reserve's Flow of Funds and Survey of Consumer Finance. Saving measured by the Flow of Funds differs conceptually from the more closely followed saving rate from the Bureau of Economic Analysis. The BEA saving rate can't be calculated for different demographic groups.

3. Middle- to upper-middle income households are defined as those with incomes below 20% and above 40% of the population.

4. This includes households with incomes in the bottom 40% of the income distribution. That is, 60% of households make more.

5. This includes households with incomes in the top 20% of the income distribution; 80% of households have less.

6. U.S. imports from China include parts and material produced elsewhere in Asia but assembled and shipped from China.

7. President Clinton worked to promote homeownership through tougher enforcement of fair lending and mortgage discrimination laws, as well as more favorable tax treatment of home sales. President George W. Bush pushed homeownership through his "ownership society" programs.

8. Before they were put into conservatorship by the government in 2008, Fannie and Freddie were private businesses with government charters. Fannie Mae was spun out of the government in 1968, to separate its borrowings for home finance from the public debt then being increased to fund the Vietnam War.

9. Most fundamentally, the government's backstop means it will make investors in mortgage securities whole if things go wrong. Investors still take some risk based on whether interest rates rise or fall but do not need to worry that borrowers may default. Indeed, during the Great Recession, the government made sure investors got their money even as mortgage losses were making Fannie and Freddie insolvent. Thirty-year fixed-rate mortgages are possible because the government takes responsibility for the credit risk. The government collects a fee for this.

10. The FHA made few mortgage loans during the housing bubble but made approximately one-third of all home purchase loans during the recession and afterward.

11. An additional tax break passed in 2008 during the crash freed underwater homeowners who sold homes for less than the mortgage value from having to pay tax on any debt forgiven by the lender.

12. Research has shown that the mortgage interest deduction mainly raises house prices and thus does little to improve housing affordability and homeownership. See "The Mortgage Interest Deduction and Its Impact on Homeownership Decisions," Hilbert and Turner, August 2010. http://www.k-state.edu/economics/staff/websites/turner/hilberturnerv024.pdf

13. This was done through raising the insurance premiums the FHA, Fannie, and Freddie charged homebuyers to guarantee that investors who invested in these loans would be made whole if homebuyers defaulted.

14. This is based on the Census Bureau's annual report of income, poverty, and health insurance coverage. http://www.census.gov/prod/2011pubs/p60-239.pdf

15. Wealth is distributed even more unequally. According to the Federal Reserve Board's 2010 Survey of Consumer Finance, families in the top 10% of the distribution owned some 75% of the nation's wealth. http://www.federalreserve.gov/pubs/bulletin/2012/pdf/scf12.pdf

16. To be considered unemployed by the Bureau of Labor Statistics, a person must be actively searching for a job. People are counted as underemployed if they work part time but would take a full-time job if offered.

17. This was reflected in an increase in the structural or full-employment unemployment rate, which most estimates put at close to 5% before the Great Recession but closer to 6% after the recession.

18. With emergency unemployment insurance, workers in states with high unemployment rates could receive up to 99 weeks of benefits. Disability benefits received as part of the Social Security program surged during and after the Great Recession.

19. Student loan debt tripled to near $1 trillion in the 10 years to 2012. Credit card debt outstanding at the time totaled less than $500 billion, and auto loan debt totaled just more than $500 billion.

20. Student loans were excluded from bankruptcy protection on the theory that otherwise lenders would charge high interest rates to compensate for the risk because students generally have no income and few assets. The bankruptcy exception also protects taxpayers because the federal government is by far the largest U.S. student lender.

21. The euro zone was formed in 2000 and by the time of the debt crisis included 17 European countries.

22. The Europeans used fiscal stimulus to support their economies but significantly less than did the United States. The European Central Bank was not nearly as aggressive as the Federal Reserve Board in managing monetary policy; the ECB even tightened monetary policy in early 2011.

23. The European Union includes 27 European countries, including the 17 euro zone nations. The European Commission is the EU's policymaking arm. http://europa.eu/about-eu/index_en.htm

24. The IMF is funded by contributions from member nations. The United States, the largest global economy, is the largest contributor to the IMF. http://www.imf.org/external/about.htm

25. This deal was struck in the 1992 Maastricht treaty, which limited nation's deficit-to-GDP ratio to 3% and its debt-to-GDP ratio to 60%. http://www.cvce.eu/obj/european_navigator-en-2c2f2b85-14bb-4488-9ded-13f3cd04de05

26. The figure shows unit labor costs for a number of European nations since the introduction of the euro in 2000. Unit labor costs measure labor compensation per unit of output and thus is a good measure of labor costs and an economy's overall competitiveness.

27. An important caveat is that troubled countries that devalue their currencies may never make the fiscal and structural changes needed to ensure they don't go down the same path.

28. The ECB's aggressive actions were due in no small part to its change in leadership in summer 2011 when Mario Draghi replaced Jean-Claude Trichet as president.

9

Getting Our Groove Back

Business cycles, the economy's ups and downs, have a regularity to them. During boom times, when the economy is firing on all cylinders, euphoric households tend to spend and borrow too much. Businesses overbuild, overstock their inventories, and add too many workers to their payrolls. Banks let down their guard and make too many loans. Job seekers find they can be choosy about wages and working conditions. And with the economy running flat-out, prices for most goods and services rise quickly.

The Federal Reserve responds to higher inflation by first tapping and then invariably stomping on the monetary brakes. The resulting higher interest rates leave overextended households and businesses vulnerable. Any sort of mishap can trigger a setback; in recent history, such triggers have included spiking oil prices, the 9/11 attacks, and the failure of Lehman Brothers. When things like that occur, economic hubris evaporates and panic quickly takes hold, causing firms, families, and financial institutions to pull back all at once. Businesses go into cost-cutting mode, slashing inventories, investment, and jobs to get their profit margins back up. Banks quickly reverse course and tighten their lending standards. Households hunker down and cut spending. The economy descends into recession.

With the economy and inflation in full retreat, the Federal Reserve pushes on the monetary accelerator, causing interest rates to fall. Households and businesses receive financial relief from lower taxes and more government aid—both are built automatically into federal policy. Worried politicians invariably add additional fiscal stimulus. The monetary and fiscal boost temporarily lifts sales and confidence, and when combined with businesses' lower cost structures, profits revive. Sensing a turn in businesses' fortunes, investors bid up stock and bond prices in anticipation of what they hope will be better times ahead.

Yet at this point in recent business cycles, the U.S economy has confronted a chicken-and-egg problem: Will consumers step up their spending when unemployment is still high, and businesses have not yet begun hiring in earnest? Or will businesses hire and invest more before consumers begin spending with conviction? The impetus for stronger growth has been slow to materialize, giving rise to the term *jobless recovery*. This uncomfortable period has dragged on for several years after recessions have ended.[1]

Although the causality has been difficult to disentangle, it appears that businesses lead the way out of this economic netherworld.[2] Managers realize they can't continue to cut their way to more profits, and without continued strong earnings growth, they can't maintain their stock prices for long. Businesses typically have been planning throughout the downturn and recovery to introduce new goods and services, hoping to expand when the time is right. There is more than a bit of faith involved; a kind of *Field of Dreams* sentiment that "If you build it, they will come."

What causes firms to finally take this leap of faith is difficult to discern and varies from cycle to cycle. But after one CEO decides to take the leap, and begins to ramp up investment and hiring, competitors quickly follow. Companies all fear losing market share because regaining it can be costly. It is as if a light is switched on in corporate boardrooms across the country; suddenly the economy is off and running. The business cycle starts anew.

I regularly speak to corporate boards in a variety of industries. By summer 2012, 3 years after the Great Recession officially ended, I had yet to see the lights go on.[3] To be sure, the tenor of boardroom discussions had changed. During the recession, companies worried about obtaining the credit they needed from the crumbling financial system. As the recovery evolved, boards focused on cutting costs; healthcare and pension expenses were big topics. But even 3 years on, although boards were considering ways to grow and in some cases acting on those plans, most companies were still sitting on their hands.

My anecdotal observations of boardroom decision making were supported by the data. GDP and employment were growing, but only slowly. Unemployment, which had touched double digits soon after the Great Recession ended, was still above 8% (see Figure 9.1). The underemployment rate, which includes those working part time but not by choice, was nearly double that. And almost one-half the unemployed had been out of work longer than 6 months, a point when many begin to lose skills and marketability, adding to the deeper problem of structural unemployment.[4] This was stacking up to be the weakest economic recovery in the nation's modern economic history.[5]

A Painfully Weak Economic Recovery

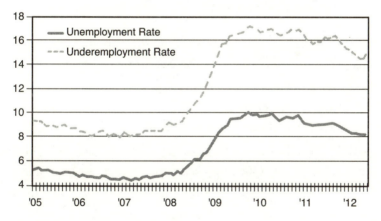

Figure 9.1 Percentage of labor force.

Sources: Bureau of Labor Statistics, Moody's Analytics

One partial explanation for what was happening was the still very depressed housing market. Housing normally leads the economy out of recession. It is the part of the economy most sensitive to interest rates; home sales, homebuilding, and house prices generally perk up when the Federal Reserve begins to ease monetary policy and mortgage rates fall. Not so after the Great Recession. The housing bust was ground zero for the recession, and housing was still flat on its back well into the recovery.

In business cycles after World War II, housing accounted for about 1 percentage point of real GDP growth per year in the first 3 years of economic recoveries, on average. That equals almost one-fourth of the overall economic growth during this period. Three years into the recovery after the Great Recession, however, housing had cut almost one-half percentage point from annual growth. If housing had simply performed as it did in the average post-World War II recovery, unemployment would have been almost 2 percentage points lower 3 years in. The economy would have still been far from normal, but it wouldn't have been nearly as dysfunctional.[6]

This Time Is Different

Another explanation that gained popularity was that the painfully subpar economic recovery was the predictable consequence of a financial crisis. Looking at economic disruptions around the globe as far back as the 1400s, economists Carmen Reinhart and Kenneth Rogoff concluded that those that began with a financial shock had been especially hard. England's King Henry VIII, for example, set off major shockwaves in the 1500s by systematically shaving his realm's silver coins to debase their value.[7] Such financially based downturns are deeper, with weaker and more halting recoveries, than those with nonfinancial roots. In this narrative, economies hit with financial recessions typically take years if not decades to return to the stronger growth rates that prevailed precrisis. A "new normal" takes hold, often leaving the economy permanently weaker.[8]

Reinhart and Rogoff document various types of financial crises through the ages, but they all involve excess borrowing and lending during the good times, producing enormous losses and failures when times turn bad. Financial crises are especially economically debilitating because they choke off credit, the lifeblood of economic activity; without credit, commerce stops. Households cannot buy homes and cars, businesses cannot invest or trade, and governments can't finance themselves. Recovery is slow because overladen borrowers must reduce their debts—a process called *deleveraging*—and surviving lenders must write off problem loans and raise fresh capital.

Governments, meanwhile, cannot stand by and watch their banks collapse. National financial systems really are too big to fail, and the public sector must use all its resources to ensure that they don't. Government budget deficits thus balloon and debt loads rapidly increase. If its backstop is insufficient, the government too can default on its financial obligations. In Ireland and Spain, for example, many banks failed during the European debt crisis, requiring so much capital that the Irish and Spanish governments were overwhelmed. Both required massive bailouts from the European Union, adding to the EU's own serious financial problems.

All this resonated ominously in the United States. The proportion of public and private debt in the economy, which had been stable since the Great Depression, began to rise quickly in the early 1980s. The amount owed by households, nonfinancial businesses, and the government surged as a proportion of GDP, rising more than 100 percentage points between 1980 and the start of the Great Recession (see Figure 9.2). Some of the increase could be explained by falling interest rates, which meant that the share of household income or business profits needed to pay interest, and principal didn't rise nearly as much.[9] Another factor was financial deepening—consumers and firms who had historically been ignored or shut out by lenders found a much friendlier credit environment. But the lending became much too friendly, and the economy's debt load grew much too heavy.

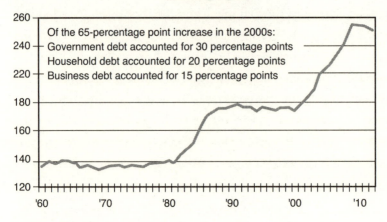

Figure 9.2 Debt to GDP ratio, %.

Sources: Federal Reserve, Moody's Analytics

U.S. companies over-borrowed during the technology bubble of the late 1990s, and the stock market and economy were hit hard when that bubble burst (see Figure 9.3). There were some notable accounting scandals and a few colossal corporate failures—including the energy trading firm Enron, telecommunications company World-Com, and accounting firm Arthur Anderson—but banks and the rest of the financial system were relatively unscathed, with plenty of capital to cushion against the losses.

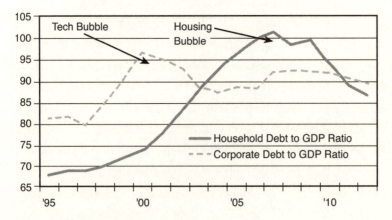

Figure 9.3 Debt to GDP ratio, %.

Sources: Federal Reserve, Moody's Analytics

Households over-borrowed in the housing bubble of the 2000s. By 2007, the sum of mortgages, credit cards, auto loans, student loans, and other consumer credit exceeded annual U.S. GDP.[10] The bursting bubble produced financial carnage as millions of homeowners couldn't meet their mortgage payments—and this time the financial system didn't have enough capital to absorb the losses.[11]

On cue, just as Reinhart and Rogoff suggested, the U.S. government bailed out the financial system. The federal government's budget deficit soared to nearly 10% of GDP, and federal, state, and local government debt ballooned from 70% of GDP to well over 100%.[12] Policymakers had no other option—stepping aside to let the economy sort itself out would have cost much more—but the rescue still was enormously costly.

The title of Reinhart's and Rogoff's book, *This Time Is Different,* was a sarcastic reference to the refrain heard often in response to bubble worriers. But "this time" is rarely different, and given the U.S. economy's lackluster performance following the Great Recession, it appeared that history was indeed repeating itself. Many economists became deeply pessimistic, believing the U.S. economy was in for a long, difficult slog. They feared it would take years for the economy to work through all the busted loans and for businesses, banks, households, and the government to deleverage.

The U.S. economy could not escape history, but it made history by deleveraging in record time. Between early 2009—the depth of the Great Recession—and summer 2012, households cut up nearly 100 million credit cards, and significantly cut back on car and home loans.[13] Exceptionally low interest rates allowed households to refinance or pay off higher cost loans, freeing up cash that had been going to debt payments. Household debt service, which had soared to a record high during the housing bubble, fell back to its level of 30 years earlier (see Figure 9.4).

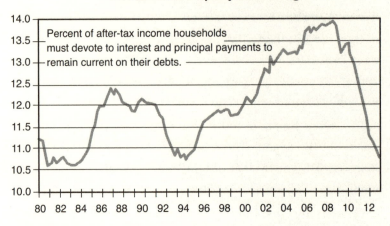

Households Rapidly Deleverage

Percent of after-tax income households must devote to interest and principal payments to remain current on their debts.

Figure 9.4 Debt service burden, percentage of after-tax income.

Source: Federal Reserve

Households also began making their payments on time. The delinquency rate on credit cards had never been lower, and delinquencies on auto and consumer finance loans weren't far behind. Some student borrowers had trouble making payments, but they were a relatively small group. Millions of troubled mortgage loans were also languishing in or near foreclosure, but even these problems were shrinking fast. The number of first mortgages that were 1 or 2 months late had fallen back to prerecession levels, and even the number of loans 3 months late was falling fast. The credit future looked increasingly bright, particularly if this last bulge of foreclosed property could be resolved without undermining the housing market.

This seemed likely. The U.S. financial system had already written off most of its troubled loans and was raising enough capital to withstand future losses. Indeed, much of the household deleveraging had not occurred voluntarily, but because banks and other creditors had simply written off bad debt.[14] It would have been preferable if more households could have avoided default, but the process was nonetheless financially therapeutic. Households' credit scores suffered initially, but in many cases recovered quickly. Many lenders, moreover, were willing to overlook lower scores as a product of the recession, rather than a reflection of households' dependability as borrowers.

Loan write-offs would have been a serious problem during the recession when banks were undercapitalized, but not by summer 2012. Banks' capital cushions were as thick as they had been since the 1930s (see Figure 9.5). The government's stress tests had forced banks to prepare for depression-scale losses, much greater than those they actually suffered in the Great Recession. Bank profits also improved sharply as the write-offs abated. Financial institutions were less profitable than they had been prior to the recession—and because of much stiffer regulations they probably would remain so—but they were hungry to make money again. Credit quality had improved, as had the margins between their interest rates on loans and deposits; thus their only way to grow was by making more and bigger loans.

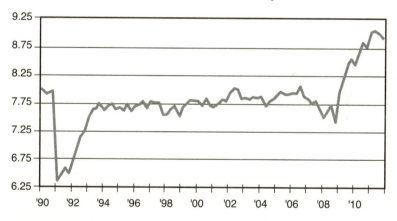

Banks Raise Lots of Capital

Figure 9.5 Commercial banks, ratio of core capital to assets, %.

Sources: FDIC

All this stood in stark contrast with the unfolding events in Europe. European banks, which had not been subjected to such rigorous stress testing, were still choking on their losses, requiring bailouts from the

European Central Bank and European Union to stay afloat. They had no choice but to deleverage, but because they didn't have enough capital and weren't able to raise more, they could do so only if they sold valuable assets and stopped lending. The U.S. banks viewed this as an opportunity to expand their market shares, particularly in loans to U.S. companies, where European banks had once been formidable competitors.[15]

U.S. banks were especially excited because U.S. businesses were in tip-top financial shape. It isn't hyperbole to say American corporations had never been so healthy.[16] If the Great Recession produced anything positive, it was the significant rise in business productivity. During the downturn, labor productivity posted one of its strongest gains ever.[17] This went straight to businesses' bottom lines in the form of record profit margins.[18] Margins were so wide that even a modest pickup in sales, which happened early in the recovery, pushed corporate profits above their prerecession peaks. There was no "new normal" in profits.

Businesses also greatly reduced their debts, borrowing cautiously and refinancing what they already owed to take advantage of the exceptionally low interest rates. Interest payments fell, and when combined with their surging profits and cash flow, a record low share of firms' cash was needed to service debt (see Figure 9.6). Much business debt also came with interest rates fixed for as long as a decade, meaning that even if market rates rose significantly, firms would be largely insulated for a long time. Businesses also had a record amount of cash to meet short-term obligations; they were extraordinarily liquid. The issue was less and less whether companies could invest and hire more aggressively, and more and more whether they were willing to. The question, in other words, was confidence.

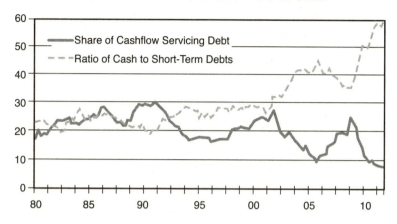

Business Balance Sheets Were in Order

Figure 9.6 Nonfinancial corporate businesses, %

Sources: Federal Reserve, Moody's Analytics

Of Sharks and Black Swans

This reminds me of a shark. More than 25 years ago, my wife and I honeymooned on the Caribbean island of St. John. One morning we rented a sailboat for a day of snorkeling, eventually making our way to a spit of land where the wildlife was teeming. As we rounded the end of the peninsula, the land became a cliff and the water suddenly deepened. The ocean bottom was no longer visible, even through the crystal clear water.

I looked up, searching for my bride, but instead saw a beady-eyed shark no more than 10 yards away. It might not have been a Great White, but it certainly looked like one to me. It definitely wasn't a hammerhead or barracuda, which would have been scary enough. I suppose the appropriate response would have been to remain calm, but I was anything but, as I choked on a mouthful of ocean. As soon as I could catch a breath I looked for my wife, but she was nowhere to be found. Not knowing what to do, I took off for the boat. Trying to outswim the shark made little sense, but I was spooked.

I made it back to the boat unscathed. (It turned out that my wife had tired of snorkeling long before and was safely back on board.) Yet to this day, I cannot snorkel or even swim in the ocean in mental peace. At every turn, I'm still looking for that shark. I know in all likelihood that I will never encounter another shark in such a close personal way, but I'm uncomfortably skittish nonetheless.

Why do I tell this story? Because years after the Great Recession officially ended, businesses were like me in the water; they couldn't shake the nightmares that the downturn had produced. And unlike me, what they had seen was a bona fide Great White shark; their experiences had been truly life-threatening. Long into the recovery, managers remained scared and dispirited. The Great Recession had emasculated those "animal spirits" that John Maynard Keynes explained were so vital to risk-taking and economic growth.[19]

Wall Street was further demoralized by the beating it took from policymakers and the media. Many who worked in the financial system had obviously stumbled badly, and some had violated reasonable ethical standards and even the law. Most had not, but they were being vilified nonetheless. This was not surprising, nor unprecedented; Americans have viewed New York bankers with suspicion since the nation's founding.[20] Critics also took umbrage at how the bankers lobbied against the Dodd-Frank financial regulatory reform, using all their financial might to sway policymakers. President Obama explicitly noted this when he spoke to financial industry leaders during the fight over the regulatory reform bill early in 2010.[21] Although the verbal bashing could be explained, it was in many respects counterproductive, as bankers retreated to their bunkers and lending remained moribund.

Adding to the business community's deep unease were a string of 'black swans'—rare events of potentially catastrophic consequence.[22] The European debt crisis was especially nerve-wracking, revealing deep structural flaws in the euro currency union that at times appeared irreparable. Round after round of turmoil in financial markets forced European policymakers to take steps toward a tighter fiscal and political union, but these seemed never enough. The crisis that began in spring 2010 with revelations about Greece's deteriorating fiscal situation was still raging in mid-2012.

The European situation was especially troubling, because it was all but impossible to assign a probability to whether the euro zone would fracture. There was no consensus on how things would play out. It wasn't difficult to envisage a dark scenario if the euro zone did fall apart, moreover. Europe and the entire global economy could conceivably experience a downturn more severe than the Great Recession. With interest rates near zero and government finances already stressed in most developed economies, monetary and fiscal policymakers would not be able to respond. Even if the odds of a euro zone crack-up were small, the prospect was frightening.

In the United States, political brinkmanship over an increase in the Treasury debt ceiling in summer 2011 had also been disconcerting. President Obama and the Republican-led House of Representatives faced an August deadline to increase the government's legal borrowing authority, or the Treasury would be unable to pay all its bills. The federal government's cash flow was sufficient to make timely payments on the nation's debt, but it wasn't clear if the Treasury had the legal authority to prioritize debt payments among the government's countless obligations. Treasury officials argued that they did not.

Defaulting on the national debt would have been cataclysmic. The U.S. Treasury is traditionally the one constant in the global financial system. When times are bad anywhere, investors flock to U.S. Treasury bonds, knowing they will get their money back. This flight to quality had pushed U.S. interest rates to record lows and was vital to keeping the U.S. economy afloat. Yet this benefit had been earned over more than 2 centuries by adhering to the bedrock principle that the United States always pays its bills on time. One missed payment and the United States would see higher interest rates for years, perhaps for generations.

A fractious Congress reached agreement just as time was running out, raising the debt ceiling high enough to last through the 2012 presidential election. But the drama unnerved business managers, who concluded that Washington was dysfunctional. It was entirely plausible that next time lawmakers wouldn't strike a midnight deal. This wasn't a setting conducive to taking chances and increasing investment and hiring.

Business managers are adept at dealing with problems related to their own companies or industries. They size up the challenges, consider their options, and make changes to improve their firms' success. But such skills are less useful in dealing with macroeconomic black swans. Managers were unnerved by events they were completely unable to control.

In most times sentiment reflects economic conditions, it doesn't drive them. But at key junctures in the business cycle, the causality reverses; how consumers, investors and managers feel drives the economy. Summer 2012 was one of those times. Everyone was on edge, still troubled by the nightmare of the Great Recession, the finger-pointing that followed, and the real possibility that policymakers at home and in Europe would falter and send the global economy back into the abyss.

Regulators and Lawyers

It also didn't help that the business environment was so unsettled. Nothing is for sure, but the more certain things are, the easier for businesses to calculate the return on any investment, and thus the more likely they will expand. In the wake of the Great Recession, it was hard to calculate anything. Massive reforms were underway in finance and healthcare; lawsuits littered the post-recession business landscape, and U.S. tax and spending policy was a maze of temporary measures that might or might not be extended. With so much up in the air, banks and businesses were quick to pause, postpone, or cancel plans to lend, expand, or hire.

The Dodd-Frank financial regulatory reform created an upheaval. Reform had been inevitable after the financial system's collapse, but Dodd-Frank had many moving parts that had yet to be put in place long after the reform had become law.[23] Given its complexity, the law's slow implementation was understandable, even desirable. It would have been worse if regulators had simply dictated changes, unmindful of unintended consequences. Regulators had to perform a tricky balancing act: They needed to listen carefully to what bankers said about the new rules while remaining true to the law's intent. And they had to do it expeditiously, so banks could get on with making loans.

I saw some of this first hand when regulators were crafting new rules for securitization.[24] Dodd-Frank had decreed that anyone involved in turning loans into securities must retain an ownership stake, as an incentive to ensure that the underlying loans were made prudently. The idea was simple, but designing rules to achieve it turned out to be quite difficult. The more inflexible the rules, the more likely they would undermine the economics of securitization. The issue still had not been settled in summer 2012, more than 2 years after Dodd-Frank was passed. Until these so-called "skin-in-the-game" rules were clearly defined, the market for securitization wouldn't revive, and a key source of capital for private residential mortgage loans would remain choked off. The federal government would thus continue to be the nation's dominant mortgage lender. No one wanted that.

The financial services industry was also tied up in lawsuits over responsibility for defaulting mortgages, beginning with Fannie Mae and Freddie Mac. As the system had been set up, firms that sold mortgage loans to Fannie and Freddie were supposed to stand behind the information they provided, regarding both the borrowers and the properties they purchased. If that information were later proved inaccurate or fraudulent, Fannie and Freddie could make the lenders buy the loans back.

This so-called putback risk amounted to hundreds of billions of dollars during the housing bust. Until it became clear just how much the mortgage originators would actually have to pay Fannie and Freddie, and how the putback rules would be enforced in the future, originators would be reluctant to issue new mortgages. The uncertainty dragged on for years, adding to the housing market's troubles.

Regulators and government lawyers also jumped into the fray. On a day when I was visiting one of my large bank clients, it received notice that it was being sued by the Federal Housing Finance Agency—Fannie Mae's and Freddie Mac's regulator—for selling bad mortgage securities.[25] The FHFA thought Fannie and Freddie deserved compensation. Although the bank's stock price fell a bit on the news, the CEO's visible anger over the suit seemed over the top; the money involved was modest in the context of everything else that was going on. However, he explained that as long as he was being sued by the government, his stock price would never recover, and until it did, he wouldn't know how much it would cost him to raise money for new lending. The uncertainty meant less credit would be available, ironically at a time when policymakers were asking this banker and others to lend more.

State attorneys general also teamed up to sue the big mortgage companies over the robo-signing scandals that came to light in late 2010. Concern that millions of homeowners weren't being treated fairly in foreclosure boiled over when it was learned that banks hadn't followed the laws before ordering families evicted. The suit prompted lengthy investigations and negotiations that slowed foreclosures to a crawl in much of the country, before it was finally settled early in 2012.

The mortgage companies ultimately paid a hefty $25 billion penalty, agreeing to various changes in their foreclosure processes, but the suit did nothing to speed loans through the bulging foreclosure pipeline.[26] The suit had been necessary to correct some major errors, but it also extended the housing slump and delayed the economy's recovery.

The Affordable Care Act of 2010—popularly called Obamacare—also created a firestorm of concern among businesses nervous about the cost of healthcare. Although most big corporations provided health insurance to their workers, many smaller businesses did not. The ACA established a new and confusing system of tax credits, health insurance exchanges, and penalties to induce employers to cover their workers. A firm's incentives depended on its size and its use of part-time employees and would change as various aspects of the reform came into effect.[27]

Given numerous legal challenges to the law and the reticence of some state governments to cooperate in the exchanges or other aspects of the law, businesses were nervous about the whole thing. Healthcare is a large and growing part of business costs, and at least until many more questions were answered, Obamacare had made it more difficult to determine those costs.

Approaching the Fiscal Cliff

Businesses also grappled with the broader policy environment, which became steadily less certain as the 2012 U.S. presidential election approached. The next congress and president would face some big issues early, including the so-called fiscal cliff—the massive tax increases and government spending cuts scheduled to hit in 2013 if legislators didn't act. Scheduled to expire were the Bush-era personal income tax cuts and the 2011–12 payroll tax holiday, and spending was set to fall under terms of the summer 2011 deal to raise the Treasury debt ceiling. Emergency unemployment insurance was also coming to an end, along with a number of other temporary tax and spending arrangements that had been routinely extended by Congress for several years running (see Table 9.1).[28] If policymakers did nothing and the nation went over the fiscal cliff, the combination of tax increases and spending cuts would send the economy back into recession.

Table 9.1 Sizing Up the Fiscal Cliff: Cost of Expiring Tax Cuts and Spending Increases
(*Calendar Year 2013*)

Fiscal Policy	Billions $
Bush Era Tax Cut (Below $250k Income)	198
Alternative Minimum Tax Patch	120
Payroll Tax Holiday	115
Automatic Spending Cuts (Sequestration)	100
Bush Era Tax Cut (Above $250k Income)	83
Emergency Unemployment Insurance	40
Affordable Care Act (Obamacare)	20
Medicare Doc Fix	20
Tax Extenders	20
Bonus Depreciation	12
Total	**728**
% of GDP	**4.6**

Sources: CBO, OMB, Moody's Analytics

Lawmakers also needed to lay out a credible plan for fiscal sustainability. Over the long term, taxes and spending needed to result in budget deficits small enough to stabilize the relationship between the national debt and GDP. The Great Recession had caused debt to double in proportion to GDP, and without big changes to long-term fiscal policy, it would continue to rise.[29] Credit agencies would likely lower their ratings of U.S. Treasury debt, triggering downgrades of state and municipal governments and important financial institutions as well. This would force some money market funds and other investment firms that are pledged to hold only the highest quality bonds to sell their holdings. More fundamentally, a failure by Washington to make progress toward fiscal sustainability would signal to financial markets that nothing would change without a crisis, with the budget spiraling out of control.

Hanging over Washington lawmakers as well was the Treasury debt ceiling, which would need to be raised again early in 2013. After the political brawl that broke out over this in 2011, it was hard to imagine that there wouldn't be a similar fracas, with the economy suffering significant damage this time around. Businesses weren't about to take a leap of faith and increase their investment and hiring under those circumstances.

Regulatory, legal, and policy uncertainty was holding business back. Much of it was the inevitable fallout from the carnage of the Great Recession. The economic impact was amplified by the nation's fragile psychological state, and it kept the nation's animal spirits bottled up. By summer 2012, some worries were beginning to fade as more of the Dodd-Frank rules were written and the Supreme Court upheld most of the Affordable Care Act. Legal wrangling also wound down as parties came to terms. But with the nation's political divisions growing wider as the presidential election approached, worries over the nation's tax and spending policies mounted.

Endnotes

1. "Jobless recovery" was first used to describe the weak economic recovery coming out of the recession in 1990–1991. This was when corporate layoffs first became a common part of the economic landscape. Economic growth was similarly weak after the 2000 recession and even more so after the Great Recession of 2008–2009.

2. This observation is based on my experience observing three full business cycles as a professional economist and examining all those since the 1930s.

3. I also serve on the board of MGIC, a publicly traded mortgage insurance company, and The Reinvestment Fund, a nonprofit, community development financial institution that combines public and private capital to invest in low-income neighborhoods and communities.

4. The structural unemployment rate, also known as the full-employment unemployment rate, is that unemployment rate consistent with stable inflation. Prior to the Great Recession, the structural unemployment rate was widely thought to be near 5%, but 3 years into the recovery, it was likely closer to 5.5% and rising. Some good economists argued it was even higher. The CBO's estimate of the structural unemployment rate is available here: http://www.cbo.gov/publication/42912

5. This includes the period since the 1930s Great Depression.

6. The unemployment rate in summer 2012 was hovering just above 8%. If housing had performed as it had on average in past recoveries since World War II, the unemployment rate would have been closer to 6.5%, approximately 1 percentage point higher than the estimated 5.5% full-employment unemployment rate.

7. *This Time is Different: Eight Centuries of Financial Folly*, Reinhart and Rogoff, 2011, Princeton University Press. http://press.princeton.edu/titles/8973.html

8. This is what bond investor Bill Gross of PIMCO considered to be the fate of the U.S. economy in the wake of the Great Recession. See "On the Course to a New Normal," Bill Gross, September 2009, PIMCO. http://www.pimco.com/EN/Insights/Pages/Gross%20Sept%20On%20the%20Course%20to%20a%20New%20Normal.aspx

9. Interest rates peaked in 1980. The 10-year Treasury yield peaked above 15%, and fixed mortgage rates rose as high as 18%. Aggressive monetary tightening by the Paul Volker-led Federal Reserve broke the back of high inflation during this period, allowing rates to fall steadily over the next 3 decades.

10. As a ratio to households' after-tax income, total liabilities peaked at close to 135% of GDP. In 1980, this ratio stood at 70%.

11. By mid-2012, the realized losses on residential mortgage debt originated during the housing bubble approached $1 trillion. This includes losses on first and second residential mortgage loans and residential mortgage-backed securities. See Table 9.1.

12. U.S. government deficits and debt were rising even before the housing bubble burst because of the wars in Afghanistan and Iraq, the Bush-era tax cuts, and the costs of adding a prescription drug plan to Medicare.

13. Total household debt fell by $1.5 trillion or 12% between early 2009 and summer 2012. This is based on credit file data from credit bureau Equifax. The data differs from the more widely used Federal Reserve Board's Flow of Funds, but it is likely more accurate. Regardless, both the Equifax and Fed data tell a similar story.

14. Although there isn't enough data to determine what proportion of the reduction in household debt was voluntary and what proportion due to write-offs, an econometric analysis suggests that $1.2 trillion of the $1.5 trillion reduction in household debt from its peak to summer 2012 was the result of write-offs.

15. At its apex, lending by foreign banks accounted for almost one-fourth of all U.S. commercial and industrial loans outstanding, according to the Federal Reserve.

16. This statement is based on comprehensive profit and balance sheet data available back to World War II.

17. According to the Bureau of Labor Statistics, labor productivity grew more than 6% during the year ending in the first quarter of 2010. Productivity has rarely grown this strongly and never during a recession. Generally in recessions, productivity suffers as businesses cut output more than employment. The Great Recession was unique in that panicked businesses slashed employment more than output.

18. According to the Bureau of Economic Analysis' National Income and Product Accounts, profit margins for all nonfinancial corporations nearly tripled after the early 1980s, nearing 18% early in 2012. The average corporate profit margin since World War II is a little more than 10%.

19. Keynes appears to have borrowed David Hume's term for spontaneous motivation, which itself comes from the Latin *spiritus animals*—a term for the spirit that drives human thought, feeling, and action. The original passage from Keynes' book *The Theory of Employment, Interest and Money: Even apart from the instability due to speculation, there is the instability due to the characteristic of human nature that a large proportion of our positive activities depend on spontaneous optimism rather than mathematical expectations, whether moral or hedonistic or economic. Most, probably, of our decisions to do something positive, the full consequences of which will be drawn out over many days to come, can only be taken as the result of animal spirits—a spontaneous urge to action rather than inaction, and not as the outcome of a weighted average of quantitative benefits multiplied by quantitative probabilities.*

20. Thomas Jefferson didn't hide his disdain for New York bankers such as Alexander Hamilton, who Jefferson felt exploited the true source of wealth, namely farmers such as himself.

21. Remarks by the President on Wall Street Reform, Cooper Union, New York, New York, April 22, 2010. http://www.whitehouse.gov/the-press-office/remarks-president-wall-street-reform

22. Nassim Nicholas Taleb introduced the concept of black swans in the context of financial events in his 2004 book *Fooled by Randomness: The Hidden Role of Chance in Life and Markets*, Random House.

23. According to law firm Davis Polk, as of early July 2012, almost 2 years after Dodd-Frank had become law, no more than one-third of the nearly 400 rulemaking requirements in the legislation had been finalized by regulators.

24. I was asked to estimate the impact of these risk-retention rules, a.k.a. "skin-in-the-game" regulations, on mortgage rates and on the size of the mortgage market, going back and forth with regulators, bankers, and others over the fine details. Other issues that had not been settled long after Dodd-Frank became law included the definition of a qualified mortgage, the Volker rule, rules for the derivatives markets, and guidelines for money-market mutual funds.

25. The FHFA filed suit against 17 firms on September 2, 2011 http://www.fhfa.gov/webfiles/22599/PLSLitigation_final_090211.pdf

26. According to Equifax credit data, close to 3.5 million first mortgage loans were in or near foreclosure when the suit was filed in late 2010. The same number of loans were in this situation when the suit was settled early in 2012.

27. Tax credits and penalties varied depending on whether the firms had fewer than 50 employees, between 50 and 100 employees, or more than 100 employees. For small businesses it also mattered whether the employees were full or part time.

28. This includes such things as an annual inflation adjustment to the alternative minimum tax, Medicare reimbursement rates for doctors, and tax credits for research and development.

29. Publicly traded Treasury debt rose from approximately 35% of GDP in fiscal year 2007 to 70% in fiscal year 2012.

10

Don't Bet Against the United States

The Great Recession posed the most serious threat to the national and global economy since the Great Depression of the 1930s. At its worst, the turmoil in late 2008 brought the financial system near collapse. Stock and bond markets cratered, and one blue-chip financial firm failed after another. By early 2009, businesses of all kinds and sizes were slashing jobs, and unemployment surged. Years later, the nightmare of that time remained vivid in the minds of investors, businesses, and consumers.

The crisis began as a fairly ordinary financial hiccup. Sharp swings in stock and bond prices happen regularly, and even major financial institutions fail from time to time. But this time disruption bred panic, with devastating economic consequences as policymakers underestimated the financial storm. The Federal Reserve thought housing was experiencing a modest downturn and began cutting interest rates only after the crash became obvious. Regulators handled foundering financial institutions erratically and inconsistently, alarming and confusing the markets. Bear Stearns was folded into JPMorgan Chase; Fannie Mae and Freddie Mac were nationalized; Lehman Brothers was thrown into bankruptcy. It was unclear if or where the government would backstop the financial system. Investors and creditors rushed for the exits en masse.

Botched policymaking ignited the panic, but the policy response to the economic crisis was massive, unprecedented, and ultimately successful. When Federal Reserve policymakers realized the crisis's magnitude, they rapidly pushed interest rates to zero and flooded the financial system with liquidity, buying trillions of dollars in bonds. The Federal Deposit Insurance Corp. expanded its safety net by raising limits on insured deposits and guaranteeing the debt issued by banks. The Treasury forced too-big-to-fail financial institutions to raise enough capital to withstand losses as big as those suffered in the 1930s.

Congress established the Troubled Asset Relief Program to shore up teetering banks unable to raise enough capital from private investors and to bail out the auto and housing industries. The fiscal stimulus of temporary tax cuts and increased government spending also played a vital role, as it has in every downturn since the 1930s. Strapped unemployed workers received additional aid, as did state and local governments working to avoid cutbacks in public education, safety, and healthcare. More money went to infrastructure projects. Personal income and payroll taxes were reduced; home and auto buyers received lucrative tax breaks, and businesses received tax benefits for making timely investments.

The Bush administration was slow to respond to the crisis at first, but ultimately invented TARP and fired the first round of fiscal stimulus via personal tax rebates. President Obama took office when the economy was in free fall and responded aggressively, using the TARP to help the auto and housing industries and enacting the Recovery Act, the largest fiscal stimulus program since the New Deal. Despite partisan sniping—first from Democrats faulting President Bush for moving too slowly and then from Republicans complaining that President Obama had overstepped—the government's response to the Great Recession was roughly bipartisan, at least early on. Republicans disliked the Recovery Act but did not actively block its passage.

The response was particularly rapid after policymakers went into crisis mode. Within 6 months of Lehman's failure, the Fed and Congress had fully deployed all the usual weapons against economic downturns, including easy money and fiscal stimulus. They also used some new ones, such as the Fed's quantitative easing and the government's equity stakes in auto companies and banks.

Policymakers also experimented. Some steps didn't work and were shelved, such as the Bush administration's short-lived plan to save structured investment vehicles and the Obama administration's public-private investment program.[1] Experimentation had its downside, adding to uncertainty; changing programs and rules made it tough for businesses to figure out what worked and how. The private sector's anxiety rose as it became clear policymakers didn't have it all figured out. If Washington didn't understand what was happening, who did?

But the willingness to try new policies resulted in some big successes. The bank stress tests, invented on-the-fly, were an immediate salve on the financial system. The Cash for Clunkers tax credit provided an unexpectedly large boost to the automakers at a critical time when they were exiting bankruptcy. Efforts to untangle the mess in mortgage markets helped lenders and homeowners come to terms on many more home loan modifications and refinancings than they would have otherwise.

Policymakers learned from the calamity of the 1930s. The 4 years between the 1929 stock market crash and President Franklin Roosevelt's inauguration were characterized by inaction or worse, counterproductive action. The Federal Reserve raised interest rates to defend the gold standard. President Hoover's administration focused on balancing the budget, raising taxes even as the economy's problems deepened.[2] In his 1932 budget message, Hoover asked Congress not to embark on any "new or large ventures of government," asserting that although "the plea of unemployment will be advanced as reasons for many new ventures...no reasonable view of the outlook warrants such pleas." The prevailing wisdom favored letting the economic wildfires burn—which they did, leaving a scorched landscape by the time Roosevelt became president.

Because policymakers didn't dither this way during the Great Recession, the nation was spared another depression. After it became clear that the government would backstop the financial system, the selling stampede halted, businesses stopped slashing jobs, and consumers stepped out of their bunkers. Any one aspect of the government's response could be justifiably criticized; the policy mix wasn't anyone's ideal prescription. But given the speed with which policymakers were forced to act and the intense political crucible in which they worked, what they came up with performed remarkably well. The Great Recession ended, and the recovery began much sooner than it would have otherwise.

Righting the Fiscal Ship

Even so, the downturn exacted a tremendous cost. Millions of jobs were lost, millions of families were displaced and trillions in wealth vanished. The public cost of fighting the downturn was enormous, totaling $1.8 trillion. Approximately $1.4 trillion paid for the fiscal stimulus, $200 billion covered Fannie and Freddie's losses, and the rest went to clean up the banks and bail out the auto and housing industries. The final bill to taxpayers was huge, exceeding 12% of GDP.[3]

The bill would have been higher still if policymakers had stepped aside and let the downturn rage on.[4] The weaker economy would have further undermined tax revenues and prompted even more government spending through automatic stabilizers—existing programs that expand on their own whenever the economy stumbles, such as unemployment insurance, foods stamps, and welfare. Nonetheless, the cost of the government step-up was enormous. Treasury debt doubled relative to GDP in the 5 years between fiscal years 2007 and 2012, from approximately 35% to more than 70%.

The nation ran up a larger debt burden during World War II, but that shrank quickly as peace returned, defense spending fell, and the economy boomed (see Figure 10.1). Policymakers in 2012 couldn't expect similar results from the winding down of the Iraq and Afghanistan wars, or count on a much stronger economy to stabilize the nation's fiscal situation. Even under the best of circumstances, the nation's debt burden was set to keep rising.

Heaviest National Debt Load Since World War II

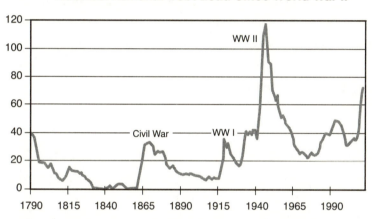

Figure 10.1 Federal government public debt-to-GDP ratio, %.

Sources: Treasury Department, Moody's Analytics

Global investors were willing to overlook this for a while. Policymakers had put the nation's fiscal house in order after past disruptions, and given the debt crisis in Europe and the risks of emerging economies such as China, Treasury bonds still looked to be the world's safest investment. With the Federal Reserve also buying Treasuries through quantitative easing, interest rates fell. By summer 2012, when the "flight to quality" was especially intense, 10-year Treasury yields fell below 1.5%, a record low.

But global investors weren't going to look away forever. And judging by the experience of other nations that had suffered sovereign-debt problems, it was impossible to know precisely when or why investors would lose faith.[5] It was clear, however, that such faith could vanish almost instantly, and that once gone it would never return, at least not with the fervor it had before. The offending nation would pay higher interest rates forever.

Credit rating agencies were already changing their views of the U.S. Treasury. Standard & Poor's dropped its AAA rating of Treasury debt in summer 2011, as Congress made a political spectacle of itself before raising the Treasury's debt ceiling. The two other big rating agencies—Moody's (my employer) and Fitch—suggested they would do the same if policymakers didn't present a credible plan to make the nation's finances sustainable, with budget deficits small enough to stabilize the nation's debt-to-GDP ratio.[6] The agencies appeared willing to wait until after the 2012 elections, but if there were no progress then, they too would likely downgrade the nation's credit status.[7]

An across-the-board downgrade would likely bring a nasty reaction in financial markets, something that had not happened when S&P acted alone. Many investors had discounted the S&P downgrade as premature. The deal policymakers struck to increase the debt ceiling wasn't all smoke and mirrors as the S&P downgrade suggested. Most important, Democrats and Republicans had agreed on how much future deficits would have to shrink to achieve fiscal sustainability—about $4 trillion over the subsequent decade.[8] Reaching consensus on the target was a significant accomplishment.

Policymakers also came to terms on specific spending cuts, totaling $1 trillion over a decade, and on a budget mechanism, called *sequestration*, that cut spending by an additional $1 trillion over 10 years. The sequestration arrangement meant that, beginning in 2013, defense and nondefense programs would be cut by equal amounts. Although there was reasonable doubt that lawmakers would actually let the cuts take place, it was credible to expect something close to the agreed upon $2 trillion in cuts, if only because it would take new legislation to avoid them. Policymakers were halfway home.

Halfway wasn't good enough, however, and unless policymakers found additional ways to shrink the deficit soon after the elections, all the rating agencies would likely issue downgrades, with dangerous consequences for financial markets. Federal agencies that rely on the Treasury's credit backstop, such as Fannie Mae, Freddie Mac, and the Federal Home Loan Banks, would also suffer downgrades. So would systemically important financial institutions, those seen as too big to fail and thus reliant on Uncle Sam to help them out in a pinch. Even state and municipal governments could see the ratings on their debt fall. Mutual and pension funds, insurance companies, and other financial institutions whose charters limit them to top-rated investments could be forced to sell securities of these institutions. Bond prices would fall and interest rates would rise, affecting the entire economy.

Avoiding all this would be a daunting challenge for the next president and Congress but not impossible. As it happened, significant tax increases and government spending cuts were slated to take effect in 2013. In addition to those spending cuts agreed to as part of the 2011 debt ceiling deal, the law called for personal income tax rates to rise as temporary cuts passed under President Bush expired. Simultaneously, the so-called "inflation patch" on the Alternative Minimum Tax was slated to end, subjecting more taxpayers to higher AMT rates, and Medicare reimbursement rates for doctors would fall. The combined budget effect of these changes would comfortably exceed the $4 trillion target for cutting the deficit over the coming decade. Indeed, if all the tax and spending changes actually took effect, deficits would fall enough to quickly reduce the nation's debt load during the second half of the decade (see Figure 10.2).[9]

The Nation's Fiscal Problems Were Solved Under Current Law

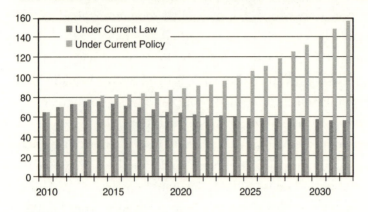

Figure 10.2 Federal government public debt-to-GDP ratio, %.

Sources: Treasury Department, Moody's Analytics

Nobody believed this would all actually happen, however. Regardless of who won the election, the president and Congress would not allow the nation to go over this fiscal cliff. Doing so would bring on a new recession and force wrenching long-term changes to tax and spending policy that neither party actually supported. But to change the law required compromise between Democrats and Republicans, something that was happening less and less. In these circumstances, however, compromise seemed possible because both parties had significant negotiating leverage. The Democrats could threaten to allow the Bush-era tax cuts to expire and draconian cuts to defense spending to kick in. Republicans could counter with the sequestration cuts set to shrink the nondefense budget. Then there was the debt ceiling, which the Treasury was set to hit again in early 2013, providing leverage to whichever side could block action in the House or Senate.[10]

Moreover, for all that divided the two parties, some common ground existed. Neither wanted the AMT to expand or Medicare reimbursements to fall, and many in both parties were uncomfortable with the across-the-board spending cuts forced by sequestration. Neither party wanted tax rates to go up for all Americans. The Republicans didn't want any tax increases—many had signed a politically binding no-tax pledge—and President Obama wanted rates to rise only for households earning more than $250,000 annually. Tax reform that involved scaling back deductions, credits, and loopholes to make the tax code simpler and fairer had broad support. Moreover, neither party wanted to take the nation over the fiscal cliff or to default on the nation's debt. Whatever else was done, the 2013 cliff would be scaled back and the debt ceiling raised again.

There was also a growing consensus in support of a budget plan laid out by the National Commission on Fiscal Responsibility and Reform—the so-called Simpson-Bowles commission.[11] The panel was established by President Obama in spring 2010 to devise a sustainable budget plan. Its 18 members were equally split between Republicans and Democrats; if 14 could agree, Congress was to vote the plan up or down in its entirety, without amendment.[12] Ultimately, only 11 members signed on to the final recommendations. Nonetheless, the commission solidly established the goal of fiscal sustainability and outlined the tax and spending reforms necessary to achieve it.

Of course, Congress could put off the tough decisions yet again. It could prevent taxes from rising and postpone spending cuts for a few months or even a year. The debt ceiling could be increased just enough to avoid default. That would dodge the fiscal cliff at the start of 2013 and buy time for policymakers to work on a comprehensive deal. But punting would jeopardize the nation's credit rating, risk a major disruption in financial markets, and elevate uncertainty among businesses and households to dangerous levels. Executives and consumers would conclude, rightly, that Washington wouldn't agree until disillusioned global investors brought on a financial crisis. The economy's prospects would erode.

In the months before the presidential election, the consensus held that regardless of the results, Washington would take the path of least resistance and punt. But the political stars looked likely to align in early 2013 in ways that could allow the next president and Congress to break with the recent past. A serious stumbling block to a budget agreement was the Republicans' no-tax pledge. Democrats insisted that more tax revenue be part of any deal. The Simpson-Bowles commission suggested that about one-third of any deficit reduction plan consist of increased taxes. Finally, tax rates were poised to rise for everyone at the start of 2013, without Congress having to vote for it. If that happened, Republicans could then leave the new rates in place for higher income households, act to lower them for everyone else, and insist they had successfully cut taxes.

A politically conceivable budget agreement would also include spending cuts along the lines proposed by the Simpson-Bowles commission and an understanding on reform of corporate and personal income tax codes. Changes would be phased in over several years, easing the impact of tighter fiscal policy on the economy. With just a bit of good luck and some deft political leadership, the nation stood a good chance of achieving fiscal sustainability.

Navigating the Monetary Shoals

The Federal Reserve was on a mission in mid-2012 as perilous as that of the president and Congress. The central bank's first concern was to ensure the economic recovery continued. The approaching fiscal cliff and the interminable European debt crisis were serious threats, forcing the Fed to keep its foot on the monetary accelerator and prepared to press even harder. More quantitative easing might be needed, and if lawmakers took the nation over the fiscal cliff or if the euro zone cracked up, the Fed's creativity would be tested again.

Europe's woes were beginning to affect the United States more tangibly. Trans-Atlantic trade was flagging, and European banks, which had been big lenders to American businesses, were pulling back.[13] More significantly, Europe's problems were becoming a major worry for American business leaders. Decision makers knew that if the euro zone fell apart, the economic damage would be global. It was all but impossible to attach a probability to this scenario, but even contemplating the possibility caused businesses to recoil. They didn't lay off more workers, but they hired more cautiously, and job growth came to a crawl.

Even if the euro zone stayed together, more financial turmoil seemed certain. Stock, bond, and commodity markets gyrated over esoteric news such as the Greek elections or interest rates on Spanish and Italian bonds. Without such market pressure, however, it seemed unlikely that Europe's leaders would summon the political will to make the difficult fiscal and economic choices required to sustain their union. German voters likely wouldn't ante up the funds needed by the strapped periphery countries, and the voters in those periphery countries wouldn't give up control of their budgets as demanded by the Germans in exchange. But the market turmoil kept everyone on edge, including American companies. The Fed had no choice but to remain on high alert.

The odds favored the Europeans staying together. With each round of financial market anguish, they took concrete steps toward deeper fiscal and political union. They were grudging steps but substantive ones overall. Most important, Germany, the only country with the resources to support the euro zone, appeared increasingly committed to it. Germany effectively backstopped the European Central Bank and its own central bank, the Bundesbank, and these institutions were at risk of losing trillions of euros if the currency union fell apart.[14] The ECB and Bundesbank had invested in the troubled periphery countries in various ways, buying troubled sovereign debt, lending to wobbly banks, and financing governments' current account deficits. If the euro zone fractured, moreover, a big part of the European banking system would collapse, bringing Germany widespread economic damage. Thus the cost to Germany of backing out of the euro zone or forcing out another country, such as Greece, was too great.

This economic logic notwithstanding, it wasn't difficult to imagine how Europe's thorny politics could lead to a breakdown, and the Fed had to be ready. In such a scenario, unconventional policies such as Operation Twist, quantitative easing, or market guidance on monetary policy wouldn't be enough. The Fed would have to take "unconventional unconventional" steps.[15] Among the most likely of these was nominal GDP targeting. Instead of setting monetary policy based on the inflation and unemployment rates, the Fed would set it based on nominal GDP, the sum of inflation and real GDP. In such a setup, the Fed would use massive doses of QE or even charge banks to hold their reserves, via a negative interest rate, to induce them to keep lending in the hope of preventing deflation and a deep recession.[16, 17] Federal Reserve Chairman Bernanke had openly criticized Japanese central bankers for being too timid and tied to policy orthodoxy to escape their country's deflationary trap in the 1990s. Bernanke was unlikely to make the same mistake himself.

The more unconventional the Fed was forced to be, the more difficult it would be to gracefully unwind its efforts when the time came. The Fed's critics worried that the more it did to keep the recovery intact, the more likely its actions would ignite uncontrollable inflation down the road. Critics believed that even if the Fed had the policy tools needed to drain the liquidity it had poured into the financial system—and they questioned whether it did—the central bank would wait too long to pull the plug. The timing would be especially problematic given the inherent difficulty of gauging the economy's direction and speed. Plus, the Fed was predisposed to err on the side of easy money, critics said; in its desire to make absolutely sure the economy was off and running, policymakers would wait too long to hit the monetary brakes.

These were sensible concerns. The Fed's timing was unlikely to be perfect; at some point inflation probably would rise above the central bank's 2% target. But prospects for real runaway inflation were low. The Fed battled high inflation in the 1980s and had won resoundingly. Inflation in the 1990s and 2000s had been precisely on target. Policymakers would have no reservations about tightening monetary policy aggressively to rein in inflation if it were clearly too high. Given the experience of the 1970s and 1980s, the view that low and stable inflation is a necessary condition for sustainable long-term economic growth was ingrained in the DNA of the world's central bankers. Nevertheless, many policymakers believed, correctly, that taking a chance on slightly above-target inflation was clearly preferable to suffering another deflationary downturn.

Getting Out of the Mortgage Business

The government's backstop of the economy during the Great Recession forestalled another depression, but it entrenched government in the nation's economic life as deeply as it had been since World War II. Much of the financial system had been on life support provided by the Federal Reserve and FDIC, and the federal government had taken big ownership stakes in many of the nation's financial institutions as well as its giant automakers.

Many of the government's interventions expired by design as the financial system and economy found their footing. Banks weaned themselves off the Fed's and FDIC's support as financial markets calmed. Repaying the government's TARP investments became a badge of honor for financial institutions. The government also sold its stake in Chrysler and many of its shares in GM and AIG. Several years after the recession ended, the government still held small ownership stakes, but only because it hoped the recovery would enable it to get better prices when they were sold.

More problematic was the continuing federal presence in housing finance. Fannie Mae and Freddie Mac had been taken over, and the FHA had expanded in the wake of the private market's collapse, effectively making the government the nation's residential mortgage lender.[18] The mortgage business had been nationalized, and there was little chance this would change soon.[19] Washington couldn't just cut back its lending activities; the housing market was still too fragile, and the economy too dependent on it. Still, few were comfortable with the government's outsized role.

The Obama administration argued for phasing out Fannie and Freddie and significantly scaling back its role in mortgages—not quickly, but over time in a clearly defined way that would allow private lenders time to re-establish the market. The administration outlined several paths for a future mortgage finance system, with different degrees of government involvement.[20] Even the most expansive of these proposals called for private lenders to provide most of the nation's mortgage credit; government would agree to backstop them, making up catastrophic losses but only in crises on the scale of the Great Recession. The guarantee would work much like FDIC deposit insurance worked for banks, deterring runs by panicked mortgage investors. As banks do for deposit insurance, mortgage lenders would pay a fee for the government's backstop and would pay more if those fees became insufficient to cover the industry.

The administration's proposal began a long debate over the future of the mortgage finance system that would continue after the 2012 presidential election. But regardless of the election's outcome, it was likely that the system would include a catastrophic government guarantee.[21] This was the only way to preserve the popular 30-year fixed-rate mortgage, a type of loan that would quickly fade in a fully privatized system without a government backstop. The FHA introduced this type of mortgage during the Great Depression, a time of mass foreclosures. The recent foreclosure crisis provided a stark reminder of why fixed-rate mortgages were established because the bulk of foreclosures involved adjustable-rate loans.

Financial institutions have historically found it difficult to manage the interest rate risk on fixed-rate mortgages: as the cost of funds changes, the rate received from homeowners remains fixed. The savings and loan industry collapsed largely because of the mismanagement of this interest rate risk during the 1980s, and even Fannie and Freddie got into trouble using inappropriate interest-rate hedging techniques to manage their earnings in the early 2000s. It thus is not surprising that 30-year fixed-rate mortgages are rare overseas; in most countries, lenders must manage interest rate risk without government support. Indeed, it is likely that a U.S. market without a catastrophic government guarantee would come to resemble overseas markets, primarily offering adjustable-rate mortgages.

Mortgage rates would also be lower with a government catastrophic guarantee than with no government backstop, particularly if private investors actually believed the government would never intervene during a crisis.[22] Such insurance would be too costly for private insurers to provide. A fully privatized market would also be fractured, much like the private-label mortgage securities market was before the recession, when Wells Fargo securities traded differently than those from Citibank or other issuers. Markets in such nonstandarized securities are thinner, and thus interest rates are higher. Moreover, under a fully privatized system, each securitizer would bear the cost of operations, administration, reporting, and auditing. Given these high fixed costs, there were significant scale economies that would be lost without a significant government role in the market. Could private industry participants come together to set tight standards on securities and achieve some economies of scale? Possibly, but that hadn't happened before.[23]

Catastrophic government insurance would also ensure that mortgage credit remained ample in the bad times, and it would reduce the odds of bad lending in good times because the government insurance would be offered at reasonable prices only to good-quality mortgages. Because private financial institutions would put up the system's capital, there would be significant incentive to lend prudently and, given the competition in the mostly private system, to innovate as well. Taxpayer bailouts would also be less likely because homeowners and private financial institutions would be required to put substantial capital in front of the government's guarantee.

A potential downside of any government backstop is moral hazard: If private investors believe the government will bail them out if things go badly, they will take inappropriate risks. But the government backstop could kick in only if losses were catastrophic, so private investors would still suffer big losses before receiving any support. There would still be a sufficient incentive for private investors to make sound loans. Moreover, moral hazard exists even in a fully privatized system. History strongly suggests government would not allow the housing market to fail; no matter what lawmakers pledge today, investors know political winds change at times of economic stress. Taxpayers would be better off if the government explicitly acknowledged this and collected an insurance premium in exchange for its guarantee.

A transition from a nationalized mortgage system to a private system with a government catastrophic backstop would take years and raise many issues. Mortgage rates would be higher than they were in the past, and borrowers would face larger hurdles to obtain mortgage loans. Given the nation's fiscal challenges, the federal government couldn't afford to continue large subsidies for homeownership. These subsidies weren't effective in any event, as was clear from the foreclosure crisis. Nonetheless, it was critical that the mortgage finance system be better designed, or the costs for future prospective homeowners would be prohibitive, and the costs to taxpayers in the next financial crisis would be overwhelming. And if mortgage finance reform were done right, the American dream of homeownership would remain in reach for most.

The debate over the future mortgage finance system was symptomatic of a broader debate over the role of government that raged after the recession. Some believed the government had intervened too aggressively in the economy. Passage of Dodd-Frank and the Affordable Care Act, which gave government new powers to regulate the financial services and healthcare industries, caused those sentiments to boil over, and the Tea Party was born. In certain respects this was therapeutic; it is important to constantly question government authority. Still, one of government's most fundamental purposes is to support its citizens in times of crisis. This includes wars, terrorist attacks, natural disasters, and also economic calamities such as the Great Recession. Only government can adequately meet society's needs in such trying times. Moreover, without the knowledge that if things go badly wrong the government will ultimately step in, few would take the risks necessary to power a well-functioning economy. Government should be compensated for providing this vital service, but only government can provide it.

Where Will the Jobs Come From?

The economy in mid-2012 had come a long way since the Great Recession. Three years of growth had brought both GDP and corporate profits back to their pre-downturn levels; stock prices were within a few percent of their all-time highs; and even house prices were rising again. Nearly 4 million more Americans had jobs than at the worst point of the recession, and most industries were adding to payrolls.

Yet, despite the progress, it didn't feel much like a recovery. Consumers and small business managers were still depressed, producing confidence index readings more typical of recession troughs than of recoveries (see Figure 10.3). The unemployment rate was stuck above 8%, and almost half of those unemployed had been out of work for more than 6 months, with many idle much longer than that. The number of Americans with jobs was still nearly 5 million below what it was before the recession. By many measures, this recovery was the weakest of any since World War II.

Still Feeling Depressed

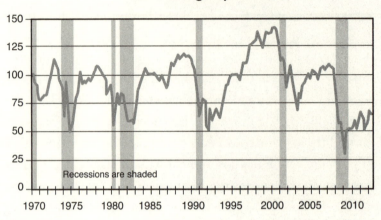

Figure 10.3 Consumer confidence, index: 1985 = 100.

Source: Conference Board

It was also unclear what would spur faster job creation, or where the new jobs would come from in the future. There had been little net U.S. employment growth for more than a decade, and much of what had occurred before the recession was in the bubble-juiced real estate and financial services industries. When the bubble burst, these jobs vanished, and the extent of America's jobs deficit became clear. Scared businesses in nearly every industry and corner of the country used the downturn to overhaul their labor forces. Workers who weren't top producers lost jobs and were never replaced.[24]

But out of this economic morass, a leaner, more competitive economy was rising. American companies in nearly every industry had restructured. They had significantly increased productivity and reduced their cost structures, shed their debt loads, and raised lots of cash. Unit labor costs, which track worker productivity and are the best measure of global competitiveness, had fallen back to levels seen in the mid-2000s. In manufacturing, unit labor costs were back to their late 1980s' level, besting the performance of nearly every other global economy (see Figure 10.4).

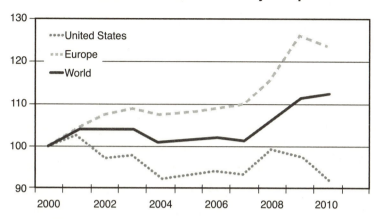

Figure 10.4 Unit labor costs, index: 2000 = 100.

Sources: OECD, Moody's Analytics

When the Moody's Corporation purchased my firm, Economy. com, in late 2005, it asked us to help determine where else in the world Moody's should expand. The only requirement was an educated workforce. Speaking English was a plus, but not a prerequisite. Not surprisingly, India offered by far the most promising expansion opportunities. Lots of multinational companies saw the same thing, and foreign investment in India grew rapidly. Labor costs there subsequently rose, and when we updated our analysis after the recession, although India remained competitive, it was no longer as compelling a place to grow. This time, surprisingly, the best place to locate was suburban Philadelphia, my home. This sounds self-serving, but the region has a highly educated workforce, competitive wages and living costs, and we speak English pretty well. It was no longer obvious that economic logic would push U.S. businesses to move operations overseas.

This was clearly true for manufacturing, particularly the high value-added activities in which the United States had become a leader.[25] Any American manufacturer that survived the Great Recession had to be doing something well, keeping costs low, selling a unique technology, or catering to a specific market niche. But although manufacturing employment rose solidly in the recovery, the goods-producing sector of the economy was too small and too productive to employ the millions of workers who would need jobs in the future.

Inevitably, the bulk of those jobs would have to come from the many service-oriented industries in which the United States had long exceled. Those ranged from accounting and legal services to advertising and entertainment; engineering and management consulting to computer software, data management, education, and healthcare. Despite the black eye of the financial panic, even banking, insurance, and money management remained American specialties. Domestic firms had been producing these services for the home market for decades; now they were turning attention overseas, where the growing wealth of emerging markets offered huge opportunities. After Chinese, Brazilian, and Russian households acquired cars and mobile phones, they wanted to send their kids to the best schools, hear the latest music, and receive a high return on their savings. Americans had been producing these services for decades, and no one was better at it. And with the possible exception of the British, no other nation was doing it on a scale that could encompass the globe.

My own business at Moody's Analytics offered a good example. Our most rapidly growing line of business was constructing the econometric models that global banking institutions used to stress-test their portfolios. Regulators around the world were requiring banks to determine how they would fare if the economy faltered. This created a need for economic scenarios to run through the models. Banks in London, Frankfurt, São Paulo, Toronto, and Sydney were using the tools we had constructed. We hired the best and the brightest from all over the world to work in our suburban Philadelphia office.

Producing services like these requires highly skilled workers— the United States' global comparative advantage—and lots of them. The effect of this could already be seen in the growing demand for educated workers. Early in the economic recovery, the number of workers with college degrees surpassed those with less education for the first time in the nation's economic history (see Figure 10.5). Unemployment, moreover, had been markedly less severe for those with college degrees, peaking at 5%—half the 10% overall rate that afflicted the economy during the recession's worst months. Joblessness among educated workers fell more quickly during the recovery, moreover, and it was not long before employers reported shortages of skilled workers.

College Is Required to Get a Job

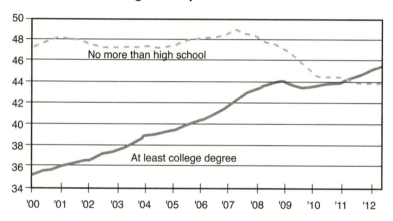

Figure 10.5 Millions of jobs, 12-month moving average.

Source: Bureau of Labor Statistics

Export-oriented service activities could provide the millions of jobs the United States economy would need in the future. But there was no guarantee they would. Global competition in these industries would assuredly heat up. America's antiquated educational system and immigration laws needed significant overhauls to provide qualified workers. Colleges and universities were under financial pressure, and it wasn't easy for talented foreign students who graduated from U.S. schools to remain in the country. This needed to change if the United States were to retain its comparative advantage and put its economic potential to work.

Pessimism came easy in mid-2012. America had been through a tough time and it showed, in our outlook and attitudes. We had more than enough to worry about: It wasn't clear how the euro zone would keep itself together or how Washington would avoid a fiscal nightmare. Left or right, few were comfortable with the idea of the federal government owning part of General Motors or serving as the nation's principal mortgage lender. And some had begun to believe the United States might indeed be doomed to slower economic growth and increasing economic inequality for years or decades to come.

This gloomy view was tempting but incorrect. Those who bet against American success have lost throughout our history, and they are likely to be wrong again. Fixing the economy would require some reasonably good choices by the Federal Reserve, Congress, and whoever occupied the White House in 2013. The process would surely be nerve-wracking, but policymakers had done what was necessary during the Great Recession, and they were likely to again. Most important, the resilience and ingenuity of American businesses and workers could never be discounted. Whatever the challenge, they would adapt.

Endnotes

1. Structured investment vehicles borrowed money by issuing short-term debt and using the funds to buy longer-term securities, such as residential mortgage-backed bonds, that carried higher interest rates. What made the SIVs dangerous was that many of the nation's largest banks owned them but did not report their earnings or losses on the banks' balance sheets. Citicorp's SIV was the first to crash in the Great Recession. Fearing that collapsing SIVs would undermine the system, the Bush administration proposed that banks fund a "super SIV" to buy assets from troubled SIVs. The idea went nowhere.

2. The Revenue Act of 1932 raised tax rates across the board, including personal income, estate, and corporate income taxes beginning with the 1932 tax year. http://en.wikipedia.org/wiki/Revenue_Act_of_1932.

3. This estimate is as of June 2012. Adding in nearly $750 billion in lost revenue and increased spending prompted by the weaker economy, the crisis cost the federal budget an estimated $2.55 trillion, approximately 18% of GDP in 2012 dollars. For historical comparison, the savings-and-loan crisis of the early 1990s cost some $350 billion in 2012 dollars: $275 billion in direct costs plus $75 billion due to the associated recession. This equaled almost 6% of GDP.

4. This is documented in "How the Great Recession Was Brought to an End," Alan Blinder and Mark Zandi, Moody's Analytics Special Study, July 27, 2010. http://www.economy.com/mark-zandi/documents/End-of-Great-Recession.pdf

5. Sovereign debt is the debt issued by national governments, which promise to pay investors interest and, eventually, to repay principal.

6. Under reasonable assumptions, federal government budget deficits between 2% and 3% of GDP will result in a stable relationship between the government's debts and the size of the economy.

7. I am employed by Moody's Analytics, an independent subsidiary of Moody's Corp. that is legally distinct from the credit rating agency, Moody's Investors Service. I take no part in the decisions of the rating agency, although I pay close attention to what it says publicly.

8. This was consistent with analyses done by the nonpartisan Congressional Budget Office.

9. This is according to the Congressional Budget Office's current law baseline budget outlook. CBO's January 2012 budget outlook can be found at http://www.cbo.gov/sites/default/files/cbofiles/attachments/01-31-2012_Outlook.pdf

10. An increase in the Treasury debt ceiling requires a majority vote in the House, and, because of its filibuster rules, 60 votes in the Senate.

11. Alan Simpson was a former Republican senator from Wyoming, and Erskine Bowles was a Democrat from North Carolina who served as President Bill Clinton's chief of staff. The commission's recommendations can be found at http://www.fiscalcommission.gov/

12. This structure was fashioned from the Base Realignment and Closure Commission, which had helped close unneeded military facilities across the country. BRAC gave legislators a way to avoid being blamed for base closings in their districts. A similar device, it was hoped, would enable Congress to vote for fiscal sustainability.

13. Before the European debt crisis hit, Europe purchased almost one-fourth of U.S. exports, and large European banks accounted for approximately one-fifth of U.S. commercial and industrial loans—loans from banks to businesses.

14. As of June 2012, this lending totaled approximately €1.875 trillion, of which €225 billion were ECB purchases of the sovereign debt of periphery countries, €125 billion in emergency lending from the ECB to mostly Greek banks suffering deposit runs, €1 trillion in ECB lending to European banks through long-term repurchase agreements, and €525 billion in lending by the Bundesbank via the Target 2 interbank funding system to periphery countries running trade deficits with Germany.

15. Any monetary policy tactic other than adjusting interest rates is considered unconventional. An "unconventional unconventional" policy would be one never before tried by the Fed.

16. This is the policy prescription of *market monetarism*, a term coined by Danish economist Lars Christensen, in a September 2011 paper, "Market Monetarism: The Second Monetarist Counter-Revolution." http://thefaintofheart.files. wordpress.com/2011/09/market-monetarism-13092011.pdf

17. An even more unconventional unconventional policy, proposed by the IMF's chief economist Olivier Blanchard, among others, would have the Fed target a higher inflation rate—3% or 4%—instead of 2%, to make it easier for debtors (including the U.S. Treasury) to repay what they owed.

18. Approximately 90% of first mortgage loans originated between 2009 and mid-2012 were government-backed loans by Fannie Mae, Freddie Mac, and the FHA.

19. In 2005 the private market accounted for more than half of all mortgage originations. This share fell nearly to zero after the panic. In mid-2012, a few big lenders were making mortgage loans to preferred individual borrowers, but there was no private loan securitization.

20. The Obama administration's whitepaper describing options to reform the mortgage finance system was issued in February 2011. http://www.treasury.gov/initiatives/Documents/Reforming%20America%27s%20Housing%20Finance%20Market.pdf

21. This is similar to the hybrid mortgage finance system proposed by Zandi and deRitis in "The Future of the Mortgage Finance System," Moody's Analytics Special Study, February 7, 2011 (http://www.economy.com/mark-zandi/documents/Mortgage-Finance-Reform-020711.pdf). Similar proposals were made by the Housing Policy Council, the Mortgage Bankers Association, and the Center for American Progress.

22. Zandi and deRitis show that under reasonable assumptions, mortgage rates would be almost 90 basis points lower in a government-backstopped system than in one that was fully privatized. A typical borrower with a $200,000 30-year loan at 6% would pay $1,199 in principal and interest each month, saving $118, or nearly 10%. Borrowers with lower credit scores or those with higher loan-to-value ratios would likely save even more. The greater the risk, the more a borrower would be penalized under the privatized system.

23. The American Securitization Forum, the trade group for private securitizers, issues guidelines but has little authority to audit or enforce them.

24. According to the Bureau of Labor Statistics, the share of layoffs that were permanent rose to a record high of 45% during the recession. In nonrecessionary times, fewer than 25% of layoffs, on average, are permanent.

25. Aerospace, machine tools, sophisticated materials and chemicals, microchips, computer technology, and construction and agricultural equipment are good examples.

INDEX

A

Affordable Care Act of 2010, 213

AIG (American International Group), collapse of, 21, 162

American Recovery and Reinvestment Act, xix, 92, 111, 136

asset bubbles, role of Federal Reserve, 51-54, 57-58

asset-backed securities. *See* mortgage-backed securities

author, economic qualifications of, xxviii-xxx

auto industry

 bailout after Great Recession of 2008/2009, xvii-xviii, 71-75

  details of, 82-86

  reasons for needing, 78-82

  TARP, role of, 37

 origin of financial problems, 75-78

 role in recovery from Great Recession of 2008/2009, 86-88

B

banking industry bailout after Great Recession of 2008/2009, xvi-xviii, 23-26. *See also* financial regulatory reform after Great Recession of 2008/2009; financial system

 FDIC, role of, 31-34

 Federal Reserve, role of, 28-31

 results of, 42-43

 stress-testing, 39-42

 TARP, role of, 34-38

bankruptcy

 of automakers, 83

 for financial institutions, 155

 mortgage loan modifications in, 121

Barr, Michael, 145-146

Bear Stearns, collapse of, 2-3, 15-16

Bernanke, Ben, 34-35, 47-49, 54-66, 98

Big 3 automakers. *See* auto industry, bailout after Great Recession of 2008/2009 "broke the buck," 20, 162

bubbles, role of Federal Reserve, 51-54, 57-58

budget deficits after Great Recession of 2008/2009, xxii-xxv

business cycles, 197-200

businesses, reaction to regulatory changes, xxii

C

cash, influx into economy, 4-6

Cash for Clunkers program, 74, 85-86

CBO (Congressional Budget Office), 110

CDOs (collateralized debt obligations), 14, 27

CDSs (credit default swaps), 14, 27

CFPB (Consumer Financial Protection Bureau), xxi, 145-146

Chrysler. *See* auto industry, bailout after Great Recession of 2008/2009

collateralized debt obligations (CDOs), 14, 27

college loans, 187

confidence in financial system
after Great Recession of 2008/2009, 171-173, 207-210
regulatory changes and, 210-213
role in Great Recession of 2008/2009, 26-28

Congressional Budget Office (CBO), 110

Consumer Financial Protection Bureau (CFPB), xxi, 145-146

consumer spending decline after Great Recession of 2008/2009, 175-178

Cramer, Jim, 48

credit
in financial system failure, 150-153
in gap between rich and poor, 187
role of, 28

credit default swaps (CDSs), 14, 27

credit spreads, 13

credit-rating agencies
mortgage-backed securities, high ratings of, 11-12
U.S. Treasury bonds, 224-225

criticism
of fiscal stimulus plan, 96
of government role in economy, xxv-xxvi

D

debt
after Great Recession of 2008/2009, xxii-xxv
raising debt ceiling, 209-210, 215
relationship with GDP, 214-215

debt ceiling, raising, 209-210, 215

debtor-in-possession financing, 73

deficit after Great Recession of 2008/2009, xxii-xxv

deflation, 55-57

deleveraging, 94, 200-207

Dodd, Chris, 145

Dodd-Frank Act (financial regulatory reform), xx-xxii, 145-149

    effect on financial crisis, 164-166

    Financial Stability Oversight Council (FSOC), 154

    Office of Financial Research (OFR), 154-155

    resolution authority in financial system failure, 155-158

    shadow banking system, 161-164

    slow implementation of, 211

    success of, 166-167

    too-big-to-fail problem, 158-161

E

economic cycles, 197-200

economy

    damage from Great Recession of 2008/2009, xiii-xiv

    government role after Great Recession of 2008/2009, xiii-xxviii, 219-222

        auto industry bailout, xvii-xviii, 71-75

        budget deficits, xxii-xxv

        criticism of, xxv-xxvi

        exit strategy for Federal Reserve, 66-67

        Federal Reserve, role of, 47-51, 58-66

        financial regulatory reform, xx-xxii, 145-149

        financial system rescue, xvi-xviii, 23-26

        fiscal stimulus plan, xviii-xix, 91-96

        housing market reform, xix-xx, 119-124, 231-235

        policy decisions in 2011, 222-228

        support for, xxvi-xxviii

    influx of cash in, 4-6

    recovery from Great Recession of 2008/2009, xiv-xvi

Elmendorf, Doug, 91

emergency UI (unemployment insurance), 102-105

European debt crisis

    ending fiscal stimulus plan after, 112-113

    Federal Reserve policies, effect on, 228-229

    lack of confidence in financial system, 209

    reasons for, 189-193

    stress-testing, 41

F

Fannie Mae

    homeownership support, 180

    nationalization of, 1, 19, 132-135

    role in housing market crisis, 16-19

FDIC (Federal Deposit Insurance Corp.), 25
  as insurer of last resort, 31-34
  resolution authority of, 156-158
Federal Housing Administration (FHA), 123, 179-180
Federal Housing Finance Administration, 134
Federal Reserve
  banking industry bailout, 24
  Ben Bernanke's leadership of, 54-58
  failure to regulate housing market, 10-11
  housing bubble, role in, 51-54
  Lehman Brothers collapse, 20
  as lender of last resort, 28-31
  low interest rates, housing market and, 6-7
  mortgage-backed securities, purchase of, 135
  policies after recovery from Great Recession of 2008/2009, 228-231
  role in business cycles, 197-198
  role in Great Recession of 2008/2009, 47-51, 58-67
  sale of Bear Stearns, 16
  transparency, 63-66
FHA (Federal Housing Administration), 123, 179-180
FHA Secure loans, 131
financial crises, slow recovery following, 200-207

financial regulatory reform after Great Recession of 2008/2009
  business confidence and, 210-213
  Dodd-Frank Act, xx-xxii, 145-149
    effect on financial crisis, 164-166
    Financial Stability Oversight Council (FSOC), 154
    Office of Financial Research (OFR), 154-155
    resolution authority in financial system failure, 155-158
    shadow banking system, 161-164
    slow implementation of, 211
    success of, 166-167
    too-big-to-fail problem, 158-161
  reasons for needing, 150-155
Financial Stability Oversight Council (FSOC), 154
financial system
  bailout after Great Recession of 2008/2009, xvi-xviii, 23-26
    exit strategy for Federal Reserve, 66-67
    FDIC, role of, 31-34
    Federal Reserve, role of, 28-31, 47-51, 58-66
    results of, 42-43
    stress-testing, 39-42
    TARP, role of, 34-38

confidence in

after Great Recession of 2008/2009, 171-173, 207-210

regulatory changes and, 210-213

role in Great Recession of 2008/2009, 26-28

Dodd-Frank Act. *See* Dodd-Frank Act (financial regulatory reform)

reasons for failure, 150-155

resolution authority, 155-158

shadow banking system, 161-164

too-big-to-fail problem, 158-161

fiscal cliff, 213-215, 222-228

fiscal stimulus plan after Great Recession of 2008/2009, xviii-xix, 91-96

amount spent, 100-99

emergency UI (unemployment insurance), 102-105

ending, 112-114

infrastructure spending, 107-108

multipliers, 102-105

reasons for needing, 96-98

results of, 108-112

state and local government aid, 105-106

tax cuts, 99-101

foreclosures. *See* housing market, reform after Great Recession of 2008/2009

foreign investors, influx of cash from, 4-6

forwarding sales, 78

Frank, Barney, 145, 159

Freddie Mac

homeownership support, 180

nationalization of, 1, 19, 132-135

role in housing market crisis, 16-19

FSOC (Financial Stability Oversight Council), 154

Furman, Jason, 91

G

gap between rich and poor, 182-188

gasoline prices, effect on auto sales, 75-76

GDP (gross domestic product), relationship with national debt, 214-215

GM (General Motors). *See* auto industry, bailout after Great Recession of 2008/2009

government

role in economy after Great Recession of 2008/2009, xiii-xxviii, 219-222

auto industry bailout, xvii-xviii, 71-75

budget deficits, xxii-xxv

criticism of, xxv-xxvi

exit strategy for Federal Reserve, 66-67

Federal Reserve, role of, 47-51, 58-66

financial regulatory reform, xx-xxii, 145-149

financial system rescue, xvi-xviii, 23-26

fiscal stimulus plan, xviii-xix, 91-96

housing market reform, xix-xx, 119-124, 231-235

policy decisions in 2011, 222-228

support for, xxvi-xxviii

spending

    cost of increases, 213-215

    policy decisions in 2011, 222-228

government-sponsored enterprises (GSEs). *See* Fannie Mae; Freddie Mac

Gramlich, Ned, 155

Great Depression, 54-55, 221

Great Recession of 2008/2009

damage to economy, xiii-xiv

government role after, xiii-xxviii, 219-222

    auto industry bailout, xvii-xviii, 71-75

    budget deficits, xxii-xxv

    criticism of, xxv-xxvi

    exit strategy for Federal Reserve, 66-67

    Federal Reserve, role of, 47-51, 58-66

    financial regulatory reform, xx-xxii, 145-149

financial system rescue, xvi-xviii, 23-26

fiscal stimulus plan, xviii-xix, 91-96

housing market reform, xix-xx, 119-124

policy decisions in 2011, 222-228

support for, xxvi-xxviii

job growth after, 235-240

mortgage-backed securities, role of, 8-10

origins of, 1-3, 26-28

panic, start of, 19-21

recovery from, xiv-xvi

    auto industry role in, 86-88

    deleveraging, quickness of, 200-207

    Federal Reserve policies after, 228-231

    fiscal stimulus plan role in, 108-112

    lack of confidence in financial system, 207-210

    legal and regulatory issues, 210-213

    weakness of, 198-200

results of, 171-175

    consumer spending decline, 175-178

    European debt crisis, 189-193

    gap between rich and poor, 182-188

homeownership decline, 181-182

pessimistic economic mood, 193-194

risk-taking, results of, 12-16

Greenspan, Alan, 6-7, 52-54, 58

GSEs (government-sponsored enterprises). *See* Fannie Mae; Freddie Mac

H

Hamilton, Alexander, xxviii, 145

HAMP, 138-139

HARP, 139-140

Henry VIII (king of England), 200

Home Affordable Mortgage Program, xx

homeownership

after Great Recession of 2008/2009, 173-174, 181-182

reasons for rise in, 178-181

Hoover, Herbert, 221

Hope Now, 131-132

housing bubble

boom and bust of, 125-130, 181-182

Federal Reserve, role of, 51-54

housing market

confidence in financial system, 26-28

failure to regulate, 10-11

Fannie Mae and Freddie Mac, role in crisis, 16-19

government role in mortgages, 231-235

homeownership after Great Recession of 2008/2009, 173-174

low interest rates, effect of, 6-7

reasons for rise in homeownership, 178-181

reform after Great Recession of 2008/2009, xix-xx, 119-124

Fannie Mae and Freddie Mac, government take-over of, 132-135

foreclosures, reducing, 137-140

loan limits and tax credits, 135-137

mortgage loan modifictions, programs for, 130-132

reasons for needing, 125-130

TARP, role of, 37

weak economic recovery and, 200

HSBC, collapse of, 14

hysteresis, 97

I

income disparity between rich and poor, 182-188

inflation target, 65-66

infrastructure spending in fiscal stimulus plan, 93, 107-108

insurer of last resort, FDIC as, 31-34

interest rates, zero-interest-rate policy, 50, 58-59

J

Japanese banks, 41, 55-56

Jefferson, Thomas, xxviii

job growth after Great Recession of 2008/2009, 235-240

job loss from auto industry liquidation, 81

L

legal and regulatory issues after Great Recession of 2008/2009, 210-213

Lehman Brothers, collapse of, 3, 20, 157-158

lender of last resort, Federal Reserve as, 28-31

Libor-Treasury spread, 15-16

loans. *See* mortgage loan modifications

low interest rates, housing market and, 6-7

M

Making Home Affordable Program, 122, 138

Merrill Lynch, sale of, 21

monetary policy. *See* Federal Reserve

Moody's Analytics, xxix

moral hazard, 120, 234

mortgage loan modifications, xx
   in bankruptcy, 121
   foreclosures, reducing, 137-140
   programs for, 130-132

mortgage-backed securities
   Dodd-Frank Act (financial regulatory reform) and, 163-164
   failure to regulate, 10-12
   Federal Reserve purchase of, 135
   foreign investment in, 5-6
   mortgage loan modifications and, 131-132
   risk-taking, results of, 12-16
   role in Great Recession of 2008/2009, 1-2, 8-10, 26-28

mortgages. *See also* housing market, reform after Great Recession of 2008/2009
   "2-28" loans, 130
   foreclosures, reducing, 137-140
   government role in, 231-235
   losses in, 127
   subprime mortgages, role in financial system failure, 153-155
   30-year fixed-rate mortgages
      origins of, 179-180
      role of government in, xxvii, 232-233

multipliers of fiscal stimulus, 102-105

municipal government aid in fiscal stimulus plan, 105-106

N

Nardelli, Robert, 72

National Commission on Fiscal Responsibility and Reform, 227-228

national debt
    after Great Recession of 2008/2009, xxii-xxv
    raising debt ceiling, 209-210, 215
    relationship with GDP, 214-215

New Deal, xxviii

O

Obamacare, 213

Occupy Wall Street, 182-183

OFR (Office of Financial Research), 154-155

Operation Twist, 63

P

Paul, Ron, 47

Paulson, Henry, 19, 34-35, 134

PDCF (Primary Dealer Credit Facility), 30

Pelosi, Nancy, 35

pessimistic economic mood, 193-194

Primary Dealer Credit Facility (PDCF), 30

Primary Reserve Fund, "broke the buck," 20, 162

Q-R

QE (quantitative easing), xvii, 49-50, 56-57, 59-63

ratings of mortgage-backed securities, 11-12

recession. *See* Great Recession of 2008/2009

recovery from Great Recession of 2008/2009, xiv-xvi. *See also* American Recovery and Reinvestment Act
    auto industry role in, 86-88
    deleveraging, quickness of, 200-207
    Federal Reserve policies after, 228-231
    fiscal stimulus plan role in, 108-112
    lack of confidence in financial system, 207-210
    legal and regulatory issues, 210-213
    weakness of, 198-200

refinancing mortgage loans. *See* mortgage loan modifications

regulators, failure to regulate mortgage-backed securities, 10-12

regulatory changes. *See also* financial regulatory reform after Great Recession of 2008/2009
    business confidence and, 210-213
    businesses' reaction to, xxii
    reasons for needing, 150-155
    resolution authority, 155-158

shadow banking system, 161-164

success of, 166-167

too-big-to-fail problem, 158-161

Reid, Harry, 35

Reinhart, Carmen, 93, 200

resolution authority in financial system failure, 155-158

results of Great Recession of 2008/2009, 171-175

consumer spending decline, 175-178

European debt crisis, 189-193

gap between rich and poor, 182-188

homeownership decline, 181-182

pessimistic economic mood, 193-194

risk-taking

in financial system failure, 153-155

after Great Recession of 2008/2009, 171-173

role in Great Recession of 2008/2009, 12-16

Rogoff, Kenneth, 93, 200

Romer, Christina, 92

Roosevelt, Franklin, 221

Roosevelt administration

bank holiday, 39

New Deal, xxviii

S

sales forwarding, 78

saving versus spending after Great Recession of 2008/2009, 175-178

second liens, mortgage loan modifications and, 132

securitization. *See also* mortgage-backed securities

in financial system failure, 152

mortgage loan modifications and, 131-132

risk-taking, results of, 12-16

role in Great Recession of 2008/2009, 1-2, 8-10, 26-28

sequestration, 224

shadow banking system, 30, 147-148, 161-164

"shovel-ready" projects, 93, 107-108

SIFIs (systemically important financial institutions), 154, 158-161

Simpson-Bowles commission, 227-228

spending

government spending increases, cost of, 213-215

versus saving after Great Recession of 2008/2009, 175-178

state and local government aid in fiscal stimulus plan, 105-106

Steele, Bob, 119-120

stimulus plan after Great Recession of 2008/2009, xviii-xix, 91-96

  amount spent, 100-99

  emergency UI (unemployment insurance), 102-105

  ending, 112-114

  infrastructure spending, 107-108

  multipliers, 102-105

  reasons for needing, 96-98

  results of, 108-112

  state and local government aid, 105-106

  tax cuts, 99-101

stress-testing, xvii, 23-24, 39-42

student loans, 187

subprime mortgages

  "2-28" loans, 130

  role in financial system failure, 153-155

Summers, Larry, 91

support for government role in economy, xxvi-xxviii

systemically important financial institutions (SIFIs), 154, 158-161

T

TAF (Term Auction Facility), 29

TARP (Troubled Asset Relief Program), xvi-xvii, 25-26, 34-38, 82-83

tax code, homeownership support in, 180-181

tax credits in housing market reform, 135-137

tax cuts

  cost of, 213-215

  in fiscal stimulus plan, 99-101

  policy decisions in 2011, 222-228

Taylor, John, 101

Taylor rule, 52

Term Auction Facility (TAF), 29

Term Liquidity Guarantee Program (TLGP), 33

Term Securities Lending Facility (TSLF), 30

30-year fixed-rate mortgages

  origins of, 179-180

  role of government in, xxvii, 232-233

This Time Is Different (Reinhart and Rogoff), 203

TLGP (Term Liquidity Guarantee Program), 33

too-big-to-fail problem, 154, 158-161

tranches, 14, 27, 131-132

transparency in Federal Reserve policies, 63-66

Treasury bonds, credit rating of, 224-225

Treasury Department

  Lehman Brothers collapse, 20

  raising debt ceiling, 209-210

Troubled Asset Relief Program (TARP), xvi-xvii, 25-26, 34-38, 82-83

TSLF (Term Securities Lending Facility), 30

"2-28" loans, 130

U-V

unemployment insurance in fiscal stimulus plan, 102-105

unemployment rate

American Recovery and Reinvestment Act and, 92-93, 111

gap between rich and poor, 184-187

job growth after Great Recession of 2008/2009, 235-240

unemployment target, 66

U.S. economy. *See* economy

U.S. government. *See* government

Volker rule, 149

W-Z

Wachovia, sale of, 21, 32-33, 157

Wagoner, Rick, 83

Washington Mutual, sale of, 21, 32-33, 157

Wilson, Charles, 82

zero-interest-rate policy, 50, 58-59

FT Press
FINANCIAL TIMES

In an increasingly competitive world, it is quality
of thinking that gives an edge—an idea that opens new
doors, a technique that solves a problem, or an insight
that simply helps make sense of it all.

We work with leading authors in the various arenas
of business and finance to bring cutting-edge thinking
and best-learning practices to a global market.

It is our goal to create world-class print publications
and electronic products that give readers
knowledge and understanding that can then be
applied, whether studying or at work.

To find out more about our business
products, you can visit us at www.ftpress.com.